# MOUN
# BIKE (

G000039275

# Mountain Bike Guide

# Wiltshire

by

## Ian White

THE ERNEST PRESS

Published by The Ernest Press 2000
© Copyright Ian White

ISBN 0 948153 60 1

A CIP catalogue record for this book is available from the
BritshLibrary

Typeset by Stanningley Serif
Produced by Colorcraft

**Disclaimer**

Whilst every effort has been made to achieve accuracy in the
production of material for use in this guide book, the author and
publisher can take no resposibility for trespass, irresponsible
riding or any loss or damage to persons or property suffered as a
result of route descriptions or advice offered in this book.

The inclusion of a route in this book does not guarantee that the
path/track will **remain** a right of way. If conflict with landowners
occurs, please be polite, leave by the shortest available route and
then check on the situation with the relevant authority.

It is worth emphasising that riders should give way to pedestrians and horse riders, and should make every effort to warn others
of their presence.

## ACKNOWLEDGEMENTS

I would like to thank all those who have helped in making this book possible; Derek Purdy for giving me the idea and inspiration; my wife Barbara for putting up with my frequent absences while I was out having fun riding the routes, and for the many unsociable evenings I've spent locked away with the word processor; to the Rights of Way staff at Wiltshire County Council for helping me to use the Definitive Map, and those at Dorset, Hampshire, Oxfordshire and West Berkshire Councils for answering my enquiries about rights of way in their areas. Thanks also to the Longleat Estate for permission to include the track from Shearwater to Nockatt's Hill in route 7.

# CONTENTS

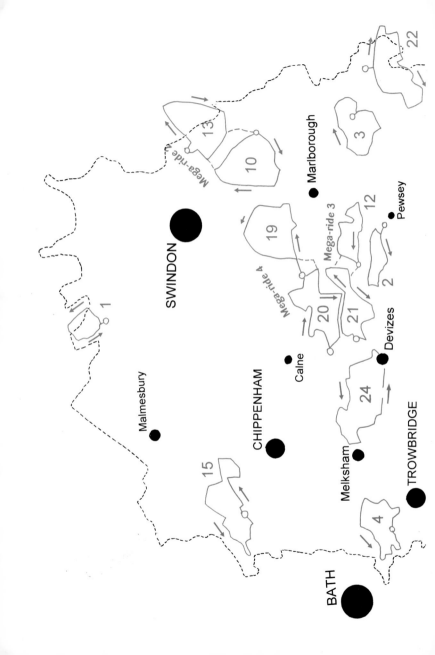

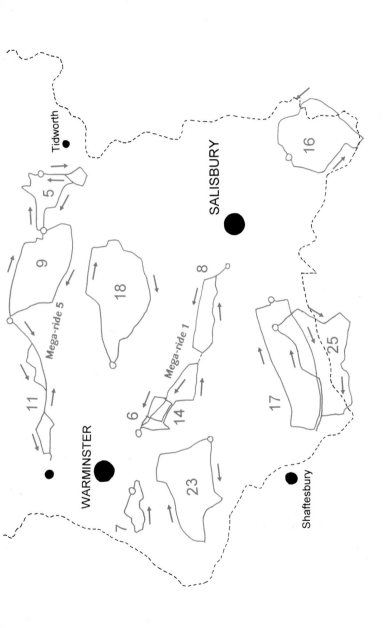

# INTRODUCTION

Welcome to Wiltshire!

When I moved to Wiltshire several years ago and took up mountain biking, I was surprised that despite the variety of good rides I discovered, there didn't seem to be any guide books to help show the way or suggest new routes. It was also sometimes frustrating to find that the ride I had planned carefully on the Ordnance Survey map included chunks that, although clearly marked as bridleways or tracks on the map, seemed to exist only in the imagination of the cartographer. I mentioned this apparent gap in mountain bike literature to Derek Purdy, a friend from my days in the north-east who is a regular contributor to mountain bike magazines and who wrote the guides to Northumberland and Durham in this series, and his response was that I should write the guide myself! Suitably inspired, I decided to take up the challenge, and this book is the result.

The aim of the book is twofold – to act as an introduction to off-road biking for those who would like to try out the challenge, and to give ideas and a bit of local knowledge for more experienced riders, either living in or visiting Wiltshire, who want to explore new areas.

I've tried to cater for a range of abilities, with rides of differing lengths and over easy and more difficult terrain, but the basic idea has been to minimise the amount of tarmac and maximise the length of the off-road sections. This inevitably makes it difficult to guarantee the level of difficulty – read the section about grading on page 22, and always make allowance for the unexpected when estimating the time and effort involved. Some of the shorter routes are suitable for family rides, but don't underestimate the stamina needed for riding off-road, and take an Ordnance Survey map so that you can plot an alternative way back if anyone in the group finds the going too tough.

Once you've tried some of the routes, you'll no doubt want to try your own variations – or perhaps be inspired enough to make up some of your own. See you on the Downs!

## ABOUT WILTSHIRE

### Geography

If you've only seen Wiltshire from the M4, or from a train speeding between London and Bristol, you might be surprised by the variety of scenery that is packed into a relatively small area. The expression 'as different as chalk and cheese' originated here – 'chalk' referring to the broad sweep of the Downs grazed by flocks of sheep (or nowadays often clothed with fields of wheat or barley) and the wide empty expanses and open skies of Salisbury Plain; and 'cheese' being the clay lowlands of the north, with their more intimate small fields of lush green grass and dairy cattle, and a side industry of raising pigs for bacon using the leftovers. These differences were reflected in the way people lived, in compact villages in the 'chalk' – for example Chitterne in the middle of the Plain, or the strings of villages along the valleys radiating from Salisbury – and in more scattered settlements with lots of small hamlets and farmsteads on the 'cheese'. Even the religion was different, with Church of England dominating in the villages of the south while nonconformism flourished in the claylands, leaving a reminder in the numerous Methodist and Baptist chapels still to be seen as you travel around.

Chalk and cheese is not the whole story however, and to add even more variety the Cotswolds extend down into the north-west of the county, past the showpiece village of Castle Combe to Bradford-on-Avon, with it's attractive Georgian terraces overlooking the river, rather like a miniature version of Bath. In the far east, beyond Marlborough, clay-with-flints overlays the chalk giving rise to the wooded, undulating landscapes of Savernake Forest. In the west, along the border with Somerset, a ridge of greensand gives yet another variation, with steep-sided valleys, wooded hills and delightful villages of Olde-England stone cottages. In the far south-east you could almost be in the New Forest (in fact you very nearly are!), with sands and clays supporting a mixture of attractive deciduous woodland and bordering onto the heathlands of Hampshire.

All of this makes for a good range of biking opportunities, and each of the different areas brings its own challenges and rewards. Many of the routes I've described are on the chalk downlands, which are well blessed with a good choice of byways and bridleways. These are often grassy or stony tracks, offering relatively easy riding, although some sections (particularly where there are trees) can get rather muddy in wet weather and can be badly churned up by horses. Beware also of the ruts left by 4-wheel drives and farm vehicles, which can make the going difficult if the track is not wide enough to avoid them.

The hills you'll encounter are not mountains – we're in the south, after all! – but there'll generally be a stiff climb onto the ridge. Once you're up, the chances are that there'll be a good long ridgeway path with glorious views to compensate for the effort, and an exhilarating descent at the other end! One final word of warning in rainy weather – wet chalk is lethal! Watch out for white patches of exposed chalk, which will be like an ice rink, and will have you off your bike faster than you can imagine if you aren't careful.

The sands of the New Forest borderlands, and the greensands around Longleat in the west, give some good rides, although bridleways are harder to find! The mud here is generally less sticky, and although it might slow you down and dirty your posh new cycling kit it should at least wash off relatively easily afterwards.

Not so with the clays and the Cotswold muds of the north and north-west, which after wet weather can be seriously frustrating, sometimes to the point of stopping progress altogether. I've found myself reduced to lifting the bike onto my shoulder – complete with what seems like a sizeable proportion of the Wiltshire countryside still immovably attached to the wheels – and carrying the whole business half a mile or more to where the mud is slightly less gluti-nous and a slow, grinding progress can be resumed. If you do find the clay beginning to ball up round the brake blocks, first try riding on the grass on the edge or middle of the track (if there is any). If you can't avoid the mud, it's probably best to try and keep going, pedalling a high gear to try and blast your way through. Scraping the mud off rarely seems to work (until you're out of the worst of it), and once you stop it's very hard to get going again. Pushing is even more difficult than riding, as the mud just clogs up even faster! The best advice is to save these rides for dry summer weather – unless you're after a particular sort of challenge!

### History

Wiltshire has a long history of settlement, so there will be plenty to see and think about on your rides! Stonehenge is the most famous of its ancient monuments, but there are many other Neolithic rem-nants, such as the Avebury stone circle, Silbury Hill, settlements and causewayed enclosures like Windmill Hill, and countless tumuli, including the Long Barrow at West Kennett where you can enter the burial chambers inside the mound. The chalk areas – where Neolithic settlement was densest and where remnants have been preserved by the lack of subsequent ploughing – are literally scat-tered with reminders of Stone Age man, and a quick glance at the

Ordnance Survey map will reveal tumuli, field systems and earth-works galore.

Later civilisations have also left their mark on the landscape. In the Iron Age, the need for defence led to the construction of hilltop forts or 'camps' – ditches and earth ramparts surrounding a flat central area which might have been used as a permanent or temporary settlement, or perhaps as a meeting area or tribal headquarters. Many of the best vantage points on the chalk downs were used in this way, so you'll often find a hillfort on your route, now providing a good place for a pause to rest and admire the view!

The Romans were here too, leaving a legacy of long straight roads, such as the Fosse Way which cuts across the north-west corner of the county on it's way from Exeter to Lincoln, or the 'Lead Road' which runs along the crest of Great Ridge on it's way from the Mendips to the south coast. After the Romans came the Dark Ages, a period about which relatively little is known and which bequeathed enigmatic linear earthworks such as the Wansdyke and Grim's Ditch, thought to be defensive lines built by the Saxons to protect Wessex from the Danes. These ditches are now followed for most of their length by bridleways which make excellent scenic biking routes.

More recent history has also provided much of interest to see and wonder at as you ride through the county. Mediaeval hunting forests such as Cranborne Chase, Savernake Forest and Selwood Forest have left a typical landscape of small fields, areas of relict woodland and scattered settlement; there are places, such as Hindon, that were established as 'new towns' in the Middle Ages but are now no more than villages; many villages have attractive churches dating from Saxon, Norman, Mediaeval or more recent times, and perhaps a tithe barn where the clergy stored their share of the village's agricultural produce; and wherever you go you will see country houses large and small, and any number of attractive villages and hamlets built in the local stone or brick. The Industrial Revolution has left its mark too, for example in the old woollen mills and cottage weaving legacy of the west Wiltshire towns; and in the Kennett and Avon Canal, which runs across the county from east to west and which has in recent years been rescued from dereliction and reopened as a navigable waterway through the heroic efforts of the K&A Canal Trust. And of course I couldn't finish without a mention of Wiltshire's famous White Horses, several of which you will see carved into the chalk hillsides as you follow the rides later in this book.

As well as adding interest to the rides, history has a more direct relevance for the mountain bike enthusiast through its influence on today's network of roads and paths. Many of yesterday's main roads are now little-used byways or tracks which make ideal routes for exploring by bike. The oldest of these are probably the old ridgeway routes along the crests of the chalk downs, the most famous of which is now followed by the Ridgeway Long Distance Path. This runs from near Avebury to Ivinghoe Beacon in Buckinghamshire, and is believed to be one of the most ancient tracks in the country, forming an easy line of communication for Neolithic tribes moving from the south-west to the Midlands and East Anglia at a time when the clay lowlands would have been densely forested and difficult to travel through. South of Avebury the prehistoric track is believed to have crossed the Vale of Pewsey and linked with the ridgeway path along the north slope of Salisbury Plain, past Urchfont Hill.

Many of the other chalk ridges have also been used in the past as important lines of communication, and until relatively recently many main road routes followed the downs rather than the valleys where today's traffic is concentrated. In the seventeenth and eighteenth centuries, several of these routes over the Downs were upgraded as turnpike roads and were used by the mail coaches on their way between Bath and London, Bristol and Southampton, and so on. Other routes remained toll-free, and were favoured by the drovers who, in the days before the railways, supplied London and other big cities with meat 'on the hoof', walking their beasts slowly over a period of several weeks the hundreds of miles from Wales or the south-west to the markets of London and the Midlands. Nowadays most of these old roads have lost their economic importance, but remain as excellent routes for exploring by bike. You can often still see the mileposts by the side of the track, standing deserted by traffic but still proclaiming the distance 'Sarum XVII miles' to passing sheep and the occasional walker or biker.

I've included a brief mention of some of the most interesting historical features you'll see in the introduction to each of the rides. If you want to find out more, several good books on Wiltshire history are available from local book shops. As a starter, I'd recommend *Exploring Historic Wiltshire* by Ken Watts (vol. 1 covers the north and Vol. 2 the south of the county). These slim volumes focus on particular areas, including many of the hillier areas covered by the rides in this book, and describe their history through the remains still visible in the landscape today. There are also references to more erudite local history books for those with a real interest in delving into the past.

Practical Information

With so much good biking country, it's surprising that Wiltshire isn't busier with visitors. In many areas you can ride all day without meeting another biker. However, this is beginning to change, as local cyclists begin to discover the hills at their back door, and as the local authorities begin to promote Wiltshire as a destination for the discerning visitor who wants to explore the beauties of the unspoilt countryside. The County and District Councils produce a range of useful and informative leaflets on things to see and do, including some specifically aimed at off-road and on-road cyclists. These are available from the Tourist information Centres listed below. The T.I.C's can also provide information on how to get to Wiltshire (by car or by public transport), and details of a wide variety of accommodation from campsites to luxurious hotels. Accommodation guides are available from all of the T.I.C's, most of which also offer an accommodation booking service.

Tourist Information Centres;
Amesbury – Redworth House, Flower Lane. (Tel. 01980 622833)
Avebury – The Great Barn (Tel. 01672 539425)
Bradford on Avon – 34 Silver St. (Tel. 01225 865797)
Chippenham – The Citadel, Bath Road (Tel. 01249 706333)
Devizes – Market Place (Tel. 01380 729408)
Malmesbury – Town Hall, Market Lane (Tel. 01666 823748)
Marlborough – George Lane Car Park (Tel. 01672 513989)
Melksham – Church St. (Tel. 01225 707424)
Mere – The Square (Tel. 01747 861211)
Salisbury – Fish Row (Tel. 01722 334956)
Swindon – 37 Regent St. (Tel. 01793 530328 / 466454)
Trowbridge – St. Stephen's Place (Tel. 01225 777054)
Warminster – Central Car Park (Tel. 01985 218548)
Westbury – The Library, Edward St. (Tel. 01373 827158)

Taking your bike on public transport

Although capacity on modern trains is limited, it is easier to travel by rail with your bike now than it was a few years ago. The train operators know there is a demand, and most allow bikes to be carried.

You may have to make a reservation in advance, and there may be a small charge for this. The rules vary depending on the train operator and the type of rolling stock used – it's important to check these out before you plan your journey. Phone National Rail Enquiries on 0345 48 49 50 , who can answer timetable and fares queries about all operators' services.

Buses are not generally able to carry bikes, but an experimental rural minibus service with a rack for two bikes – the 'Wiltshire Wigglybus' –  has recently begun in the Pewsey Vale, serving the area between Devizes, Pewsey and the villages to the east. This could be used to link with routes 2,3,5,11,12,21 and 22. Phone 01380 860100 for information.

If you can't take your bike with you, another option is to hire one when you get to Wiltshire. For details of local bike hire, ask at the Tourist Information Centres listed above.

## EQUIPMENT AND SAFETY

### The Bike

I'm not going to tell you how to choose a bike – there are plenty of others more qualified than me to do that. If you haven't got a suitable machine, read the magazines to get an idea of what is available and then visit a good bike shop and ask for help. Explain what sort of riding you intend to do. Although you don't need a top-notch machine to enjoy yourself, if you intend to do much off-road riding you should look for something capable of taking the strain. Choose a bike that is fit for the purpose for which it will be used – not one that looks good as a fashion accessory!

## Maintenance

Do it! A badly maintained bike is not only dangerous, but will let you down just when you don't want it to, usually at the furthest point of the route, or when it's just started to pour with rain. Always check the brakes and tyres before you start. Also check that there's no wobble in the wheels or front forks, and occasionally check for play in the bottom bracket. After the ride clean the bike well – particularly take care to clean and dry around all moving parts, cable housings and the chain, and spray these with lubricant to keep them running sweetly. While cleaning the bike, take the opportunity to check it over for loose, worn or damaged parts, and fix these ready for your next outing. Look for any thorns in the tyres – it's surprising how often the air doesn't leak out until you get home and pull the offending spike out. Look carefully, you'll find that off-road punctures are like London buses and always come in twos or threes!

## Clothing

Again, I'm not going to tell you what to wear. There's an enormous range of kit available these days, and the magazines are full of reviews of the latest gear. You don't need to spend a fortune on expensive clothing, but you will need something to keep you dry and warm, and padded shorts are certainly more comfortable than ordinary trousers or shorts on a long ride. Expect to get muddy and wet – if you come back with clean shoes you haven't been trying hard enough! If you can afford it, a good pair of off-road shoes with rigid soles and a flap protecting the laces is a good investment. The only essential is a helmet. You only have one life, and riding without a helmet is one way to lose it. Please wear one!

Things to carry

You don't need to turn your day out into an expedition – it's more comfortable to travel light – but there are some things you will need to take with you;

   * a bike pump, puncture repair kit and tyre levers – for obvious reasons!

   * a spare inner tube – replacement can be faster than trying to mend a double or treble puncture on the spot

   * a basic tool kit – either take one of the multi-purpose tools now available, or a mini-adjustable spanner, mini-pliers, small screw-driver, and a selection of Allen keys to fit your bike. A chain tool can also be useful.

   * map(s) – take the relevant Ordnance Survey Landranger or Explorer maps. The 1;50000 Landranger maps are ideal; the 1;25000 Explorers show more detail, but you'll need more to cover the same area.

   * a compass – essential if you venture into the remoter areas of Salisbury Plain or the Marlborough Downs in misty weather, but can also be reassuring even in easier conditions if you find yourself temporarily misplaced!

   * food and drink – it's important to drink plenty in hot weather, particularly if you're working hard. Carry a water bottle, or if you're really keen invest in a special back-mounted drink sac.

   * money – for emergencies

   * a basic first-aid kit – plasters and antiseptic cream at least

   * personal identification – also tell someone where you're go-ing, in case of accidents

   * lights and reflectors if you might be riding in the dark

RIDING OFF-ROAD

Rights of Way

All of the routes in this book are on rights of way on which a legal right to cycle exists; or in the few cases where there is no public right of way, access has been checked with the landowner. If however you want to devise your own routes or variations, you will need to be able to recognise the differences between the different types of rights of way;

* *Bridleways* are open to walkers, cyclists and horse riders, and are often marked by waymark signs with blue arrows

* *Byways* are open to cyclists, walkers and horse riders, but also to vehicular traffic. They are often marked by red waymark arrows.

* *Roads Used As Public Paths* are also open for use by cyclists and walkers and horse riders, though not necessarily by vehicular traffic (these are gradually being reclassified as byways or bridleways)

* *Footpaths* **cannot** be used by cyclists – if you have to follow a section of footpath, **get off and push**.

Although the Ordnance Survey maps are usually accurate, to be absolutely certain of the legal status of a route you'll need to check it against the Definitive Map, which is held by the County Council. The Definitive Map is available for inspection at the relevant County headquarters (for Wiltshire this is County Hall in Trowbridge), and copies are also often kept at the main District Council offices and some of the larger public libraries.

The Salisbury Plain Training Area

The Army uses large areas of Salisbury Plain as live firing ranges, and although the public rights of way across these areas are closed when firing is taking place, the Army encourages access at other times. This gives an opportunity to visit a unique area, which has been protected from modern agriculture and development, and which is a refuge for many rare species of plants, insects and other creatures. If you plan to ride on the rights of way which cross the ranges, make sure to check in advance whether access is permitted on the day you want to visit. Information is published in the local press, on parish notice boards, or can be obtained by telephoning the SPTA Headquarters on **01980 620819**. The Army also issue a monthly News Sheet which not only gives full details of firing days and other military activity, but also gives a brief topical summary of the flora and fauna to look out for at that time of year. Write to SPTA Headquarters, Westdown Camp, Tilshead, Salisbury, Wilts. SP3 4RS.

**On no account enter the ranges when the red flags are flying**. When in the training areas;

    * comply with the Bylaws displayed on the Range Warning Noticeboards, and with the instructions of the wardens

    * do not approach or pick up any metal objects

    * keep away from all buildings unless marked otherwise

Kennet & Avon Canal

The towpath in Wiltshire is **not** a public right of way, but British Waterways allow cyclists and walkers to use it. However, since 1997 cyclists have been required to pay for a pass for the privilege, and towpath rangers are employed to check that passes are being carried. The current charges for an annual pass are £12.50 if purchased in advance (£15 if bought on the towpath from a ranger), and for a monthly pass £4 in advance (£5 from a ranger). Passes are free for under 16's. Apply for your pass by post from the British Waterways

Board, Bath Road, Devizes SN10 1HB; by telephone from BW Customer Services on 01923 201120 (quoting your credit card details); or from one of BW's agents – usually shops, pubs and boatyards along the canal, and local Tourist Information Centres.

The introduction of passes caused considerable local opposition, but despite the protests there have not, at the time of writing, been any changes to the scheme.

Mountain Bike Code of Conduct

Always be courteous and considerate, both to those who live and work in the countryside and to other visitors. Mountain bikers have gained a bad reputation in some areas due to the behaviour of a minority – so be sure to ride respectfully, and don't spoil things for yourself or for other bikers who may follow. Whenever you're out riding, **you** are an ambassador for the sport, so always follow these simple rules;

* follow the Country Code; enjoy the countryside, and respect its life and work

* stay in control of your bike, particularly downhill – make sure you can stop in time if anything unexpected happens

* don't cycle on footpaths

* slow down and give way to walkers and horse riders (a cheerful greeting costs nothing and is worth a fortune!)

* take your litter home with you

THE ROUTES

I've chosen the routes that follow to suit a range of abilities, and also to take in a wide variety of the different types of scenery that Wiltshire has to offer. If you're interested in history, wildlife or landscape, read the introductory notes to the rides; if what turns you on is the challenge, ignore the blurb, put your head down and go for it – there's a range of rides to test your stamina whatever your level of fitness. And for the super-fit, I've included five 'Mega-Rides' which link shorter routes to give a real day out!

The routes are graded as easy, moderate or hard. This should be treated as a rough classification only. Conditions change quickly, and what may be an easy ride in summer can be very hard in winter – particularly where wet clay is involved! Seasonal changes in vegetation can also make a big difference – tall grass, nettles and growing crops can make some paths difficult in summer, and newly ploughed fields can also make the going difficult at other times of the year.

As a general rule, 'easy' routes should suit relative newcomers, or more experienced riders wanting an easy day out; 'moderate' routes are generally longer and over more difficult terrain, and require more stamina; while 'hard' routes are for fit and experienced riders only. I haven't tried to give an estimate of riding time, as this will vary tremendously depending on individual fitness and stamina, the conditions, and how fast you want to go! However, if it has been wet expect everything to be much slower and more difficult, and plan a shortcut back to the start in case you run out of time or energy. If you're not sure of your abilities, start with one of the easy routes and see how you get on before progressing to a more difficult one.

I've described the routes as I found them. However, things can change quickly so don't be surprised if you find my description doesn't match what's on the ground from time to time. Vegetation in particular can change, as can the appearance of paths and tracks. While writing this book I found on at least two occasions that my original description was out of date on a second visit, and had to be revised – in one case an area of thick rhododendrons had been cleared, completely changing the appearance of the wood and making a bridlepath virtually impassable; and in another, what I had described as a very badly rutted byway had been improved and is now a good firm track! Bridleways across fields are also very prone to change, and may disappear under the plough (or even crops) if not properly reinstated by the farmer. So, take the relevant Ordnance Survey map with you, and use it to follow the route as you go. If you find the description doesn't seem to fit, don't panic, but use common sense and the map to guide you. If you have real difficulty with a right of way that has been obliterated or become impassable, contact the local Rights of Way Warden based in the County Council (Wiltshire County Council has a freephone telephone number for reporting all highways-related problems, including those to do with Rights of Way – ring 0800 23 23 23).

## LIST OF ABBREVIATIONS

R – right
L – left
RH – right hand
LH – left hand
TJ – T junction
X-rds – crossroads
X-tracks – cross-tracks
sp. – signposted
m – metres (altitude)
km – kilometres
N, S, E, W – north, south, east, west
(**A**), (**B**) etc. – location points in text (bold) agreeing with letters (red) on maps

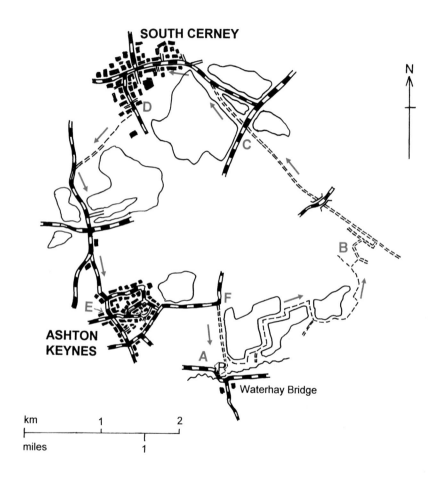

**SOUTH CERNEY**

N

D

C

B

F

ASHTON
KEYNES

E

A

Waterhay Bridge

km          1          2

miles                1

# 1) ASHTON KEYNES & THE COTSWOLD WATER PARK

Grade; Easy
Length; 14 km (8·5 miles)
Terrain;   9 km hard/stony track
            5 km tarmac
Map; OS Landranger 163 Cheltenham and the Cirencester area
Ref Points; GR 060933 Waterhay Bridge carpark (start & finish)
                080948 old railway line (bridleway)
                049970 South Cerney
                047941 Ashton Keynes
Facilities; shops and pubs in South Cerney and Ashton Keynes.
Nearest rail station; Kemble 7 km

Background

The area around Ashton Keynes is unique in Wiltshire, and is the product of many years of large-scale extraction of gravel and sand from the flat river valley of the upper reaches of the River Thames (the river rises not far to the west of here, near the village of Kemble). This has left a strange landscape with a mixture of active gravel workings, areas of quicksand surrounded by fences and warning notices, and large shallow lakes which cover entire areas of the map, separated by narrow strips of land followed by the roads and foot-paths that cross the area.

Out of this peculiar man-made landscape has been created the Cotswold Water Park, which now attracts visitors from a wide area to sample all manner of water-dependent activities. Some of the lakes have been set aside for water skiing, power boating or jet ski-ing, some for sailing or wind surfing, some for fishing, while others are quiet havens for wildlife. As well as the bird life that you would expect on a large area of inland water, the meadows are home to many flowering plants, including rarities such as the snake's-head fritillary.

Ashton Keynes itself is an attractive village which has several times won Best Kept Village awards. South Cerney also has a heart of Cotswold stone houses, although with a fringe of industry mainly related to the aggregate extraction which surrounds it.

This ride is one of the shortest in the book, has no hills, and being mainly on hard tracks or tarmac roads is one that can be undertaken at any time of year. It's certainly worth it for the experience of cycling through Wiltshire's own Lake District!

### Route Description

Waterhay Bridge to South Cerney

There's a visitors' carpark at Waterhay Bridge (**A**), where the ride starts and finishes. Take the bridleway that leads from the rear of the car- park, then after a few hundred metres turn R by the signpost 'Thames Path'. This path winds around several lakes, including a large one frequented by fishermen – ignore any turns off, and continue to follow the main bridlepath. After about 2·5 km the path leaves the lakes behind, and you'll come to a track junction among trees (**B**). Take the L fork, sp. 'Public Bridlepath to South Cerney'. Follow this through the woods, then at the next path junction turn R, sp. Cricklade (**don't** take the left turn to South Cerney – this leads onto the road before long).

After 300 metres the track bears L, then comes to a TJ. Turn L, this time following the South Cerney signs, onto the straight bridleway that follows the old railway line. Keep going for just over 2 km, finally coming to a level crossing with the road (**C**). This is the main 'spine road' through the Water Park, so beware as the traffic moves quite fast! Cross straight over, and continue to follow the old railway path which now runs on a narrow strip of land between two lakes, one used for sailing and the other surrounded by holiday chalets.

At the far end, turn L onto the road and into South Cerney.

South Cerney to Waterhay Bridge

Follow the road into the centre of South Cerney village, and by the stone cross turn L into Broadway Lane. By the last house on the way out of the village (**D**), turn R into a narrow bridleway, sp. to Ashton Keynes. Follow this straight on to meet a road after 1 km.

Turn L onto the road.

At the next X-rds, go straight across towards Ashton Keynes, then fork L into Ashton Keynes village. In the village, turn L by the 'White Hart' (**E**), then soon bear L again into Fore Street (following the sp. to the village shop). At the end, turn R into Kent End, then turn L into Rixon Gate. This narrow road leaves the village and passes more gravel quarries. After nearly 1 km, near the quarries, the road bends left. Turn R into a bridleway (sp. Waterhay) on the corner of the bend (**F**). This track will lead you back to the carpark.

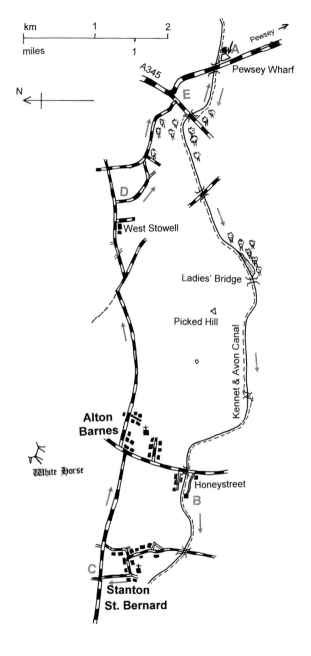

km 1 2

miles 1

N

Pewsey

A

Pewsey Wharf

A345

E

D

West Stowell

Ladies' Bridge

Picked Hill

Kennet & Avon Canal

Alton
Barnes

White Horse

Honeystreet

B

C

Stanton
St. Bernard

## 2) PEWSEY WHARF AND HONEYSTREET

Grade; Easy in dry conditions, but the canal towpath can get very
muddy in winter
Length; 17 km (10·5 miles)
Terrain;   8 km canal towpath (grassy)
          9 km tarmac
(Don't forget that to cycle on the Kennet & Avon Canal you need
a towpath permit - see page 20  for details)
Map; OS Landranger 173 Swindon & Devizes
Ref Points; GR 157611 Pewsey Wharf (start and finish)
                101617 Honeystreet (Barge Inn)
                093623 Stanton St. Bernard
                137624 West Stowell
Facilities; Tea Rooms at Pewsey Wharf (in season). Drinks and
food at the Barge Inn (Honeystreet). Pewsey itself has all the
facilities you'd expect in a small town.
Nearest rail station; Pewsey 750 metres


Background


In summer this route is a pleasant canal-side amble, returning to
Pewsey along minor roads following the foot of Wiltshire's highest
downland. In the depths of a wet winter it can be altogether a different proposition, with glutinous clay mud that sticks to your tyres,
balls up around your forks and eventually makes all progress im-
possible!

Pewsey Wharf, where the route starts and finishes, is as its name
suggests where  boats on the Kennet & Avon Canal used to load and
unload their wares. Nowadays there's a small carpark, and tea rooms
run by the K & A Canal Trust, who have restored and reopened the

canal so that it can once again be navigated for its whole length from Bath to the River Thames.

Perhaps more surprising is that Honeystreet, despite being in the middle of the Vale of Pewsey miles from any town, was once a more important canalside centre than Pewsey, with industries such as timber yards and fertiliser manufacturing springing up alongside the wharf. There was even a ferry across the canal for animals using the drove road on their way to the livestock fair that used to be held on Tan Hill. The Barge Inn, next to the canal, used to house a bakery and general store for the wharf as well as acting as the 'local'.

As you cycle along the towpath from Pewsey, about half way to Honeystreet, the canal suddenly widens and takes on the appearance of an ornamental lake, backed by woods. Just past this is an overbridge, but instead of the usual functional brick or stone blocks, this one is decorated in ornate stonework. The reason it was built like this was to please the Lady of Wilcot Manor, who made it a condition of her permission for the canal to cross her land that it should be appropriately 'landscaped'. 'Ladies Bridge', as it is known, is reckoned to be haunted – so don't get caught out here after dark!

On the way back towards Pewsey look out for the White Horse carved into the flank of Milk Hill. This is the largest White Horse in Wiltshire, and was carved in 1812 by a local farmer.

### Route Description

Pewsey Wharf to Honeystreet

Quite straightforward really – just turn L onto the towpath by the Tea Rooms (**A**) – sp. Wilcot – and follow the canal to the Barge Inn (**B**). (6·5 km in total). On the way you'll have to cross onto the other side of the canal at Bristow Bridge, not far out of Pewsey, and then back onto the south side about 2 km short of Honeystreet. Watch out for Ladies Bridge on the way. The Barge Inn is at the far end of Honeystreet, right next to the canal, so you can't miss it.

Honeystreet to Pewsey Wharf

Continue on the towpath past the Barge Inn, and leave the canal at the next overbridge (about 750 metres further on). Turn R over the bridge, and follow the road up through Stanton St. Bernard village, past the church and uphill to meet the 'main' road (**C**). Turn R, and follow the road for 1·5 km, under the foot of Milk Hill and past the White Horse, to a TJ at the end.

Turn L and then immediately R (sp. Pewsey). There's a steady climb for the next km., past the edge of Alton Priors and over the low ridge that links Woodborough Hill (to your right) to the main ridge of the Downs. Then it's downhill for another 1 1/2 km., and fork L into a smaller lane (sp. West Stowell). Keep straight on past West Stowell Farm, and past the first right turn to Wilcot. After a few hundred metres take the next turn R (**D**), and follow the road as it bends L past a driveway entrance to reach a TJ after about 1 km.

At the TJ turn R, and then go straight ahead towards Pewsey (i.e. **don't** turn immediately right again). After passing the woods of Stowell Park on your right, you come to another TJ (**E**). Turn R again. After 500 metres you'll find yourself back at Bristow Bridge – cross the canal, turn L onto the towpath and follow this back to Pewsey Wharf.

Opposite top – *Ladies Bridge and some Wiltshire mud*

Opposite foot – *Alton Barnes White Horse*

Above – *Nearly back in Great Bedwyn*

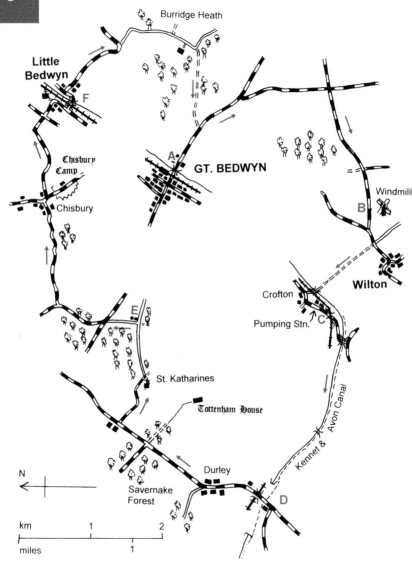

**3**

Burridge Heath

**Little Bedwyn**

F

Chisbury Camp

Chisbury

A

**GT. BEDWYN**

Windmill

B

Crofton

Pumping Stn.

C

**Wilton**

E

St. Katharines

Tottenham House

Kennet & Avon Canal

Durley

D

N

Savernake Forest

km        1        2

miles        1

## 3) THE BEDWYNS, CROFTON AND DURLEY

Grade; Easy – mainly tarmac and hard tracks, but one or two sections(including the canal towpath) can get muddy in wet weather.
Length; 22 km (13·5 miles)
Terrain; 15 km tarmac
          2 km hard/stony track
          5 km canal towpath (grassy) and grassy bridleway
Don't forget that to ride on the canal towpath you need a towpath permit - see page 20 for details)
Map; OS Landranger 174 Newbury & Wantage
Ref Points; GR 279646 Great Bedwyn (start and finish)
                275617 Wilton Windmill
                261622 Crofton Pumping Station
                238642 Durley
                277663 Chisbury
                297642 Burridge Heath
Facilities; Pubs in Wilton village (500 metres off route), Little Bedwyn and in Great Bedwyn. Great Bedwyn also has a shop / Post Office. Refreshments are served at the Crofton Pumping Station on summer weekends.
Nearest rail station; Bedwyn (on route)

Background

Although fairly short, this route passes through some delightful countryside, with narrow twisting lanes, small fields cleared from the woodlands that surround them, and scattered red brick farms and hamlets. Whilst there are no major climbs, it's an undulating landscape with quite a few hills, and new views at every twist and turn.

The plentiful woods and copses that are a feature of the country-side around here were once a part of Savernake Forest, which in the Middle Ages was an important royal hunting ground and stretched far beyond its current boundaries. The main Forest today is confined to an area just to the north-west of the route, between the Durley road and Marlborough – still a very impressive forested area, and popular with walkers and day trippers. The estate (including the road and all tracks through the forest) is privately owned, although managed by the Forestry Commission.

As would be expected, Savernake has many historical connections, including a link with the Seymour family who were much involved in the political intrigues of the sixteenth century. It is said that Jane Seymour, King Henry VIII's third wife, met Henry whilst he was on a hunting visit to the family's home at Wulfhall, not far from the route. The family later built the much larger country mansion at Tottenham House, to which you pass the entrance gates just after Durley.

The route also follows an interesting section of the Kennet & Avon Canal, including the Pumping Station at Crofton and the entrance to the tunnel near Durley. The tunnel marks the highest point on the canal, where it crosses the watershed to leave the Thames Basin, and the Pumping Station nearby provides a supply of water into the canal to feed the locks downhill in both directions, raising it from the artificial lake of Wilton Water. The Pumping Station houses two old beam engines, one dating back to the opening of the canal in 1812, which have been lovingly restored and are open to visitors in season. Check also for the dates of special open days when the engines are in steam and can be seen in action.

Another remnant of former times that you'll pass on the way round is Wilton Windmill, a traditional old wooden mill that dominates the skyline from its position on a hilltop just outside Wilton village.

Once again, the mill has been lovingly restored to working order and is open to the public in season – you can see how the mill works, read about it's history and even buy bags of locally-milled flour (if you don't mind carrying the extra weight !).

Great Bedwyn, where the route starts and finishes, is the last stop for commuter trains from London, Reading and Newbury. However, it retains the charm of a country village. It has a couple of pubs, a small shop or two, and a wharf on the Kennet & Avon Canal.

## Route Description

Great Bedwyn to Durley

Park in Great Bedwyn (**A**) (either in the middle of the village or by the railway station) and take the Shalbourne road, crossing the canal by the Wharf. Continue on this road for just over 1 km, then turn R (sp. Oxenwood). Uphill steadily for another 1 km, then turn R again at the X rds (sp. Wilton).

After almost 2 km you'll pass Wilton Windmill (**B**), and then drop down to a trailing junction with a road coming in from the right. Go straight ahead towards Wilton village, but at the edge of the village turn R along a sunken track (part of an old Roman Road leading to Cunetio, near Marlborough). This climbs for a short distance, over a ridge from which you can see the chimney of the Pumping Station ahead, and then drops quite steeply down to cross first the canal and then a level crossing over the railway. At the end of the lane, turn L onto the road and climb round the bend to pass the Pumping Station (**C**) a short distance further on.

Just after the Pumping Station the road crosses the railway again, and a bit further on turns to cross the canal. On the far side of the bridge turn R along the towpath, and follow the canal for the next 2 km., past several locks to the mouth of the Durley Tunnel. Peer into the darkness, then climb the steep path up to the L. and follow the track straight ahead over the roof of the tunnel until you reach the road (**D**). Turn R on the road and climb steadily (for about 1 km) to the scatter of houses that make up the hamlet of Durley.

Durley to Great Bedwyn

Follow the road through Durley, and past the junction about 1 km further on with the road going off to the left into Savernake Forest. 500 metres past this junction turn R into a small road (sp. St. Katharines). After 1 km, past a couple of bends, the road ends by St. Katharines Church, hidden among the trees.

Turn L into the track sp. Chisbury, and after 750 metres turn L (by the houses) (**E**) into another well-made track. Keep going to the X rds, and continue straight ahead into a tarmac lane.

After another 750 metres, turn R (sp. Little Bedwyn and Chisbury) and follow the road to the attractive hamlet of Chisbury. Here turn R, then immediately L, following signs to Little Bedwyn.

As the road curves down the hill, there are pleasant views over the fields to the tiny church at Little Bedwyn, nestling in the valley bottom. At the X rds. go straight ahead to reach the village, and follow the road as it bends round to the R by the railway. Turn L at the junction to cross the road bridge over the railway (**F**). After crossing the railway and then the canal the road bends L again. Follow it round, but then turn R (sp. Bagshot), and climb out of the village past the Harrow Inn.

At the top of the hill (1 km) turn R into a signposted tarmac bridleway to Burridge Heath. Follow this round a bend to the R, then for a further 1 km until it bends sharply to the left just past a large farm house on the right. Don't follow the tarmac round to the left, but go straight ahead on an unsurfaced track which then bends to the R. Follow this pleasant track for about 1 km, past various woods and copses, until it descends to meet the road climbing out of Great Bedwyn. Turn R, and it's not far back to the village.

*Beside the Kennet & Avon Canal, Bradford-on-Avon*

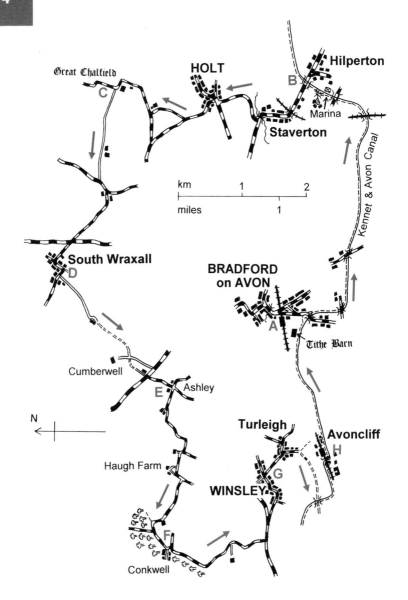

4

Great Chalfield

HOLT

Hilperton

C

B

Staverton

Marina

Kennet & Avon Canal

km 1 2

miles 1

South Wraxall

BRADFORD
on AVON

D

A

Tithe Barn

Cumberwell

Ashley

E

N

Turleigh

Avoncliff

H

Haugh Farm

G

WINSLEY

F

Conkwell

## 4) BRADFORD-ON-AVON, CHALFIELD AND AVONCLIFF

Grade; Easy. More tarmac than most of the rides in this book, and not too many hills. Good for an easier ride, or for a wet day when you don't want to get stuck in the mud!

Length; 26 km (16 miles)

Terrain; 15 km tarmac

        8 km canal towpath

        3 km hard/stony track

Don't forget that you need a towpath permit to cycle on the Kennet & Avon Canal - see page 20  for details

Maps; OS Landranger 173 (Swindon & Devizes) and 172 (Bristol & Bath)

Ref points; GR 824607  Bradford-on-Avon (start and finish)

              856610  Staverton Bridge

              861632  Great Chalfield Manor

              820631  Great Cumberwell

              793627  Conkwell

              801610  Winsley

              804600  Avoncliff

Facilities; No shortage on this route! There are several pubs and eating places around the canal in Bradford-on-Avon (including Lock Cottage, by the towpath entrance, which as well as serving food and drinks has a whole range of bikes – standard and unusual! – for hire, and also sells towpath permits). The Cross Guns in Avoncliff is  a pleasant place to rest near the end of the route, and there are also pubs in Staverton, Holt, Upper South Wraxall (1/2 mile off the route) and Winsley.

Nearest rail stations; Bradford-on-Avon and Avoncliff (both on route)

Background

There are fewer bridleways in this part of West Wiltshire than on
the Downs, but the winding lanes around Conkwell are almost as
good! There's an interesting section of the Kennet & Avon Canal
towpath to follow, with lots of canalside and boating activity around
Lock Cottage and Bradford Wharf, and the picturesque hamlet of
Avoncliff nestling in the valley of the River Avon around an imposing aqueduct, on which the canal soars over the river and railway.

Avoncliff is an odd place – a few houses, the canal, a tiny railway
platform (still in use) and the remnants of quarrying for Bath stone
and of mills formerly used for fulling wool and grinding corn –
there's an old water wheel still visible by the weir below the Cross
Guns. It's one of the few places that actually seems easier to get to
by canal or train, as the dead-end roads on either side of the valley
are narrow and steep, with limited parking.

Bradford-on-Avon is also worth a visit in its own right, and with
its rows of Georgian stone houses perched on the hillside is in many
ways more like Bath than the other towns of west Wiltshire. You
can walk up from the river through narrow lanes to discover the
'lost' Saxon church, only rediscovered in the last century by a cler-
gyman who happened to notice a cross among the jumble of rooftops
of the buildings that had grown up around, and which were hiding
the tiny old church. Down on the Town Bridge there's an old lock-
up where in days gone by those disturbing the peace were left to
cool down, and next to the canal (you pass it right at the end of the
ride) is a huge Tithe Barn in mellow Bath stone.

Another fine old building you'll pass is the magnificent Manor
House at Great Chalfield, a gem set in the middle of the country-
side. Built in the late fifteenth century, it is now owned by the
National Trust but is only open on certain days of the week. Holt

also boasts a National Trust property – The Courts, where you can wander round the gardens in the summer – although this is slightly off the route in the middle of the village.

## Route Description

Bradford-on-Avon to Great Chalfield

Start by the railway station in Bradford (**A**), where there's a big public carpark. Leave the carpark by the main entrance and turn R into Frome Road. Continue 500 metres to the canal bridge, and turn L onto the towpath past the locks and the old Wharf.

Follow the towpath for about 4·5 km, taking you out of Bradford, through the countryside and eventually past the edge of Trowbridge, to the marina at Hilperton. Just past the marina the towpath climbs a steep humpback bridge over the entrance to a canal basin, and shortly afterwards you'll come to a road overbridge (**B**). Leave the canal here and turn L onto the road (take care – can be fairly busy!). Carry on through Staverton village, past the 'Old Bear', to the bridge over the river near the Nestles factory (1 km approx.)

Immediately after the bridge take the R turn to Holt. At the TJ by the 'Tollgate Inn', turn R and then immediately L into Leigh Rd. Climb gently for nearly 1 km, then turn R into the lane signposted to Great Chalfield. After passing Holt Manor turn R again at the TJ. The road crosses a couple of fields, bends down through some trees and then climbs round a corner to reach Great Chalfield Manor (**C**).

Great Chalfield to Winsley

Passing the Manor on your left, go straight ahead into the tarmac lane signposted "bridleway to Little Chalfield". This soon becomes a good quality stony track, then tarmac again before reaching Little Chalfield. Go past the house, along a tree-lined avenue and turn L onto the road at the TJ.

Soon fork R again onto a smaller road signposted 'South Wraxall'. After 1 km go straight across at the crossroads with the Bradford–Corsham road (take care here, traffic approaches deceptively fast along this stretch). In South Wraxall, follow the road as it bends sharply round to the L, then again to the R. After another 100 metres turn L into a tarmac lane (**D**), past the 'No Through Road' signs.

After Cherry Orchard Farm (approx. 1 km) the lane becomes a rougher unsurfaced track. Bump along, ignoring turns off into the landfill site, until the track bears slightly R to pass some old farm buildings and then meets the new approach road to the Cumberwell Golf Clubhouse. Cross this, and go straight on along the tarmac track (parallel to the approach road), past some more old farm buildings to reach the main road.

Cross the main road and into a narrow lane signposted to Ashley. After 1/2 km turn R at the crossroads (**E**), and follow the winding lane through Little Ashley. After another 1 km, the road jinks R and then L by Lower Haugh, then shortly afterwards passes the drive to Rose Cottage Farm. Turn R at the signpost to Conkwell (don't turn off too soon or you'll end up in the farm). After 1 km more you'll reach the edge of Warleigh Woods, and after skirting the trees for 100 metres will come to a junction. Straight on, following the Conkwell sign again, and before long you'll find the village itself.

The road dips here, and bends round to the left. Ignore the lane down into the village (only a hamlet really, but with an attractive row of houses seeming almost to drop over the steep edge of the valley), but turn immediately sharp R following the signpost to Limpley Stoke and Bath (**F**). There's a short but steep climb, then a lovely stretch of road past Conkwell Grange Stud Farm with its fine horses, parkland setting, limestone walls and views over the Avon Valley. Ahead you can also see the flatter land around Trowbridge and, in the distance, the Westbury White Horse.

At the main road turn L (take care – busy!), then take the fork R into Winsley village.

### Winsley to Bradford-on-Avon

Now that the bypass has been completed, the road through Winsley is much quieter than it used to be. Carry on past the Seven Stars, past the Memorial Cross, and just round the bend at the bottom of the hill turn R into a narrow road signposted 'Turleigh – Unsuitable for heavy vehicles' (**G**). You'll see why as you plunge steeply downhill!

As you reach the edge of Turleigh village, turn R into Green Lane (don't worry about the sign saying 'No through road to Avoncliff' – this is for cars!). Steal a look back over your shoulder for a glimpse of some of the big old Georgian houses in this pretty village, then, where the tarmac ends, turn R into a stony bridleway and through a metal gate. From here you can enjoy the view across the Avon Valley, with the canal, river and railway winding peacefully down towards Bath, and Avoncliff nestling around its aqueduct directly below. You'll need to concentrate on the next bit though, as the track drops down a steep and bumpy hill to meet the canal at the bottom.

Cross the bridge and turn L onto the canal towpath, which soon brings you back to Avoncliff. Immediately after crossing the aqueduct, turn R, follow the road back under the arches, and then turn sharp R uphill by the 'Cross Guns' to regain the towpath on the opposite side of the canal (**H**). Turn L on the towpath, and it's 2 km back to Lock Cottage in Bradford (watch out for the Tithe Barn, which is next to the canal just before you get back).

**5**

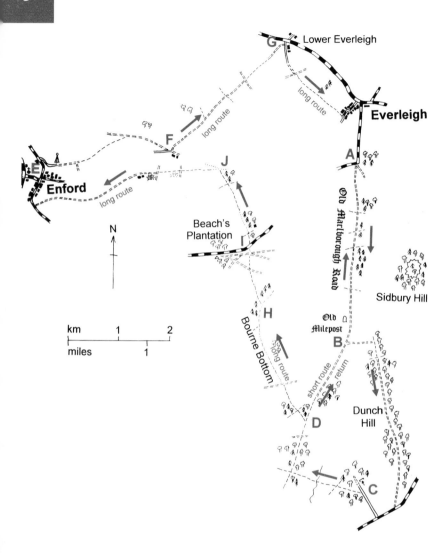

Lower Everleigh

Everleigh

long route

G

A

Old Marlborough Road

long route

F

long route

Sidbury Hill

E

Enford

long route

J

Beach's
Plantation

I

H

Old
Milepost

B

N

Bourne Bottom

short route

return

long route

Dunch
Hill

km    1    2
miles    1

D

C

## 5) BULFORD RANGES & THE OLD MARLBOROUGH ROAD

Grade; Easy or moderate, depending on which route you follow. A good chunk of both routes runs through the Bulford Army Ranges, so you'll need to plan to visit on a non-firing day. See page 20 for the telephone number to ring for details. **Don't try to enter the ranges when the red flags are flying – you may end up dead!**

Length; 29 km (18 miles) for the full route from Enford;

15 km ( 9·5 miles) for the shorter route from Everleigh

Terrain; short route 10·5 km hard/stony track

4 km rutted track or grassy/field bridleway

0·5 km tarmac

longer route 13 km hard/stony track

13 km rutted track or grassy/field bridleway

3 km tarmac

Map; OS Landranger 184 Salisbury & The Plain

Reference Points;

short route; GR 203525 road/track junction south of Everleigh (start and finish)

210483 Dunch Hill

197466 Old Marlborough Road

longer route; GR 143517 Enford (start and finish)

188546 Lower Everleigh

203525 rd/track junction south of Everleigh

210483 Dunch Hill

197466 Old Marlborough Road

185507 bridleway/road crossing near Beach's Plantation

Facilities; Pubs in Everleigh, and in Enford (long route only)

Nearest rail station; Pewsey 10 km ('Wigglybus' minibus link possible to Everleigh)

Background

One of the most unusual experiences in Wiltshire is to visit the Army ranges (on a non-firing day when there's no danger of being hit by a stray bullet!) and to explore some of the miles of rights of way crossing areas of the Plain that for much of the year are out of bounds. I've suggested two possible routes here to cater for a range of abilities and inclinations, both centred around the Old Marlborough Road as it passes through the Bulford Ranges. One is a short and relatively easy circuit around the centre of the restricted area, mainly on hard gravel tracks, while the other is a longer and tougher ride starting and finishing down in the Avon Valley at Enford.

The Army have been on the Bulford Ranges since the turn of the century, when large areas of downland were purchased to establish the Salisbury Plain Training Area. Although access is restricted, the Army's presence has protected the areas concerned from the modern farming techniques that have turned such a large proportion of southern England's downland into an arable monoculture. Today the landscape is a mixture of grassland, pasture, scrub, and woodland plantations, criss-crossed by tank tracks and range roads that seem to be constantly appearing and disappearing – take note, this can make navigation difficult, particularly if you try to rely on one of the older Ordnance Survey maps. The military presence also adds an extra dimension to your ride, as even on a non-firing day you will be quite likely to come across a platoon of sooty-faced soldiers carrying guns, or to notice an armoured battalion hiding under camouflage netting among the trees!

Despite the mock battles that rage across the Plain during much of the year, the Ranges are also a haven for flora and fauna. The Army issues a monthly news sheet giving details of firing days and other military activity, and these also give topical information about some of the unusual species that can be seen at each time of year. In March the stone curlews are breeding; April is a good time to see the many varieties of bumblebee for which the Plain is an important habitat; in May the rare green-veined and burnt-tip orchids are in flower; and so it goes on ...

Like most downland areas, the Bulford Ranges have a wealth of prehistoric remains that have survived due to the absence of ploughing over the centuries. Tumuli abound, particularly to the south (maybe due to the proximity to Stonehenge?), and the map is covered with ancient linear earthworks and field systems. Sidbury Hill, visible to your left from the Old Marlborough Road, has an Iron Age fort hidden under all those trees.

The Old Marlborough Road itself was once the main coach road between Salisbury and Marlborough, until it was abandoned in favour of the valley roads that now link the two towns – one running along the Avon valley and through Pewsey, and the other via the Bourne valley and the Collingbournes. In the middle of the open lands of the Ranges there's an eighteenth century milepost, marking the distance as 13 miles from Salisbury and 14 miles from Marlborough – sit by it for a few minutes to admire the view, and see if you can conjure up the sound of the hoof beats as the mail coach passes on it's way north ...

## Route Description

a) Short route

Park either in Everleigh, or where the minor road to Netheravon bends sharply westwards at the edge of the restricted area (GR 203525) (**A**). Where the road bends, ride straight ahead onto the Ranges, following the gravelled range road – the Old Marlborough

Road – as it runs due south and passes to the R of a small wood on the skyline. Keep on along the gravelled road past a couple of other small wooded areas, dipping to cross a couple of shallow valleys, to reach the prominent milestone (13 miles from Salisbury) which stands to the right of the track about 3 km from the entry to the ranges.

Shortly after the milepost, take the next turn L (**B**) onto a stony track which runs up to the trees on the ridge. Bear R onto the track in front of the trees and follow the ridge. Go straight across the next Army track, and follow the main track through the beech woods which line the crest of Dunch Hill. After a short while the view opens out to your right, and you can see down over the ranges as you begin to drop downhill to meet the public road at the bottom.

Turn R onto the road. After only 300 metres turn R again into a tarmac military road leading to a rifle range. Before reaching the shooting butts fork half L into an earthy bridleway leading into the woods (**C**). This runs in a straight line through the trees, then becomes a delightful stony / grassy track through scrub-covered downland, and crosses a shallow valley before climbing back into a belt of trees on the far side.

At the next X-tracks turn R into a wide, rather rutted muddy byway – this is the Old Marlborough Road again, which runs through the trees for a while before emerging into open downland and once again becoming a gravelled range road. Follow it back to the prominent milestone, and retrace your tyre marks to the start.

b) Longer route

Start in Enford – you can park just north of the village along the minor road towards East Chisenbury, where there's a small lay-by (**E**). Ride towards East Chisenbury, then turn very sharp R into a signposted tarmac bridleway that runs back uphill, bears L and then passes a radio mast overlooking the valley. Continue to follow the bridleway as it turns into a grassy track, rather rutted in places. At the signposted bridleway junction go straight ahead along the grass-covered track which winds along the side of the valley, following the contours, until it meets a gravelled Army road coming in from the left.

Bear R onto the range road, and follow it for about 1·5 km as it drops down to a cluster of farm buildings in the valley bottom (**F**). Turn L here into another range road that runs north-east along the bottom of the valley, surrounded by rough grassland. After another 1·5 km or so, the road climbs towards the head of the valley and comes to a TJ with another range road. Go straight across, and into the grassy bridleway that leads up towards the skyline. Over the crest of the hill, you'll come to a hedged track which drops down to reach the main road at Lower Everleigh.

Immediately before the TJ with the main road, turn R into a sign-posted tarmac byway (**G**). Follow this past farm buildings, to a TJ with a gravelled range road running along the valley bottom (this is not shown on older OS Maps!) Go straight across the range road and up the grassy byway that climbs quite steeply up the opposite side of the valley. Follow this, down and up (possibly overhung by nettles in places!), to reach a lane at the back of Everleigh village. Turn L along the village street to the main road, then turn R. Almost immediately turn R again (sp. Netheravon), past the Crown Inn, to join the route followed by the short ride (above) (**A**).

Follow the route description for the short ride along the Old Marlborough Road to point (**B**), over Dunch Hill, past the rifle range (**C**), and back to the point where it rejoins the Old Marlborough Road.

Turn R onto the Old Marlborough Road, still following the same route as the short ride. However, instead of keeping straight on back towards Everleigh, turn off after about 1 km at point (**D**) – watch carefully for the turn, which is a L fork onto a grassy track just after you've crossed a shallow valley (more of a dip in the track really) which coincides with a break in the trees. The fork takes you to the left of the wood on the far side of the open area, then drops down slightly to a rough X-tracks. Bear slightly L here to cross the X-tracks and follow a muddy track along the RH side of the wood opposite. This takes you over a low ridge to a TJ with a big gravelled range road. Go straight across the road and straight up the bottom of the wide valley opposite (Bourne Bottom) – there will probably be lots of tank marks churning up the ground here, and the path may not be clear to start with; persevere however, and you'll soon pick up the wide muddy / grassy track which leads up the valley bottom.

As you continue along the valley bottom, you'll pass a small wood on the RH valley side. You can also see ahead a larger wood on the LH valley side, where the main valley bends round to the right. Follow the track up the valley ignoring all tracks branching off to left or right, aiming for the gap in the middle of this pine wood. Fork L (**H**) to pass through the gap, and pick up a stony track that climbs out of the valley on the far side of the trees.

Keep straight on for about 1 km, crossing a couple of X-tracks, until you reach a public road (when I did this ride the top end of the track was fenced off – if it still is, you'll have to turn L and reach the road further west, by the trig. point and trees of Beach's Plantation. Then turn R onto the road to rejoin the proper route). Go straight over the public road (**I**) and into a rutted bridleway running along the LH edge of a small wood. Soon cross a deeply-rutted Army track, and keep straight on following the edge of another plantation, on an indistinct grassy path. After the end of the wood the path be-comes more distinct and turns into a rutted track, running across the fields and then following the LH edge of another long thin plantation.

At the far end of the trees, turn L (**J**) along a grassy track which follows the ridge westwards. Cross a gravelled range road near to an ancient burial mound, and keep following the ridge west, on a wide grassy track. This soon turns into a proper stony track which passes a barn, then sails on along the ridge for a good 2 km (over-looking Rainbow Bottom to your right) before bumping steeply down to rejoin the Avon Valley 'back road' just south of Enford. Turn R, and it's only a few hundred metres back to the welcome sight of the 'Swan Inn'!

*Crossing Milston Down*

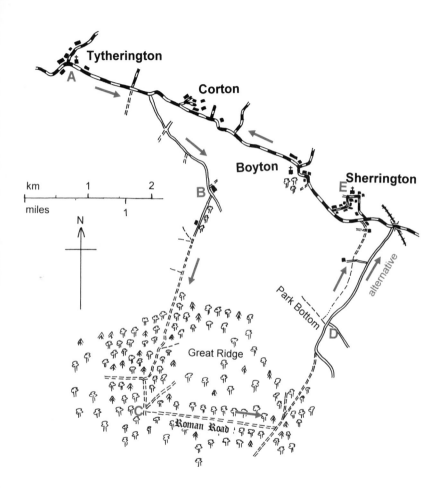

Tytherington

Corton

Boyton

Sherrington

A

B

C

D

E

km    1    2

miles    1

N

Great Ridge

Roman Road

Park Bottom

alternative

## 6) TYTHERINGTON AND GREAT RIDGE (short)

Grade; Easy/moderate. Relatively short, mostly on hard tracks or
 tarmac, but with some steady climbs.
Length; 18 km (11 miles)
Terrain;   9 km tarmac
              6 km hard/stony track
              3 km grassy track
Map; OS Landranger 184 Salisbury and The Plain
Ref Points; GR 916412 Tytherington (start and finish)
                     930364  Great Ridge
                     956374  Park Bottom
                     960392  Sherrington village
Facilities; No facilities on the route – nearest pubs to the start/
 finish are in Sutton Veny or Heytesbury (approx. 2 km)
Nearest rail station; Warminster 7 km

Background

Although only short, this route has plenty of scenic interest, from
picturesque villages and quiet country lanes to the brooding woods
which cover the Great Ridge. Although not far as the crow flies
from the villages of the Wylye Valley, Great Ridge always feels to
me to be one of the most remote areas of Wiltshire, with a sort of
mysterious silence that grows on you as you approach the long dark
line of the forest, broken only by the screech of a jay or the crash of
a wood pigeon bursting out of the trees. The crest of the ridge is
followed by the line of the old Roman road from the Mendips and
Bath to Salisbury and the south coast – a forerunner of the modern
A36 which carries endless lines of lorries and cars along the valley
several miles to the north. Away from the crest, the ridge is cut into

by a complex series of dry valleys, secluded and tree-lined, including Snail-creep Hanging, which wins my vote for the most curious place name in Wiltshire!

Back in the valley, Sherrington is a pretty village with thatched cottages and a large pond (but unfortunately no pub!), and is worth a diversion to see. Tytherington, also an attractive hamlet, has some lovely old houses, a dovecote and the 11th century church of St. James.

The route from Sherrington back through Boyton and Corton to Tytherington is on a delightful road through idyllic rural scenery. You'll probably notice the small blue signs marking the Wiltshire Cycleway, which follows the Wylye Valley 'back road' all the way from Wilton to Sutton Veny. This is part of a linked network of marked cycle routes circling the County on minor roads – there's a leaflet published by the County Council which can be picked up in Tourist Information Centres etc, or obtained direct from County Hall.

### Route Description

Tytherington to Great Ridge (Roman Road)

Take the 'back road' east from Tytherington (**A**), past St. James' Church and towards Corton. After about 1 km the road begins to climb through an avenue of beech trees – where the road bends to the left at the top of the hill, turn R onto the RUPP (road used as a public path) past a sign saying 'private road – no cars'.

Climb steadily on a stony track through the beeches, and at the X-rds go straight ahead onto the tarmac lane. This continues to climb steadily, with views of the Wylye Valley at first on your left. Ignore any turnings until, about 1 km after the X-rds, you reach some old farm buildings (**B**) & a stony track leading off R by a long row of trees. Take this turn, and follow the track and trees S towards Great Ridge.

Shortly after passing a large barn, the track deteriorates into a rough grassy bridleway for a while, until reaching a gate and becoming a wide grassy track which climbs up to the edge of the forest. Once among the trees, the track becomes more winding. Ignore a wide grassy ride that comes in from the left, and instead keep on the main track as it bends gradually to the R, then gradually L again, then more sharply to the R to a junction with a good stony track.

Turn L onto the stony track for about 500 metres. Ignore the first (sharp) L turn, but then 50 metres further on turn L onto a long straight ride – as you might have guessed, this is the Roman Road (**C**).

### Great Ridge to Tytherington

Follow the Roman Road as it runs straight as a die along the Great Ridge, a well-made track through pleasant woods which are particularly attractive in spring and autumn. After 2 km the track ends abruptly at a TJ, where you turn L onto another wide track. Before long there's a fork – take the R branch, which immediately begins to drop downhill. This is a long and fairly steep descent, and good fun – but watch out for the deep ruts cut into the path by rainwater, which can be a bit dodgy particularly in the autumn when they could be buried by fallen leaves!

At the bottom of the hill the track joins a tarmac lane, and continues on down the valley. Another 500 metres further on you come to Park Bottom where a wide side valley joins the main valley from the left, marked by a crossroads of tracks. Turn L through the gate onto the grassy bridleway that heads up into the side valley, but almost immediately turn R again along the fence towards a gate that marks the start of another bridleway that leads between hedges over the flank of the hill, parallel to the road. (If you don't like bumpy tracks, the next section can be avoided by keeping straight on  the lane at Park Bottom – this leads down after about 2 km to the road, where you turn L to rejoin the main route near Sherrington village).

If you're sticking to the 'proper' route, follow the bridleway over the flank of the hill and keep straight on, crossing a farm access road and a barn and eventually dropping to meet the road. Turn R onto the road, and immediately sharp L into Sherrington village (if you've followed the road down from Park Bottom, you'll be coming from the other direction and will need to turn R here into the village). Follow the lane as it winds through the scattered houses, bends L to pass the church (**E**) and then sharp L and R past the delightful village pond, to rejoin the 'main' road again at the end of the village. Turn R onto the road, and follow it through Boyton, past the Upton Lovell turn, past Corton and back to Tytherington.

*Tytherington Church*

*On the Roman Road by Vernditch Chase (Ride 25)*

*Dropping down towards Horningsham*

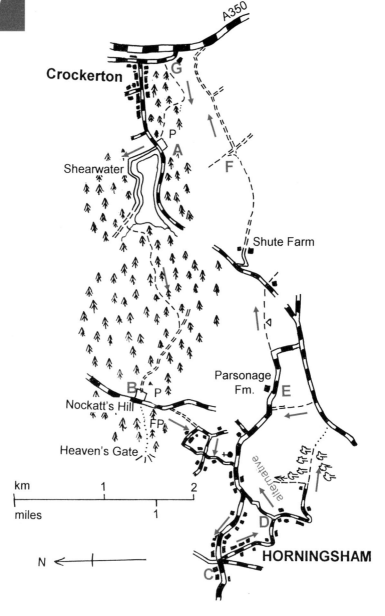

A350

**Crockerton**

G

P

A

Shearwater

F

Shute Farm

Parsonage Fm.

E

B P

Nockatt's Hill

FP

Heaven's Gate

alternative

D

km          1          2

miles          1

N

C

**HORNINGSHAM**

## 7) SHEARWATER AND HORNINGSHAM

Grade; Easy/moderate

Length; 15 km (9 miles)

Terrain;   5 km hard/stony track

             5 km grassy track/field or forest bridleway

             5 km tarmac.

*The track from Shearwater to Nockatt's Hill is not a public right of way, but Longleat Estate have kindly given permission for its use. Please make sure to give way to pedestrians and horse riders – the aggressive behaviour of mountain bikers has caused real concern for older pedestrians here on a number of occasions in recent years.*

Map; OS Landranger 183 Yeovil and Frome

Ref Points; GR 854420 Shearwater carpark (start and finish)

               828423 Nockatt's Hill carpark

               810417 Horningsham (Bath Arms)

               843412 Shute Farm

               864419 road/bridleway junction near Crockerton

Facilities; Pubs in Horningsham, and Crockerton (300 metres off the route). Shop/P.O. in Horningsham. There's also a convenient Tearooms next to the carpark at Shearwater!

Nearest rail station; Warminster 5 km

Background

Although short, this route is hilly and includes some genuine off-road bits. It's not too difficult, but slow down, take it easy and admire the scenery if you're new to the game.

There's certainly plenty to see. Shearwater Lake, surrounded by trees at the edge of the Longleat Estate, is a popular picnic spot and also hosts a sailing club. There are waymarked walks through the forest, one of which is followed by the ride as it climbs steadily towards Nockatt's Hill. Here you're not far from Heaven's Gate, the classic viewpoint overlooking Longleat Park from which the full splendours of the House and it's grounds can be taken in. Longleat House was built by Sir John Thynne (ancestor to the current owner, Lord Bath) in the 1500s. It has been extensively modified in later centuries, and the park was landscaped by the famous Capability Brown in the eighteenth century. Although there's no cycle access to Heaven's Gate, it's an easy stroll of less than 1 km each way along a path flanked with specimen trees, and if you're not in a hurry it's well worth the effort. Listen carefully while you're there and you might just hear a lion roar in the Safari Park below!

Horningsham is a gem of a village, to my mind one of the most attractive in Wiltshire. Scattered along the roads and lanes in the upper reaches of the valley in which Longleat Park sits, it's really more like a collection of small hamlets joined together, with small stone cottages and their tiny gardens tucked in among the steep contours and patches of relict woodland. The woods around here were once part of the vast Selwood Forest, which although not wholly covered by trees stretched from Stourhead and Zeals in the south, on the Dorset border, all the way to Chippenham in the north.

### Route Description

Shearwater to Horningsham

Start from the carpark opposite the entrance to Shearwater Lake (**A**). Cross the road into the entrance, past the toll booth, and follow the tarmac lane past the end of the lake and the sailing club. Continue on around the lake shore and past a barrier at the end. Before long turn L off the tarmac onto a gravel track, sp. Nockatt's Hill Car Park.

Follow the gravel path as it climbs steadily through the forest, ignoring any smaller tracks leading off it. After about 1·5 km it meets a larger track coming in from the left – bear R onto this and keep going for a further 1 km to the carpark (**B**). If you want to walk to Heaven's Gate, leave your bike here and cross the road to the well-signed footpath opposite.

To continue the ride, turn L onto the road. Before long take the first turn R into a signposted stony bridleway, and after a quick pause for the view of Horningsham nestling in the valley ahead, bounce down the steep track to the edge of the village. Keep straight on where the track joins a tarmac lane, then turn R by the red telephone box. Plod uphill, then turn sharp L at the small X-rds. A down and an up will bring you to a TJ by the church. Turn R onto the 'main' road and follow this through the village to the Bath Arms (**C**).

Horningsham to Shearwater

In front of the Bath Arms is a complicated 5-point junction. Take the first L, (sp. to the Village Stores and Post Office), and keep going past the old chapel (dating from 1556). 500 metres further on the lane bends sharply left (**D**) – instead go straight ahead, past the 'No Through Road' sign, and follow this lane a further 1 km to the field gate at the end.

Go through the gate, and keep straight on following the bridleway along the RH side of the wood. There's a muddy bit at the far end of the woods, then the path climbs to the L of the stream (another muddy bit) to reach a gate in the far corner of the field. Turn L into the road, then after 300 metres turn L again into a grassy track which after 500 metres reaches another road. Turn R to pass Parsonage Farm (**E**).

[If you want to miss out the muddy sections by the wood, keep to the road after passing Horningsham chapel. Ignore the lane with the

'No Through Road' sign, and instead stick to the road as it bends L at point (**D**). At the TJ with the main village road bear R, and follow the road past the village church again. Keep straight on, and in 1 km you'll rejoin the main route at Parsonage Farm. (**E**)]

Pass Parsonage Farm, and after 750 metres the road bends sharply right. Instead go straight ahead to follow a grassy field edge bridleway. This passes a trig. point, and then rejoins the road. Turn L. After 500 metres turn sharp R into the access road for Shute Farm. Climb steeply up the valley side, pass the farm and go through the gate into the track which continues in the same direction. This becomes a field edge bridleway – with several more gates to slow down progress!

Watch out when the track you're on appears to bend to the left (**F**), towards the forest on the skyline. You **don't** want to go this way – the track you're after (a grassy green lane running between high hedges and bracken) goes straight ahead, parallel to the forest boundary, but you'll need to turn R (onto a track running towards the valley) and immediately sharp L again to find it.

Follow the green lane (ignore the farm track going off to the right a little further on), and after 1·5 km it will drop you down steeply to meet the main A350 road. Turn L, then almost immediately turn L again, sp. Crockerton and Shearwater. Soon turn L yet again, into the signposted bridleway marked 'Longleat 1/2 mile' (**G**). Follow this up the edge of the wood. At the top of the hill it bears R into the wood (there's another muddy section here, but it's only short!), crosses the crest of the ridge and drops steeply down to the Shearwater carpark.

*Beech-lined avenue, Grovely Wood*

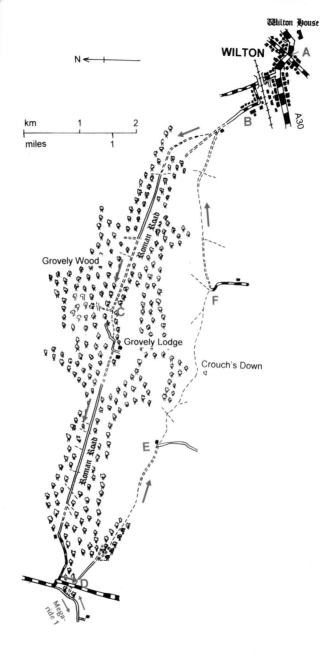

8

N ←—|—————

km    1    2

miles    1

Wilton House

WILTON

A

B

A30

Roman Road

Grovely Wood

C

Grovely Lodge

Crouch's Down

F

E

D

Mega ride 1

## 8) GROVELY WOOD

Grade; Easy / moderate. Easy going out through Grovely Wood, but tougher and more undulating on the way back along the Drove Road.

Length; 21 km (13 miles)

Terrain; 7 km hard/stony track

7 km rutted/grassy track

7 km tarmac

Map; OS Landranger 184 Salisbury and The Plain

Ref Points; GR 096313 Wilton Town Centre (start and finish)

049341 Grovely Wood

006348 road/track junction W end Grovely Wood

043327 Crouch's Down

Facilities; No facilities on the route itself, but Wilton has everything you would expect in a small town.

Nearest rail station; Salisbury 5 km

Background

This is a ride of two contrasting halves – the first being an easy spin (after the initial steep climb out of Ditchampton) along the flat and well-made hard track through the centre of Grovely Wood, and the second a more testing ride back along the old Western Drove Road, which cuts across the several dry valleys (coombes) that run south from the ridge. The scenery also offers a contrast, with quiet woodscapes and long tree-lined avenues to begin with, giving way to wider views across open farmland on the return leg.

The ride starts in Wilton, the ancient capital of Wessex and still a pleasant little town although now rather swamped by traffic. It's famous for its carpet factory, now with a big shopping village next door, and for the impressive grandeur of Wilton House, seat of the Earls of Pembroke. There's also an intriguing Italianate Church which you'll pass at the start of the ride.

Grovely is part of what was once a much larger mediaeval hunting forest, and at its western end is only separated by a couple of miles from the equally large Great Ridge woods. If you want a longer and more demanding day out, combine this ride with another – see Megaride 1 on page 197 for details!

Like Great Ridge, Grovely Wood is traversed for its full length by the old Roman 'Lead Road' from the Mendips – hence the straightness of the track you'll be following! In places you can also see remnants of Grim's Ditch, winding in a more circuitous manner through the trees. This is an old defensive earthwork, much like the Wansdyke which runs across the middle of Wiltshire and is followed by several of the other routes in this book, and the Bokerley Ditch on the Hampshire/Dorset border which features in route 25. The similarities with the Wansdyke even extend to its name, 'Grimm' being another name for the god Woden, after whom both are called.

Grovely Wood's other claim to fame lies in the ancient custom of Oak Apple Day, in which the villagers of nearby Great Wishford every year reassert their right to cut and collect wood in the forest, marching in procession to the wood and chanting "Grovely, Grovely, and all Grovely" – something to watch out for if you're in the area at the end of May!

South of the Wood lies the old Western Drove Road, which you'll follow on the way back. This is one of several old drove routes converging on Salisbury, which, lying where several ridges meet, was a natural focus. Routes led on from there to London – in these days of international food transport it's hard to think that in the days before the railways arrived, and more recently refrigerated transport, cattle used to be driven 'on the hoof' in huge herds to London and other big cities from the Somerset Levels, the Welsh Marches and other good livestock rearing areas in the west of the country. The drovers would be on the road for long periods at a time and needed food, drink and accommodation in the towns and villages along the route – you'll pass the site of an old drover's inn (the 'New Inn') by the side of the track miles from anywhere at GR 026335, although there's little to mark the spot now. You can also see the old milestones at intervals along the side of the track – for example, there's one by the junction of tracks at GR 057324, showing you that it's not too far back to the car!

### Route Description

Wilton to Grovely Wood

Park in one of the town centre carparks (**A**). There's also roadside parking in The Hollows if you prefer, cutting out the first 1 km through the town. Follow the A30 past the Italianate Church, then fork R (sp. Great Wishford). Immediately beyond the railway bridge turn L into The Hollows. Continue round the bend and past Wilton Middle School (**B**). Keep straight on at the end of the houses, where the road turns into an unsurfaced byway flanked by beech trees.

Climbing along the beech-lined track, you'll come to some farm buildings on the left. Ignore the track branching off to the left just past the farm, and then immediately fork R towards Grovely Wood along a narrower track bordered by high hedges. At the end, continue into the wood and follow the dead-straight road which runs along the centre of the forest, lined by magnificent beech trees.

This track continues as straight as a die for nearly 3 km, partly unsurfaced and partly tarmac, and then bends sharply to the right (**C**). At this bend leave the hard track and go straight ahead into a much narrower signposted bridleway which continues as single-track through the trees for about 500 metres before meeting the forest road again.

Turn L onto the tarmac, follow the bend round to the R, then where the road bends left again  towards Grovely Lodge continue instead straight ahead (past the Forestry Commission sign) into another long, straight tarmac lane which runs the full length of the western part of the Wood. Keep going dead straight for 3·5 km to the barrier at the far end of the Wood.

## Grovely Wood to Wilton

Continue straight on past the barrier, bear L past a large barn (keeping to the tarmac) and follow the lane for about 1 km to the junction with the public road. You meet the road  on the corner of a Z-bend; turn L, and spin downhill through the trees for about 400 metres to a junction with a tarmac lane on the L (**D**).

Turn L into the lane [Megaride 1 joins and leaves the route here], which runs along the edge of the wood and then across fields. After 500 metres you reach the edge of the woods again – fork R into a hard earth track, which then bears L to run just inside the edge of the wood. This bit is rather rutted, particularly where it drops downhill just before leaving the trees and turns into a grassy track along the bottom of the combe.

Passing the site of the 'New Inn' the track becomes more solid, down to a large barn by a track junction (**E**). Take the rutted muddy track straight up the slope opposite, and follow it as it widens out, over the brow of the hill. Keep going straight on, ignoring any turns off to right or left, as the Drove road winds up and down across the slopes below the edge of Grovely Wood, bearing R past the trees on Crouch's Down and then descending again to a track junction below Barford Down (GR 057324) (**F**).

Ignore the tarmac road going off to the right and the bridleway signposted left towards the woods, and instead climb the hard un-metalled track which bears slightly L ahead. Once again, keep following the Drove Road straight ahead and after another 2·5 km you'll come to a wide avenue of beech trees. This will lead you back to the track which climbs out of Ditchampton – turn R at the TJ by the farm buildings, and it's downhill all the way back to the car.

*Salisbury Plain, near Compton*

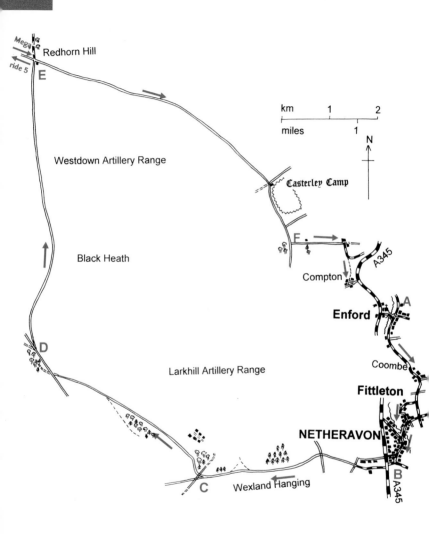

Redhorn Hill

Mega

ride 5

E

Westdown Artillery Range

km    1    2

miles    1

N

Casterley Camp

F

Black Heath

Compton

A345

A

**Enford**

Coombe

D

**Fittleton**

Larkhill Artillery Range

**NETHERAVON**

C

Wexland Hanging

B
A345

## 9) OVER THE RANGES - LARKHILL AND WESTDOWN

Grade: Easy/moderate. Mainly on hard tracks, & with no steep climbs (but several long steady grinds!). The route runs through the Larkhill & Westdown Artillery Ranges – see page 20 for how to find out about access. Make sure it's a 'no firing day' before you set out, or risk a wasted journey! If you want a longer day, see Megaride 5 (page 199) which combines this ride with route 11.

Length; 28 km (17·5 miles)

Terrain; 18 km hard/stony track

9 km tarmac

1 km grassy bridleway

Maps; OS Landranger 184 Salisbury & The Plain, and 173 Swindon & Devizes

Ref Points; GR 143517 Enford (start and finish)

147487 Netheravon

107477 junction of Army tracks

074490 junction of Army tracks

060553 Redhorn Hill (vedette)

112538 Casterley vedette

132521 Compton

Facilities; Pub in Enford, pub and shops in Netheravon.

Nearest rail station; Pewsey 10 km

Background

This ride will take you deep into the heart of Salisbury Plain, through the middle of the Larkhill and Westdown Artillery Ranges. It's an eerie place, miles of empty grassland and scrub, wind and sky, and the rusty hulks of the burnt-out tanks and army trucks that are used as targets for the big guns. The army have been on Salisbury Plain since the turn of the century, buying their first land in 1897 and then taking over larger areas between 1897 and 1902. More land was acquired during the last war, when the village of Imber (a few miles further west) was evacuated and remains a ghost village, used by the soldiers to practice close range fighting. Unlike Larkhill and Westdown where there are rights of way open for public access when firing is not taking place, the Imber Ranges are permanently closed except for one or two days a year when the former inhabitants are allowed to return and visit the village and church.

One effect of the Army's occupation of the Plain has been to preserve it from the ravages of modern agriculture. While vast areas of former chalk downland elsewhere in the country have succumbed to the plough, the Salisbury Plain Training Area is still home to many now uncommon grassland plants and creatures. There are no less than five Sites of Special Scientific Interest, and the whole of the Plain area is designated as a Special Landscape Area. The Plain is also rich in ancient monuments, with numerous burial mounds, field systems and other earthworks. The Army are becoming more aware of their heritage, and as well as encouraging access at permitted times, publish information on conservation in their monthly access news sheets.

The second part of the ride runs along the ridgeway on the north edge of the Plain. On your right are the warning notices marking the edge of the Army ranges, while to your left are views over the Vale of Pewsey to the high downs of Tan Hill and Milk Hill. Look out for the White Horse carved into the hillside opposite, above the village of Alton Barnes.

Casterley Camp, where you begin to turn south into the Avon valley, is an ancient hill settlement which has been dated to the 1st century A.D. – these days there isn't much to see except for a ring of low earthworks among fields, but it's a reminder of the days when the ridgeways were important lines of communication and defence; an important consideration in choosing where to live.

The valley of the Avon provides a contrasting start to the ride, following the quiet 'back road' through the pretty villages of Enford, Coombe and Fittleton. Before the bleak windswept expanses of the Plain, enjoy the rural tranquillity of thatched cottages, meandering river and water meadows on the first few miles down to Netheravon.

## Route Description

Enford to Redhorn Vedette

Start in the pretty village of Enford – parking is difficult in the village itself, but there is a small lay-by just out of the settlement, by the minor road which runs N to East Chisenbury. Follow the minor road S through Enford (past the Swan Inn), and continue through the hamlet of Coombe. Turn R at the sp. to Fittleton. At the end of the village turn R again and cross the river into Netheravon.

At the far end of the village (**B**), turn R (sp. Amesbury and Salisbury) to the main road. At the main road turn L, then immediately R into a tarmac lane which climbs gradually towards the Plain.

After passing the Army checkpoint (**strictly no entry beyond this point if the red flag is flying**) the lane becomes an unsurfaced track. About 500 metres beyond the checkpoint, bear slightly L to cross a wide gravel Army road, and continue to follow the unsurfaced track along the wide, shallow valley of Wexland Hanging. Surrounded by rough pasture and rectangular stands of young conifers, the landscape around here feels remote, and makes me think more of northern hills than southern downland!

This feeling increases as you wind further up the valley into the heart of the Ranges. Continue for about 2·5 km, past the wide side valley of Well Bottom to your right, until you reach a junction of tracks marked on the far side by four white concrete blocks (**C**). Before the blocks, bear R, cross another track at right angles and continue to bear slightly R to follow the track that bends round the LH end of the small wood, climbing out of the valley onto a flat plateau. Stay on this track for nearly 4 km, past the woods of Shrewton Folly on the left, to another major track junction at the far end of the ridge.

Turn R onto the big track that runs dead straight to the north-west. After 750 metres, you'll come to a fork, incongruously marked with a large white fingerpost (**D**). Follow the RH fork (sp. Devizes), which climbs gently but steadily onto the high Plain past Black Heath and Chirton Gorse. This part of the ranges is used as an impact area for artillery shells – it's a strange landscape of tall whispering grass and scrub, littered with the rusting remains of tanks, and the track is lined with signs warning you not to leave the road or touch anything, on pain of death! The track through this wilderness is well-made and solid, a mixture of rough tarmac and some unsurfaced sections, but there's a steady gradient all the way to Redhorn vedette, almost 6 km further on (**E**).

Redhorn Vedette to Enford

[Megaride 5 – page 199 – joins and leaves the route here].

Approaching the vedette (an Army blockhouse marking the edge of the artillery ranges) you'll see with relief that you've reached the highest point of the ride, overlooking the Vale of Pewsey and, beyond, the Pewsey Downs. Turn R past the vedette, and follow the hard track along the ridgeway, bowling along easily for the next 5·5 km to Casterley vedette.

Here there's another army blockhouse. Bear R past this, following the track parallel to the low earthbank that marks the west side of Casterley Camp. The track dips steeply down and up – ignore the first track to the left, but take the second track approx. 300 metres further on (sp. 'Byway, Ridgeway Path') (**F**). Follow this for 1 km. to the large barn visible on the skyline.

At the barn turn R following the tarmac lane. When the lane bends left (past a sp. 'No access to the public'), go instead straight ahead onto a bumpy grassy bridleway that drops steeply down to the hamlet of Compton. Turn L by the houses and follow the track to the main road.

Turn R along the road (take care – busy main road), and after 1 km turn L into the minor road sp. East Chisenbury/Enford. This will bring you back into Enford near The Swan.

*Near Four Barrows*

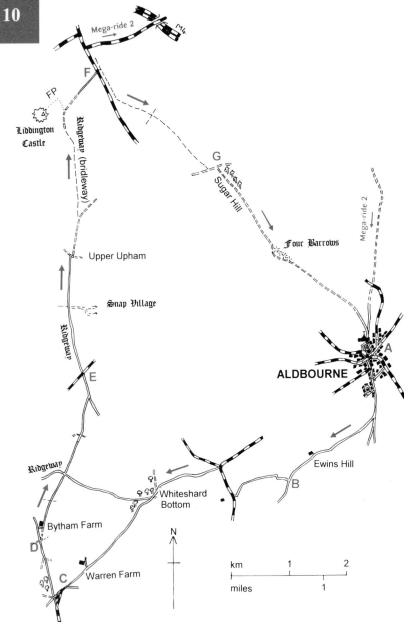

Mega-ride 2

M4

F

FP

Liddington
Castle

Ridgeway (bridleway)

G

Sugar Hill

Four Barrows

Mega-ride 2

Upper Upham

Snap Village

Ridgeway

E

Ridgeway

A

ALDBOURNE

Ewins Hill

B

Whiteshard
Bottom

Bytham Farm

N

km          1          2

miles          1

D

C          Warren Farm

## 10) ALDBOURNE, THE RIDGEWAY AND SUGAR HILL

Grade; Easy/moderate. Mainly reasonably easy going, although with several steady climbs and (as anywhere on the Downs) the possibility of sticky mud after wet weather.

Length; 25 km (15·5 miles)

Terrain;   6 km tarmac

       10 km stony track

        9 km field bridleway/grassy track

Map; OS Landranger 174 Newbury and Wantage

Ref points; GR 264757 Aldbourne village centre (start and finish)

              208729  Bytham Farm

              213797  Liddington Hill

              241785 Sugar Hill

Facilities; Pubs, shops and tea shop at Aldbourne

Nearest rail station; Swindon 10 km

Background

This route follows tracks, field bridleways and a section of the Ridgeway long distance path, and explores some of the pleasant downland to the south-east of Swindon.

Aldbourne, where the route starts, is a pleasant village which used to be famous for its bell foundry – many of Wiltshire's church bells were made here. There's a very attractive village square in front of the church, which has the largest Norman doorway in Wiltshire, and also is home to two 18th century fire engines called Adam and Eve.

The part of the Ridgeway path followed on this route is not the original ancient trackway, which runs directly across the lower ground from Barbury Castle (south of Swindon) to just north of Liddington Hill. Nevertheless, it is a fine route with good views and enjoyable riding. If you want a longer ride exploring more of the Ridgeway, Megaride 2 on page198 combines this route with ride 13.

An interesting historical curiosity not far from the Ridgeway (between Bytham Farm and Liddington Hill) is the abandoned village of Snap. There are many places in England where you can see the ridges and hollows marking the site of a village abandoned in the Middle Ages – usually as a result of the Black Death, or where the fields were grassed over to make way for more profitable sheep – but Snap is different. Here is a village abandoned at the start of the present century, a victim of the agricultural depression of the late Victorian period when cheap grain imports from America undermined British production. It's a reminder that the history of the countryside is still in the making.

At Liddington Hill we're back with ancient history again – another large and impressive Iron Age hillfort, and reputedly the site of King Arthur's victory against the Saxons at the Battle of Badon. The hill also has more recent historical connections though, as it was a favourite haunt of the nineteenth century countryside writer and local historian Richard Jefferies – standing by the trig point you can imagine his feelings when he wrote;

"By the time I had reached the summit I had entirely forgotten the petty circumstances and annoyances of existence. I felt myself. I was utterly alone with the sun and the earth."

### Route Description

Aldbourne to Bytham Farm

Starting in the centre of Aldbourne (**A**), take the minor road signposted Ogbourne and Marlborough which turns L off the Swindon road. Immediately turn L again (by the Post Office) following signs for Axford and Marlborough. Where the road bends to the R, keep straight on along the Butts, past some charming 'Olde English' thatched cottages. At the next junction go straight on again into South-ward Drive, past a playing field on the L.

Climbing fairly steeply out of the village, fork R (keeping to the tarmac byway) and cast a glance to your right as the view of Aldbourne and the Downs beyond unfolds below. Stay on the tar-mac for another 1·5 km, past the house at Ewin's Hill, and then turn R on a wide gravel bridleway through the trees (**B**).

After 1 km you will come to a minor road – turn R, and then before long (where the road bends to the R) turn sharp L following the signpost "byway to Whiteshard Bottom". This is tarmac at first, but soon turns to gravel, and there's a good fast stony descent to the valley bottom. Ignore several byways signposted off to the R (in-cluding one temptingly signed 'to the Ridgeway' – you could use this as a short-cut if you want to cheat!), and keep straight on, up and down as the byway turns several times from gravel to tarmac, and back to gravel again.

About 4 km after leaving the road you come to a fork in the track (by now tarmac again), by some large grain silos (**C**). Fork R (in practice more like straight ahead), and follow the tarmac track through the silos, to a X-rds with a gravel track. There's a wooden finger post here – turn R, following the arm pointing towards Ogbourne. Keep straight on at the next track junction, but then fork R at the signposted byway crossroads just before Bytham Farm (**D**). The next 100 metres is very muddy, but soon improves and turns back into a solid gravel track as you pass to the right of the Farm.

Bytham Farm to Aldbourne

Keep straight on again past the farm entrance, and after about 1 km the route joins the Ridgeway Long Distance Path which climbs up from the valley to the west. The navigation is easy from here to Liddington Hill – just keep straight on, following the well-marked National Trail as it crosses a minor road (**E**) (the deserted village of Snap is only a mile away to the east here), and jinks R and L to cross a byway signposted Upham. Some parts of the track around here are a bit rutted, but they are generally quite rideable!

Just before the final climb to Liddington Hill, the Ridgeway Path divides, with the route for motor vehicles forking off right down to the main road. Our way keeps to the high ground, following the grassy Ridgeway bridleway as it drops slightly and then climbs the flank of Liddington Hill. The bridleway doesn't actually go to the summit of the hill, but instead veers away to the right. There is however a permissive footpath to the trig. point, so if you want to admire the view or look at the hillfort you can leave your bike and walk – it isn't far.

Keep to the bridleway as it curves to the R and passes a clump of trees, than dives steeply down as a gravel track to reach the main road (**F**). [Megaride 2 leaves the route at this point]. Push your bike over the road and climb the stile directly opposite, turning R on the signposted bridleway to Sugar Hill. This follows the field edge parallel to the road before curving L and climbing a pleasant grassy ridge, with views opening out on all sides. Through several small gates, and continuing to climb, you eventually reach a large and rutted byway crossing the ridge. Turn L, then after 200 metres R onto another byway (**G**) which follows the edge of a wood, along the ridge of Sugar Hill. Don't dawdle here – the hill isn't named after sweetness and light, but from the old 'Shuger Waie' (Robbers' Road), where unsavoury characters would lurk waiting to attack lone travellers!

It's straightforward from here back to Aldbourne – follow the path down the ridge, after a while skirting the 'Four Barrows' (Neolithic burial mounds in which cremated remains, two skeletons, a dagger and arrow head and several other implements were discovered), then straight on along the wide grassy drove road that leads downhill to the village. Back in Aldbourne you'll pass the pretty square in front of the church, where the `Blue Boar' is a tempting stop for refreshment and recuperation.

*View from Bratton Camp*

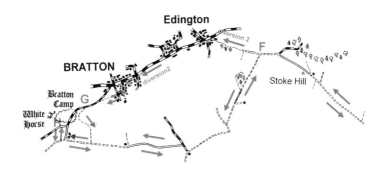

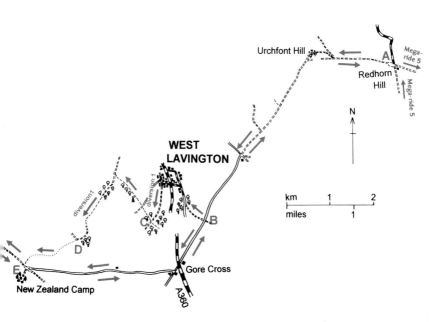

## 11) URCHFONT HILL & THE WESTBURY WHITE HORSE

Grade; Easy/moderate, or moderate/hard, as you choose
Length; 42 km (25 mls) out and back along the ridgeway path;
      46 km (29 mls) including the diversions on the way out
Terrain; there and back on the ridgeway path and Perimeter Path;
      25 km hard/stony track
      17 km tarmac
    Longer route including diversions;
      23 km hard/stony track
      16 km tarmac
      7 km rutted track or grassy/field bridleway.
Maps; OS Landranger 184 Salisbury and The Plain, and 173
    Swindon & Devizes.
Ref Points; GR 060553 Redhorn Hill (start and finish)
          999527 Strawberry Hill (long route only)
          956527 Stoke Hill
          915524 Bratton village (long route only)
          900515 Bratton Camp
          009509 Gore Cross
Facilities; Pubs in Edington and Bratton, and shops in Bratton, on
the long route. Also a pub in West Lavington – turn R on the main
road before crossing into Rickbarton. In summer there's usually
an ice cream van at Bratton Camp.
Nearest rail station; Westbury 4 km


Background


You can make this ride as easy or difficult as you want. Choose
either a straightforward out-and-back along the hard tracks of the
Urchfont Hill ridgeway and Imber Ranges Perimeter Path, or if you

want more of a challenge you can add in one or both of the 'diversions' which will take you onto less-frequented bridleways to explore some of the combes that cut into the northern edge of Salisbury Plain. The diversions don't actually add much in the way of distance, but there are several steep hills and with the rougher surfaces as well it feels a lot further! For a real killer, try Megaride 5 on page 199 which combines this with route 9.

Both the longer and shorter routes give good views in all directions. To the north are panoramas over the clay vales of central Wiltshire, scattered with villages and small towns, and with the chalk hills of the Pewsey Downs, and the wooded sandstone ridges towards Chippenham, clearly visible. To the south there are tantalising glimpses into the empty interior of Salisbury Plain, largely out of bounds due to the military training area. Many of the hilltops on the Plain are graced by attractive clumps of trees – their attractiveness is not a matter of chance, most being the result of thoughtful planting by landowners in the eighteenth century, when the 'landscape improvement' championed by Capability Brown and others like him was in vogue.

The ridgeway over Urchfont Hill is not part of the official Ridgeway Path, but is thought to be a continuation of the route used by prehistoric man which follows the line of easy movement offered by the relatively lightly-wooded chalk downland across southern England. The long-distance path today finishes at The Sanctuary, near Avebury, but is linked by roads and footpaths across the Pewsey Vale to the paths which follow the northern edge of Salisbury Plain.

At the far end of the ride, Bratton Camp is a large and well-preserved Iron Age hillfort. It's a popular spot, with a large carpark, and can get busy at weekends and in the summer. Nevertheless, it's a good spot to rest for a while, and the view from above the White

Horse must be one of the finest in West Wiltshire. There are often hang-gliders or radio-controlled model aircraft soaring and swooping above the hillslope to give added interest.

The White Horse is one of Wiltshire's best-known landmarks, and can be seen for miles around. Some claim that it's also the oldest in Wiltshire, and was carved to commemorate King Alfred's victory over the Vikings at the Battle of Ethandune in 878 A.D. – the battle having taken place near modern Edington. Others dispute this; however, whatever its age there is no doubt that the Horse was remodelled in the eighteenth century, apparently in part so as not to offend genteel society, the original being very obviously a male! These days the Horse is covered in cement for protection, and is kept bright, white and visible from afar by regular coats of whitewash.

### Route Description

Redhorn Hill to Bratton Camp along the ridgeway track and Perimeter Path (easy route)

Park at the top of Redhorn Hill, by the army checkpoint (**A**), and set off westwards along the wide stony track towards Urchfont Hill. Before reaching the circular wood on top of the hill (about 1·5 km after Redhorn) you'll come to a fork. The stony track goes straight ahead, cutting across a corner of the Army ranges, so turn **half** R onto another hard track that bends around to pass the RH side of the clump of trees and then curves back to rejoin the original track (don't take the full right turn, or you'll find yourself heading rapidly downhill!).

Follow the ridgeway track again, passing Lavington Vedette where the track becomes tarmac, and spin steadily downhill (past point **B**) to reach the main road at Gore Cross 3 km further on.

Go straight across the road into the tarmac track opposite, then immediately fork R. Climb steadily back up onto the Plain and along the ridge. Bear R where the tarmac ends, 3·5 km further on by New Zealand Farm (a small Army camp hidden in the trees) (**E**), and continue along the wide stony track for another 2·5 km to Stoke Hill. Keep straight on past the barn and trig. point, and follow the track (now tarmac again) as it descends. Where the tarmac road turns right, keep going straight ahead following the stony track. 500 metres further on there's a byway junction (**F**) – turn L here towards the wood on the skyline.

Follow the track dead straight for 1·5 km, then turn L at the TJ and almost immediately R again to follow the track along the edge of the ranges to the Army checkpoint at the head of the minor road coming uphill from Bratton.

Turn R past the checkpoint, then L again to climb back up onto the ridge (tarmac at first, then stony track). Keep going along the edge of the ranges on the Perimeter Path for 3 km, until you reach a cluster of farm buildings with a radio mast. Turn R immediately past the buildings to reach the car park at Bratton Camp (**H**).

Alternative (more difficult) route from Redhorn Hill to Bratton Camp, including 'diversions'

Follow the same route from Redhorn Hill until you're about 1·5 km past Lavington vedette. As the slope begins to steepen, you'll come to a X-tracks (**B**) next to a signboard marking the edge of the Salisbury Plain Training Area (SPTA). Turn R onto a farm track which drops downhill, joins a tarmac lane and passes through a wood to the edge of West Lavington. After passing two houses, turn L into a narrow lane and drop down to the main road.

Cross carefully, straight over the main road into Rickbarton, another narrow lane that climbs steeply past more houses. At the TJ with White Street turn L into a signposted bridleway that runs back out of the village and past cultivated fields. About 1 km further on, turn R at a signposted X-tracks (**C**) into a narrow, tree-lined bridleway. This is deeply rutted at first, and climbs to cross a stony track before passing the radio mast on Strawberry Hill and dropping down past the RH side of a wood (there's another rutted section here).

At the end of the track turn L at the TJ, and climb past the SPTA signboard along a bridleway that follows an old sunken lane up through the shrubs – engage first gear, it's a stiff climb! At the top the way follows a wide grassy track along the ridge, and then bears L down towards a small wood in the valley bottom. Just before the wood you join a steep, deeply-rutted track which passes to the R of the trees. The hard track then bends to the right (**D**) – leave it, and go straight ahead along the bottom of the valley following wheel marks in the grass. These will lead you the full length of the valley, following the valley bottom and then climbing steeply up the head of the combe. At the top, bear L and follow the fence to rejoin the main route near New Zealand Farm Camp (**E**).

Follow the main route for the next 3·5 km, past Stoke Hill to the sp. byway junction 500 metres past the end of the tarmac section (**F**).

Here the main route turns left – go straight on instead. The stony track begins to drop steeply, and deteriorates into a narrow sunken path hemmed in between hedges and deeply eroded by running water. This bit is technical, and definitely not for the fainthearted! At the bottom the path emerges into a lane – bear R to reach the main road, then turn L onto the road and follow it into Edington.

Keep going on the road to Bratton, 1 km further on. Just past the Duke Inn turn L into The Butts. At the top turn R into Upper Garston Way, and where this dips down to a X-rds with a narrow tree-lined lane, go straight across into the lane sp. 'Bridleway to Bratton Camp'.

The lane passes some houses, then becomes a narrow bridleway between hedges, and continues climbing until it joins the road which leads to Bratton Camp.

Turn L and climb steadily up towards the Camp. Just before you reach the lower edge of the earthworks you'll see a grassy bridleway forking off to the L (**G**). Take this, and follow as it contours as a sunken track around the head of the combe. Where the track starts to bend R away from the combe, spare a moment to admire the lovely view back towards Bratton – the fields in the bottom of the combe seem to lap up against the rougher valley slopes like waves against the cliffs. Then follow the track as it winds through an area of grass and rabbit warrens to a gate, leading into a fenced track heading to the interior of the Plain. This soon meets the Perimeter Path again – turn R to rejoin the main route, and after 500 metres R again by the radio mast to reach the carpark at Bratton Camp (**H**).

Return route from Bratton Camp to Redhorn Hill, along the Perimeter Path and Ridgeway (both routes)

This is the reverse of the outward route. Go back to the buildings by the radio mast, turn L, and follow the Perimeter Path to where it meets the road coming up from Bratton. Turn R, then L by the checkpoint. Further, follow the bend to the L and turn immediately R, then straight on past the wood on the left. Turn R at the TJ, (**F**) climb to Stoke Hill and keep straight on to New Zealand Farm Camp (**E**). Fork L onto the tarmac track and continue along and down to Gore Cross.

Straight over the main road, up the long steady climb past (**B**) to Lavington vedette, then straight on again along the ridge to the clump of trees on Urchfont Hill. Follow the track that curves round the LH side of the wood, and back up to rejoin the army track on the ridge. Turn L, and it's not far back to Redhorn Hill.

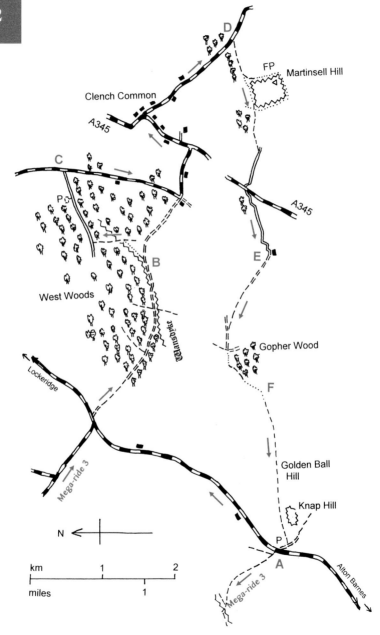

D

FP    Martinsell Hill

Clench Common

A345

C

P

B

West Woods

Wansdyke

Lockeridge

Mega-ride 3

A345

E

Gopher Wood

F

Golden Ball
Hill

Knap Hill

P

A

Alton Barnes

Mega-ride 3

N

km        1        2

miles        1

## 12) KNAP HILL, WEST WOODS & MARTINSELL HILL

Grade; Moderate. A mixture of forest tracks, minor roads and grassy ridgeway. Some bits may be muddy after wet weather.
Length; 20 km (12·5 miles)
Terrain;   8 km tarmac
           3 km hard/stony track
           9 km grassy bridleway or forest track
Map; OS Landranger 173 Swindon & Devizes
Ref Points; GR 116638 Knap Hill carpark
            156660 West Woods
            175642 Martinsell Hill (bridleway)
            130639 Golden Ball Hill
Facilities; No facilities on the route; the nearest pub to the start/finish is the Barge Inn at Honey Street (GR101616).
Nearest rail station; Pewsey 5 km ('Wigglybus' minibus link possible to Alton Barnes, at foot of Knap Hill)

Background

This route offers a pleasant contrast between the forest tracks of West Woods, and the wide open vistas of the Tan Hill Way, which overlooks the Vale of Pewsey from Martinsell Hill and the crests of Oare Hill, Golden Ball Hill and Knap Hill.

West Woods were once part of the royal hunting grounds of Savernake Forest, which in the early Middle Ages covered a much wider area than they do today. The woods are at their best in spring, when parts are carpeted with bluebells, or in autumn when the leaves turn golden and form a crisp blanket on the ground (watch out for the tree roots and ruts hidden underneath!). There is a carpark and a network of waymarked footpaths, but the woods are large enough never to seem busy, and there are several other bridleways which can be explored if you enjoy biking on forest tracks.

Like many of the hilltops in Wiltshire, Martinsell is crowned by an Iron Age hillfort, and as the hill juts out to dominate the Vale, the trig. point on the end commands a great view. The bridleway skirts the back of the earthworks, but a footpath, which you can push your bike along if you want to savour the view, follows the crest of the slope past the trig. and rejoins the bridleway further on. Martinsell Hill was once the site of an annual Palm Sunday Fair, which continued until 1860 when the tradition was abandoned after developing a reputation for rowdiness. One strange custom at the Fair was sliding down the hillside on horses' jawbones – personally I'm happy to stick with my mountain bike!

The ride over Golden Ball Hill is one of my favourites – grassy downland dotted with grazing sheep, sustained views all the way, and a swooping descent at the end past Knap Hill. Only one problem – there's a gate halfway down, which is bound to be closed.

If all this isn't enough for you, why not keep going and combine this ride with route 21? See Megaride 3 on page 198.

### Route Description

Knap Hill to Martinsell Hill

Park at the small carpark at the foot of Knap Hill (**A**) (a convenient start point which avoids the steep climb up from the valley!). There are inviting bridleways from here in all directions, but to start this route keep to the road and head north towards Marlborough. Follow the road for 3 km, to the junction with the road to East Kennett. [Megaride 3 joins the route here]

Just past the junction turn R onto a rutted byway climbing uphill towards a radio mast in the trees at the top. Follow the track straight on into West Woods – still deeply rutted at first, and with big puddles after rain, but gradually getting easier. Keep straight on as the track crosses two narrow valleys. At the top of the climb from the second, the track jinks R then L to run along the edge of the woods with an earthbank to your left (this is the Wansdyke, an ancient earthwork which features in several other rides in this book).

Before long you'll come to a path junction where the track bends to the right, and the Wansdyke curves away left into the woods (**B**). Turn off the main track and follow the bridleway alongside the Dyke, keeping the earthbank to your left. Dodge the tree roots and fallen branches until after about 500 metres you come to a TJ with a wider (signposted) bridleway. Turn L to cross the Dyke, and follow the bridleway to its junction with the main forest drive. Turn R, and whizz along the hard surface past the main carpark and picnic area and down the access drive to the public road at the entrance to the Woods (**C**).

Turn R onto the road, and follow it 2 km up the valley, round a right-angle bend to the L, and another 750 metres to meet the main Marlborough–Pewsey road. Turn L and follow the main road for 750 metres (busy road – mind the traffic!). At Clench Common turn R onto a minor road (towards Wootton Rivers) and follow this for nearly 2 km to a small carparking area on the R, just before the road begins to descend steeply down to the valley (**D**). This is the carpark for Martinsell Hill, which you can see beyond, standing proudly overlooking the Vale of Pewsey.

Martinsell Hill to Knap Hill

Turn R through the carpark and through the gate, and follow the grassy bridleway past the trees towards Martinsell. At the end of the

*Springtime in West Woods*

*The final descent past Knap Hill*

trees, the footpath to Martinsell Hill bears left uphill, but the bridle-way goes straight ahead across the grass, passing to the R of a clump of trees before bearing L uphill. When you come to the north side of the earthworks, follow these R to a gate, straight on through the gate, and straight on again at a X-tracks (sp. Oare Hill). There's a short 'technical' section through the woods (a winding single-track path through the trees), before joining a gravel road with good views over Rainscombe House nestling at the foot of the scarp.

Follow the gravel road down to the main road, and cross straight over (take care!) into another gravel track which goes round a series of right-angle bends before ending by a house (**E**). Go straight on through the gate and follow the rutted bridleway along the crest of Huish Hill until it drops down to Gopher Wood.

Cross another bridleway at the corner of the wood, and go straight ahead through the gate, up the hill (through a field parallel to the edge of the wood), and bear L on a grassy bridleway to another gate at the top. Follow the north edge of the wood, and at the next gate (at the far end of the wood) bear half–L across the grassy field to a clump of bushes on the skyline (**F**). When you reach these, turn R to follow the grassy track along the crest of Golden Ball Hill – 2 km of delightful ridge riding, before the final plunge down past Knap Hill (the earthworks on its flanks are a Neolithic Causewayed Enclo-sure, thought to be a seasonal meeting area dating back to 3500 B.C.), to the carpark.

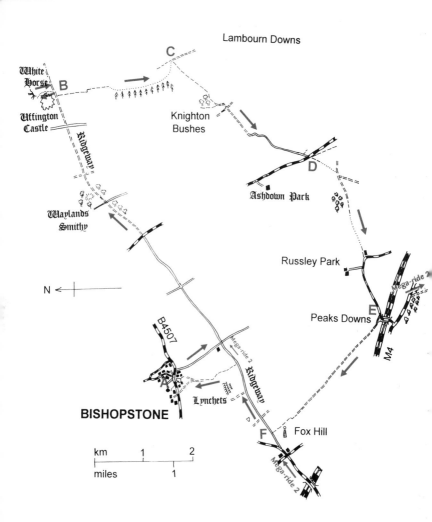

Lambourn Downs

C

White Horse

B

Uffington Castle

Ridgeway

Knighton Bushes

D

Ashdown Park

Wayland's Smithy

Russley Park

N

Mega-ride 2

E

Peaks Downs

B4507

Mega-ride 2

Ridgeway

M4

A

Lynchets

BISHOPSTONE

F

Fox Hill

km      1      2

miles        1

Mega-ride 2

## 13) BISHOPSTONE, THE RIDGEWAY AND UFFINGTON WHITE HORSE

Grade; Moderate. Generally reasonably good tracks, but several steady climbs and some bumpier sections to test your stamina.
Length; 25 km (15·5 miles)
Terrain;   3 km tarmac
            9 km hard/stony track
            13 km grassy track/field bridleway
Map; OS Landranger 174 Newbury & Wantage
Ref points; GR 245837 Bishopstone village (start and finish)
                301864 Uffington Castle
                298827 Knighton Bushes
                258794 Peaks Downs
                235816 Foxhill
Facilities; Two pubs in Bishopstone, and one 500 metres off-route at Foxhill (Shepherd's Rest, GR 231813).
Nearest rail station; Swindon 12 km

Background

A good section of this ride follows the Ridgeway Long Distance Path. (Megaride 2 combines this route with ride 10 to explore an even longer section of the Ridgeway). Reckoned to be one of the oldest trackways in Europe, the Ridgeway follows the crest of the chalk downland from Dorset, through Wiltshire and Berkshire, and eventually north-east to East Anglia. This is the way that Stone Age man travelled c.12,000 years ago, following  the easier land of the chalk ridges. The Neolithic farmers who built the Avebury monuments also penetrated England using tracks like the Ridgeway, their settlements spreading from the S Coast c.6,000 years ago. The dense forests that covered the clay lowlands were cleared long ago, and the chalk ridges are no longer important communication links – abandoning the Ridgeway to recreational walkers, the occasional 4WD vehicle, and bikers like you and me! Since the Ridgeway Path became a National Trail, the Countryside Commission have 'improved' several sections to create a hard stony surface. I confess to mixed feelings – it makes for easier cycling than on other sections with mud & ruts, but inevitably at the cost of the sense of adventure.

A parallel ancient route, the Icknield Way, follows the foot of the Downs and can be seen in the name of the main road through Bishopstone village. Bishopstone is an attractive village in which to start and finish the ride, with thatched houses built from local 'clunch' (a soft chalky building material), a peaceful millpond, and a choice of pubs. In the combe behind the village are some very well-preserved strip lynchets – mediaeval fields terraced into the hillside, so that crops could be grown on the steep slope.

Along the Ridgeway you'll pass two famous ancient sites. The first is Waylands Smithy, a Neolithic chambered long barrow similar in design to the one at West Kennett and built c.2800 B.C., which is hidden in a small wood just off the track. The curious name is much more recent, bestowed by the later Saxon settlers after their god Wayland the Smith who, according to legend, will shoe the horse of any traveller who leaves a coin on the lintel of the tomb overnight.

A couple of miles further is Uffington Castle, another of the imposing Iron Age hillforts that lie on the crest of the Downs. Just below the Castle, carved on the N-facing slope of the Downs, is the Uffington White Horse. This is thought to be the oldest chalk figure in the country, and is said to be c.3,000 years old – though as it's very difficult to date a scratch in a hillside it may be older still. To see anything of it, you'll need to go beyond the trig. point to the edge of the hill – but the best views from the valley below. Best to stay where you are and look down instead over the expansive panorama spread out in front of you.

## Route Description

Bishopstone to Uffington Castle

Park in the village (**A**) and point your bike eastwards, as if to follow the main road towards Ashbury. In the middle of the village, turn R up a tarmac lane signposted Russley Down. To get you warmed up, there's a good climb for the next 1 km, up to Ridgeway Farm.

Just past the farm buildings, turn L onto the Ridgeway Path, which provides a good hard surface for most of the way to Uffington Castle ( the ruts in the 'softer' sections can generally be avoided fairly easily). Watch out for Waylands Smithy, sheltering in the trees on your left after about 4 km, which is worth a visit.

There's a stiff climb up to Uffington Castle, which dominates the highest point on this section of the Ridgeway. Just past the earthworks there's a gate on the left (**B**) – go through this and follow the bridleway past the trig. point until you reach the edge of the hill, from where you should be able to see the White Horse directly below. There are also fine views over the Vale of White Horse to reward your efforts. When you've taken in the distant panorama, look down at the funny flat-topped hill straight ahead, just below where you're standing – this is called Dragon Hill, and according to legend is where St. George made a name for himself by slaying the beast!

Uffington Castle to Peaks Downs

Retrace your steps past the trig. point and onto the Ridgeway Path (**B**). Backtrack for a short distance past the edge of the hillfort, but almost immediately turn L onto a signposted bridleway which follows the field edge down a long ridge away from the Castle. Jink L then R, then when you reach a long line of trees bear R to ride parallel to the trees, following the short white posts that mark the edge of the racehorse gallops. At the far end of the trees bear L again, following the fence to a junction of bridleways (**C**).

Turn **sharp** R here to bounce down Whit Coombe, towards the clump of trees (Knighton Bushes) visible at the bottom. Skirt to the left of the trees, then follow the bridleway as it turns L then R. At the next junction (a crossroads of tracks) go straight ahead, following the byway sign that points uphill – this one is quite a stiff climb! At the top, the track bears L by a lone sarsen stone, levels out, and then begins to descend, gently at first and then increasingly steeply as you swoop down to the road at the bottom (**D**).

Cross straight over the road, and through the gate opposite to follow the public bridleway straight ahead (not the byway that veers away to the left). After a good start, the path becomes rather indistinct – don't worry, but keep straight on, aiming for the track that you can see climbing steeply up the hillside ahead. Much to your relief no doubt, you don't actually have to ride up this skull-splitter – at the bottom of the hill you'll meet a well-defined bridleway crossing your path from left to right. Turn R on this to run parallel to the foot of the slope, passing to the left of Botley Copse and then straight on across grassy fields for about 1·5 km.

Eventually you'll come out (by a small bungalow) onto a bend in a minor road. Turn R on the road and climb steadily to the bridge over the M4 at Peaks Downs (**E**). [Megaride 2 leaves the route here]

Peaks Downs to Bishopstone

Just before the motorway bridge, turn R onto the bridleway that

*Park Bottom*

climbs gently along the ridge towards Fox Hill. Don't be deceived by the straight, wide track and easy gradient – the whole of the next 3 km has been covered in soft woodchippings which, while good for horses, seem designed to sap the energy of cyclists!

Just before the radio masts on Fox Hill, jink R then L, and carry on past the masts over the crest of the hill to drop down to rejoin the Ridgeway (**F**).

Turn R onto the Ridgeway Path [Megaride 2 joins the route here], climb past the summit of Charlbury Hill (the trig. point visible on your left) and then whizz downhill again. At the bottom of the dip turn L through a small gate into a signposted bridleway towards the head of a steep-sided combe [unless you're following the Megaride, in which case continue along the Ridgeway]. Follow the bridleway down the bottom of the combe, eventually reaching a gate into a track. After a slight climb take the LH fork, then drop down to the road. Turn R into Bishopstone village.

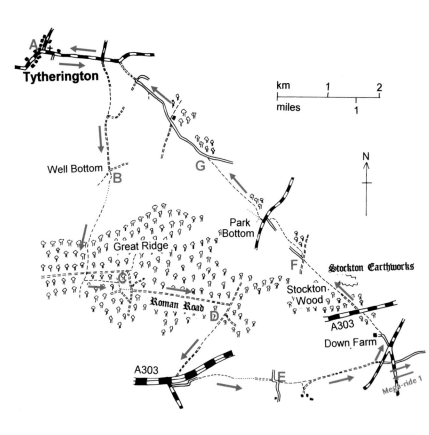

Tytherington

Well Bottom

B

G

Great Ridge

C

Roman Road

D

Park
Bottom

F

Stockton Earthworks

Stockton
Wood

A303

Down Farm

A303

E

Mega-ride 1

km          1          2
miles              1

N

## 14) TYTHERINGTON AND GREAT RIDGE (LONG)

Grade; Moderate. Longer than route 6, and with a higher propor-
tion of grassy or muddy tracks, but nothing too difficult.
Length; 25 km (15·5 miles)
Terrain; 14 km grassy track/field or forest bridleway
        6 km hard/stony track
        5 km tarmac
Map; OS Landranger 184 Salisbury and The Plain
Ref Points: GR 916412 Tytherington (start and finish)
             922364 Great Ridge (forest bridleway/track junction)
             939343 Chicklade Bottom
             980351 Down Farm
             956374 Park Bottom

Facilities; No facilities on the route – nearest pubs to the start/
finish are in Sutton Veny or Heytesbury (approx. 2 km)
Nearest rail station; Warminster 7 km

Background

The ride starts and finishes at the same place as route 6 – by the
attractive little eleventh-century church of St. James in Tytherington
– but the two routes only have a short section in common. Anyway,
I make no apologies for visiting Great Ridge twice in this book, as
it's one of my favourite areas of Wiltshire. W.H. Hudson described
it at the turn of the century as 'wild and solitary', and it still feels
like that today. Perched on the divide between the Wylye and Nadder
valleys and far from any roads (except the A303 which speeds long-
distance traffic past its eastern end), you can spend hours in the
huge wood without seeing a soul. And if you tire of the woods, there

are interesting tracks along the secluded dry valleys leading up to the ridge with occasional wide views over the valleys and Downs to the north or south. There's plenty of wildlife up here – you'll often see deer bounding away through the trees, and when recce'ing the ride for this book I came across a badger rooting by the side of the track in broad daylight. In spring the woods are carpeted with blue-bells, and later in the year the autumn colours make for a scenic ride.

Great Ridge may be remote from modern civilisation, but this was not always so. The long straight track down the centre of the woods follows the line of a Roman Road – called the 'Lead Road', because it was used to carry the produce of the Mendip mines to Salisbury, and then to the South Coast where it was shipped over to the continent to supply the Roman Empire. Later on the ride you'll also pass Stockton Earthworks, a late Iron Age settlement occupying a broad promontory backed by Stockton Wood, and commanding superb views north over the Wylye Valley.

One other piece of history worth mentioning concerns the track that you'll follow east from Chicklade Bottom. Although the first part seems like a normal field bridleway, it soon becomes a wide green lane surrounded by hedges, marching purposefully across the countryside as if it used to have more importance than it does today. It is in fact part of the Western Drove Road, which used to be a busy route for cattle on their way from the farms of the Somerset Levels to Salisbury and London. Although abandoned once the railways took over it's role of transporting animals to market, much of the old road is still traceable on the map, and often makes a great biking route. Route 8 follows the same Drove Road further east (if you want a more testing ride, you can link these two routes together as in Megaride 1 on page 197), and you'll also meet it as it runs over the crest of White Sheet Hill to the west if you attempt route 23.

## Route Description

Tytherington to Chicklade Bottom

Park by the telephone box in Tytherington (**A**), and take the road E towards Corton. After 1 km, turn R into a signposted bridleway opposite the junction with a small minor road. Follow the bridleway as it winds up a long dry valley, climbing gently towards the woods that you soon see ahead, brooding on the crest of Great Ridge. The bridleway starts as a wide track, then becomes narrower and more rutted for a while, before joining a hard stony farm track. Where the hard track ends (at an X-tracks) (**B**), go straight on, climbing steeply on a grassy bridleway that climbs up the low ridge straight ahead.

At the top, follow the RH edge of the field along the ridge towards the woods. Go downhill and then steeply up again, still following the edge of the field. Enter the woods past a signpost with a map showing the Great Ridge rights of way, and follow the bridleway through the trees (this bit can get very muddy – you'll probably have to push part of the way after wet weather).

After 750 metres you'll come to an X-tracks with a gravelled forest road. Go straight across, continuing along the muddy track, then after a further 200 metres turn L into a straight grassy ride (this follows the line of the old Roman Road). Continue for about another 750 metres to an X-tracks with a well-defined earth track (**C**), and turn R (you'll know if you overshoot this junction, as the 'Roman Road' loses it's straight alignment and begins to wind more through the trees). Just before reaching the TJ with a forest road, turn L to follow a bridleway which, after 250 metres, meets another forest road near a junction of tracks. ( This section of bridleway was difficult to follow at the time of writing due to forestry operations, but is due to be reinstated.)

At the junction of tracks, take the wide, straight track which runs straight ahead, once again following the public bridleway along the line of the Roman Road – which runs for 2 km directly through the centre of the woods. At the far end turn R at the TJ, fork R shortly afterwards at the next junction (**D**), and follow the track out of the woods into open countryside. After a glance at the view, swoop downhill across the fields to meet the A303 at Chicklade Bottom.

Chicklade Bottom to Stockton Earthworks

Cross the busy dual carriageway into the minor road opposite, then turn immediately L through a metal gate into a tarmac lane running parallel to the A303. The lane soon bends sharply to the left, but ignore this and instead go straight ahead along a field edge bridleway. (At the time of writing there were no bridleway signs marking rights of way in this area, but small white 'Monarch's Way' stickers on gateposts were a useful guide to the next section of the route). The bridleway climbs a gentle ridge, then bends gradually to the R away from the A303, keeping to the field edge. Through the gate at the top, go straight on across a grassy field, bearing slightly away from the fence on the RH edge to reach another gate at the far side (with a Monarch's Way sticker) leading into a hedged track.

The route follows this track (part of the old Western Drove Road) in more or less a straight line for the next 3 km, cutting across a tarmac farm track after about 1 km (**E**) and becoming a wide green lane between hedges, before eventually coming to a TJ with the Chilmark road [Megaride 1 leaves the route here]. Turn L onto the road for about 400 metres, then turn L again into the track leading to Down Farm.

Next to the farm go straight ahead into a grassy bridleway past the farm entrance. Follow this for 500 metres to the A303.

Cross the extremely busy road (be sure to wait for a suitable gap in the traffic, which approaches very fast!) into the track which continues on the far side, towards Stockton Wood. After a short muddy section through the edge of the woods, the track emerges through a gate onto grassy downland next to Stockton Earthworks.

Stockton Earthworks to Tytherington

The earthworks are a good place to pause for a rest, and to sit on the grass with the sheep, contemplating the peace and quiet and admiring the views over the Wylye Valley towards Salisbury Plain. When you've polished off the last of your rations and emptied your drink bottle, remount and continue along the byway, now a track across open grassland. After 500 metres this crosses a hard track which leads away downhill to the right (**F**). Go straight ahead through the gate into a tarmac lane, but immediately turn R off the tarmac and cross the grass towards the edge of the small wood. Turn L and follow the grassy path which runs alongside the fence next to the wood (this is in fact the right of way – the tarmac lane is a private farm road – and is in any case a much more interesting route).

At the end of the wood the path continues across the field, becoming a delightful sunken grassy track which starts to descend ever more steeply through the shrubs, bends to the L and rejoins the tarmac lane at the bottom of the hill in Park Bottom.

Go through the gate, turn L into the road on the far side, and then immediately R off the road and through another gate. Bear slightly R to climb the chalky bridleway up the side of the valley ahead, passing to the L of a wood as you climb. Follow the track straight ahead across the fields, along a ridge from which you can see the woods of Great Ridge across the combe to your left. After 1 km the

*The descent to Park Bottom*

track reaches a gate leading onto a farm road (**G**) – bear L onto the road and follow the tarmac straight ahead for another 2 km.

Where the tarmac turns right (at a X-tracks) keep straight on into a stony track. Bounce and rattle downhill to meet the road, turn L and spin easily back along the road to Tytherington.

*Bridge over the By Brook*

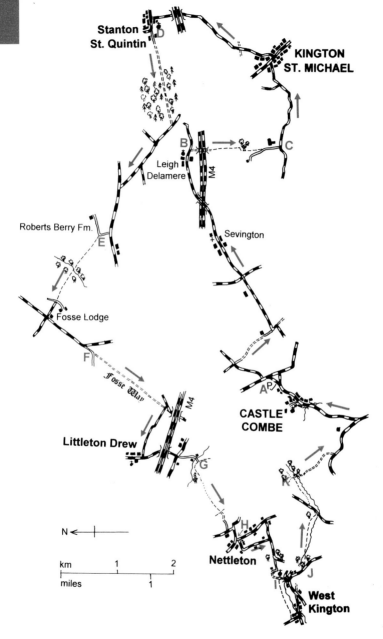

Stanton
St. Quintin
D

KINGTON
ST. MICHAEL

B
Leigh
Delamere
M4
C

Sevington

Roberts Berry Fm.
E

Fosse Lodge

F
Fosse Way

Littleton Drew
M4

CASTLE
COMBE
A P

G

K

H
Nettleton

J
West
Kington
I

N ←

km          1          2
miles              1

## 15) CASTLE COMBE AND THE FOSSE WAY

Grade; Moderate. Don't be fooled by the pretty villages and high proportion of tarmac – once off the roads it's not easy going. Not recommended after wet weather.

Length;   33 km ( 20·5 miles)

Terrain;   19 km tarmac

      4 km hard/stony track

      10 km field/wood bridleway or rutted track

Map; OS Landranger 173 Swindon and Devizes

Ref Points; GR 846777 Castle Combe Visitors' Carpark (start and finish)

           884792 Leigh Delamere

           907798 Stanton St. Quintin

           857820 Fosse Lodge

           813776 West Kington Church

Facilities; Pubs and shop in Castle Combe

Nearest rail station; Chippenham 9 km

Background

This part of Wiltshire is very different from the chalk downlands in the centre and south of the County – here you're in the southern end of the Cotswolds, with warm honey-coloured limestone oozing from every village and hamlet. Castle Combe is a showpiece village, a collection of quaint and attractive stone cottages nestling in the wooded valley of the By Brook, famous for it's market cross (which shows that it was once a more important place than today), and for the fact that it was used as the setting for the filming of 'Doctor Dolittle' – during which it masqueraded as a seaside village! The price for being an 'unspoilt' Cotswold village is, of course, that it attracts thousands of visitors from all over the globe (particularly Japanese and Americans) who make sure that it is now no longer unspoilt. Nevertheless, it's still a pleasant place to look around when you've finished your ride (did I say finish? – don't forget that Castle Combe is in a valley and there's a long steep hill back to the carpark !).

You'll pass through several other attractive villages on the way round – West Kington, Nettleton and Stanton St. Quintin all have their fair share of pretty stone cottages, as do the hamlets of Sevington and Leigh Delamere. Watch out for the old School House in Sevington – although it's many years since falling pupil numbers led to its closure, it's now been restored as a Victorian period piece and is visited by classes of Primary School children from all over Wiltshire, who dress up for the day and learn what school used to be like a hundred years ago.

Predating all the picturesque Cotswold architecture is the Fosse Way, which can be seen striding across the map on its straight line route between Bath and Cirencester. The Fosse was one of the main thoroughfares of the Roman occupation, linking the major Roman towns of Exeter, Cirencester, Leicester and Lincoln. Much of the old Roman road is still in use to this day, but in this part of north Wiltshire a long stretch has fallen into disrepair and is now a rough byway. You'll follow in the steps of the Roman soldiers for a short way between Fosse Lodge and Fosse Gate (near Littleton Drew).

The countryside in this part of Wiltshire is typical of the Cotswolds, with wide open agricultural landscapes cut into by occasional steep-sided river valleys. You'll meet the By Brook and it's tributaries a couple of times on your trip – usually with a steep hill down followed by an equally steep one up the other side! The woods and meadows along the winding and intimate valleys make an appealing contrast to the open landscapes and dry-stone walls of the limestone plateaus in between, and will also ensure that you finish the ride fitter – or at least more tired – than you were when you started!

## Route Description

Castle Combe to Stanton St. Quintin

Start from the well-signposted visitor's carpark at Castle Combe (**A**), just off the B4039 road which passes the edge of the village. Turn L out of the carpark entrance back to the B4039, turn L again onto the main road and then almost immediately R into a minor road sp. Grittleton. Continue for nearly 1 km, then turn R into a signposted byway. This starts as a good stony track, but soon degenerates into a muddy, rutted track through trees – you'll probably have to get off and push in places.

Continue at the far end into a lane, then at the junction with a minor road turn L. After 1 km there's an X-rds; go straight across, sp. Sevington and Leigh Delamere. Continue through Sevington, over the M4 motorway, to Leigh Delamere. Just past the church (**B**) turn R into a signposted bridleway which crosses back over the M4. Just beyond the bridge, there's a gate – go straight ahead down the edge of the grassy field, following the hedge. At the far end of the field go through the bridleway gate and straight on across another field. Next to the wood at the far end of this field, bear R through the gate, then bear L again to continue past the wood and on across the field in the same direction as before. The path soon meets a farm lane – follow this straight on over a cattle grid, and past a large farm to meet the public road (**C**).

Turn L and follow the road to Kington St. Michael (1·5 km). At the TJ in the village turn R, then almost immediately turn L again sp. Stanton. Follow this road to Stanton St. Quintin (2 km).

Stanton St. Quintin to West Kington

Turn L at the TJ in Stanton. Where the road bends right, by the church (D), continue straight ahead into a signposted bridleway which runs as a concrete track past Stanton Manor Farm and then becomes a stony track across the fields. It then continues straight on through the woods of Stanton Park – this bit may be slightly muddy at first, but it's fairly solid underneath and shouldn't be too much of a problem. Keep going to the far end of the woods where you rejoin the road.

Turn R onto the road. Ignoring a right and then a left turn, keep straight on to reach a TJ after 1·5 km. At the TJ turn L, then after a further 1 km (where the road begins to bend slightly to the left) turn R into a tarmac farm drive. After 250 metres the tarmac bends to the right (**E**) – instead, go straight ahead into a grassy green lane running between hedges. Continue along this track across the fields. After about 1 km there's a difficult section where the track crosses a wooded valley – the way becomes a narrow and stony single-track path through the trees, dropping steeply down to the stream, and followed by a steep and rather technical climb up the other side. I bet you'll be pushing up here!

Once out of the other side of the wood the path widens again, and continues straight on along the edge of a field before meeting the track from East Dunley Farm. Go straight on along the tarmac lane, to a TJ with the Fosse Way by the curious tower of Fosse Lodge. Turn L onto the Fosse Way, here a minor road. Follow the tarmac road straight on for 1 km, then where the road bends left continue straight ahead on the line of the Fosse Way, as the Roman Road becomes first a lane and then, when the lane bends to the right (**F**), continues straight ahead as a byway. The byway is deeply rutted at first and very muddy, but fortunately improves a bit further on –

although it is rutted all the way, you can usually avoid the worst by riding along the edge or middle of the track.

After 2 km the byway ends at a TJ with a minor road. Turn R towards Littleton Drew. At the TJ on the edge of the village turn L and continue under the M4 bridge to another TJ. Go straight across into the tarmac bridleway that drops down through the trees to a house by the river. Cross the footbridge at the far end of the yard, then turn immediately R (**G**) to follow the river bank on a grassy path that soon bears L and climbs steeply uphill past the edge of a wood. At the top go through a small gate, and bear L across the field away from the wood's edge towards a stone wall running along the skyline, following the far edge of the field. Follow the wall to another gate – go through, then continue straight across the next field on a rather indistinct path following a slight ridge in the ground. This path leads to another stone wall, which you follow to a gate hidden in the far corner of the field, next to a bridleway junction signpost. Bear L through the gate to follow the stony track which leads to the road.

Turn L on the road, then R at the TJ to Nettleton. In the village turn L (**H**), then immediately turn R again (sp. West Kington). Turn R again at the next TJ, still heading towards West Kington. Just past the West Kington village sign, turn R into the drive which leads towards the church. Follow signs for the church, which lead round to the R behind the farm buildings and then L again across the farm yard to reach the small carpark next to the church itself (**I**).

West Kington to Castle Combe

Turn R through a gate from the church carpark to cross a small paddock, leading to a field gate on the far side marked with a blue bridleway arrow. Go through this, and follow the field edge bridleway which overlooks the village of West Kington nestling in the valley below. After 1 km meet a minor road, and turn L to drop steeply downhill into the far end of the village. Turn L again at the TJ at the bottom of the hill, then climb to a trailing junction and bear L (sp. Nettleton and Burton). Descend again to the river, but just before the bridge turn R into the minor road sp. Castle Combe, and follow the road along the valley and into the woods.

After 500 metres bear L into a signposted bridleway (**J**). There's a rather muddy bit down to the river, then, after crossing the water, a grassy track across open fields along the valley bottom. Where this path meets a road crossing the valley, turn L. Halfway up the hill turn R into another signposted bridleway. This is very rough and narrow at first, but persevere – it soon improves, and although still single-track is mainly quite rideable, and runs along a delightful secluded valley. After 750 metres you come to a clearing (**K**) where the path drops down into the trees by the river. Cross the river on an old clapper bridge, then get into low gear for the long steep bridle-way climbing out of the valley on the other side. See if you can ride all the way to the top!

Breathe a sigh of relief as the gradient levels out, and follow the stony track to the road. Turn L through the woods. At the TJ 1 km further on, turn sharp L towards Castle Combe and spin easily down-hill to reach the village. Go slowly down the narrow main street, admiring the picturesque cottages and watching out to avoid knock-ing over some of the many tourists who'll be wandering along the road doing the same. If you stop for a pint, don't forget that al-though you're nearly back there's another steep hill out of the vil-lage! (to get back to the start follow the road through the village, keeping to the R of the Market Cross, and fork L at the top of the hill to find the carpark).

*Forest track near Bramshaw Telegraph*

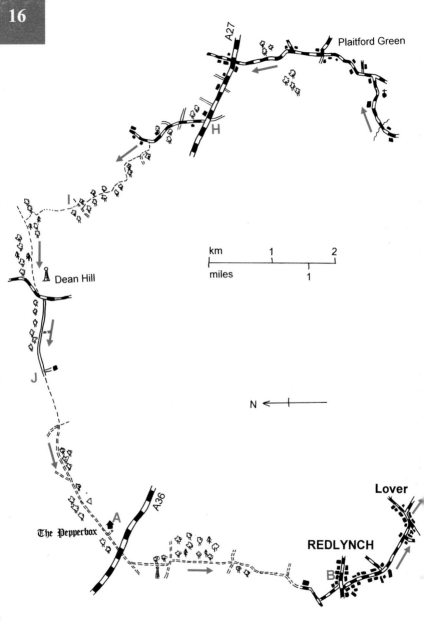

A27

Plaitford Green

H

I

km    1    2
miles    1

Dean Hill

J

N

Lover

The Pepperbox

A36

REDLYNCH

A

B

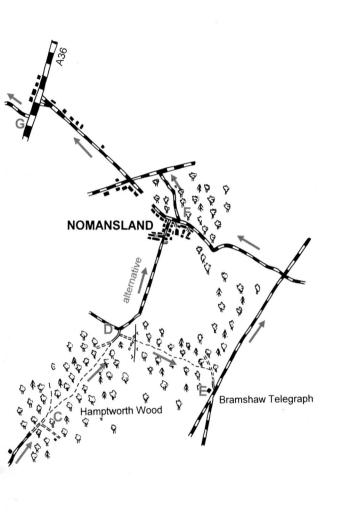

## 16) PEPPERBOX HILL AND NOMANSLAND

Grade; Moderate. A fairly high proportion of road makes the first half of this ride quite fast. The single-track section climbing up on to Dean Hill, and some muddy tracks through the woods, make the latter part more demanding.

Length;   32 km ( 20 miles)

Terrain;   18 km tarmac

     4 km hard/stony track

    10 km field/wood bridleway or rutted track

Map; OS Landranger 184 Salisbury and The Plain

Ref Points; GR 212248 The Pepperbox (start and finish)

       202213 Redlynch (Kings Head)

       228167 Bramshaw Telegraph

       253173 Nomansland (Lamb Inn)

       284226 Sherfield English P.O. (on A27)

       251259 Dean Hill

Facilities; Pubs in Redlynch and Nomansland. P.O./Stores at Sherfield English, where the route meets the A27 (the shop is just up the minor road on the opposite side of the A27).

Nearest rail station; Dean 2 km

Background

This SE corner of Wiltshire is unlike the rest of the county, and along the border with Hampshire has a New Forest feel to it. The woods here lie on sandstone rather than chalk, and in spring and early summer are colourful with purple rhododendron. At Bramshaw Telegraph you're in New Forest heathland, and in Nomansland (actually just in Wiltshire), the ponies graze on the village green against a backdrop of cool green deciduous woodland.

The geology has a more direct benefit to bikers too – although the woodland tracks can still get muddy and waterlogged after wet weather, at least it's normally sandy mud rather than the glutinous clay that binds up your wheels and brings progress to a halt!

Dean Hill is more familiar territory, being formed from a long ridge of chalk which pushes up through the sandstone. It's similar in many ways to the downland ridges further north, complete with a ridgeway track offering good views over the Test Valley, the villages of West Dean, East Grimstead and Farley nestling at the foot of the hill, and the woods – remnants of the mediaeval hunting forest of Clarendon. As you round the flank of Dean Hill on the way back to The Pepperbox, watch out for the distant view of Salisbury Cathedral's tall spire soaring gracefully skyward, and think of the tremendous skill and effort that was involved in planning and building such an impressive edifice eight hundred years ago.

Pepperbox Hill, where the ride starts and finishes, is now owned by the National Trust. The curious octagonal building near the summit was built in 1606 by the Eyre family, apparently as a gazebo from which they could observe the hunting in the valley below. It's certainly a good viewpoint, with an orientation table giving distances and directions to all the landmarks visible on the horizon – a good place for a rest at the end of the ride!

Although the route has a higher proportion of tarmac than I'd have liked – due to the frustrating shortage of bridleways in this far south-eastern corner of the County – it's not all easy going. Some of the tracks (particularly where they pass through woodland) are deeply rutted and can be muddy, and the section of single-track climbing up to Dean Hill is waylaid by tree roots and overhung by vegetation – full leg and arm cover is recommended in summer when the nettles are out! If it was smooth going all the way, though, wouldn't life be boring?

**Route Description**

The Pepperbox to Nomansland

Start from the National Trust carpark on Pepperbox Hill (**A**) (just off the A36) and ride back down to the main road. Take extreme care crossing straight over into the byway directly opposite. After 100 metres, fork L into a rutted byway to pass the radio mast and continue straight on along the hard track. A few hundred metres further on, turn L at the track TJ, then immediately R again into another rutted track that runs along the RH side of a wood.

Ignore tracks turning into the wood. After c.1 km go straight on at the X-tracks along the stony track, passing a farm after 1·5 km. Continue straight on into the tarmac lane, then before long turn L at the next junction to enter Redlynch next to the Kings Arms (**B**).

Cross straight over the main road into Princes Hill, and follow for 1·5 km to Lover (pronounced with a long 'o'). Keep straight on where the road from Woodfalls joins from the right, then soon turn R into Black Lane. This runs for 1 km past small hedged fields and pretty cottages until it enters the forest and becomes a rutted bridleway. Go straight on past a junction where the main track turns right, then watch out for a fork where the bridleway bends slightly left and a slightly smaller bridleway continues more or less straight ahead (**C**). Take the R fork (straight ahead) through the trees. The first part of this section is a delightful track winding through deciduous 'New Forest' woodlands – further on, the way becomes more deeply rutted and waterlogged, and although it's 'sandy mud' you may need to push round some of the bigger holes and puddles.

At the far end of Hamptworth Wood, join a stony track where the trees end. After 200 metres, where the track bears L, turn R into another stony track (**D**). You'll soon reach a clearing crossed by electricity pylons – go straight across onto a smaller bridleway into the woods opposite and through the trees for 1 km. At the far end the bridleway gets rather rutted, and there's a short steep climb before joining a wider stony track leading through a gate to the road (**E**).

Turn L onto the road past the carpark at Bramshaw Telegraph, overlooking the New Forest heathlands. After 2 km turn L and keep going to Nomansland.

[If you want to shorten the ride by missing out the section by Bramshaw Telegraph, follow the track out of Hamptworth Wood as it bears L at point (**D**) (don't turn R to the clearing under the electricity pylons). At the TJ with the road turn R and follow it for 2 km to Nomansland. Turn R at the TJ to reach the 'Lamb Inn' (**F**).]

Nomansland to The Pepperbox

Turn R in front of the Lamb Inn (**F**) – or L if you've taken the short cut. Follow the road through the forest (past a couple of Forestry Commission carparks). Turn L at the TJ with the main road, cross a cattle grid, and turn R (sp. Plaitford). Follow this road for 2 km, to the junction with the A36.

Turn L onto the main road. Taking great care (this is a very fast and busy road!), turn almost immediately R again into Giles Lane (G). This is much more pleasant – a winding country lane which crosses a ford (go for it!), and passes a moated farmhouse and the delightful tiny church of St. Peter, Plaitford. Past the church, turn L at the TJ and continue to wind through pleasant countryside (ignoring several even smaller roads turning off to the right) for 2·5 km until you reach another main road, the A27.

Unfortunately, there's no legal alternative to a 1 km stretch along the A27 (nowhere near as busy as the A36). Turn L and flog along, watching for a R turn into Bunny Lane (**H**). Follow the lane for 1 km.

Where the lane bends round to the right look for a signposted bridleway turning off to the L (a signposted footpath turns off to the left shortly before the bridleway). The bridleway is narrow single-track, climbing along the edge of the woods, and although there are lots of tree roots and overhanging vegetation (nettles in summer!), it's quite rideable for most of the way.

After a while there's a wider section, but not for long – where the wider track bends left, be careful instead to go straight ahead into another section of nettle-infested single-track. This climbs up through the woods, eventually coming to a TJ with a wide stony track. Turn R as far as the edge of the wood, but don't go out of the trees. Look carefully for a well-concealed bridleway arrow marking another single-track just inside the wood, and turn L into this (**I**) to continue climbing up the combe. Before long the path leaves the wood, but continues in the same direction, climbing along the edge of the field next to the trees. Follow the field edge to the top of the hill, then around to the R by the hedge until behind the old wartime observation post at the top of the field. Here there's a small wooden gate leading into the wood which lines the crest of the ridge and a firm track that marks the end of the climb and the single-track section.

Go through the wood, and turn L onto the wide grassy ridgeway track heading towards the radio mast on Dean Hill.

The track contours along the hill just below the mast – look out for Salisbury Cathedral in the distance – and meets a minor road crossing the ridge. Turn L, then R again onto the signposted byway which continues along the ridge. This is tarmac as far as the turn to Dean Hill Farm (**J**), where it continues straight ahead as a grassy bridleway. Ignore the right turn 500 metres further on, and keep straight on along the ridge past the trees (the track here is quite deeply rutted, and can get rather waterlogged after wet weather). It's not far back to Pepperbox Hill and a well-earned rest!

*Win Green – looking back along the Ridgeway*

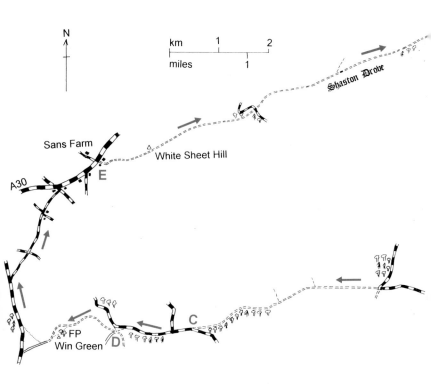

N

km 1 2

miles 1

Shaston Drove

White Sheet Hill

Sans Farm

E

A30

FP
Win Green

D

C

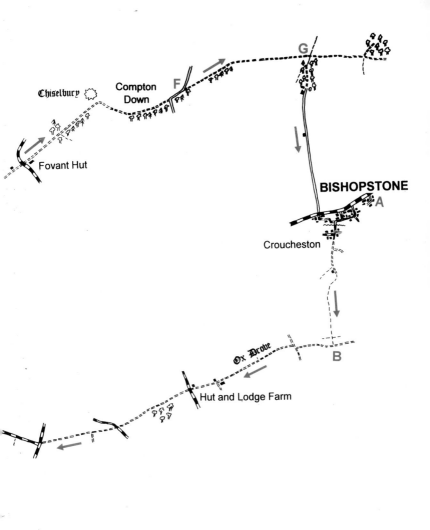

Chiselbury

Compton
Down

**F**

**G**

Fovant Hut

**BISHOPSTONE**

**A**

Croucheston

Ox Drove

**B**

Hut and Lodge Farm

## 17) ALONG THE SALISBURY RIDGEWAYS

Grade; Moderate. A longish ride, but mainly fairly easy going
Length;  41 km (25·5 miles)
Terrain;  21 km hard/stony track
              10 km rutted byway
              10 km tarmac
Map; OS Landranger 184 Salisbury & The Plain
Ref Points; GR 068258 Bishopstone (start and finish)
                    043225 Hut & Lodge Farm
                    925206 Win Green
                    943242 White Sheet Hill
                    001266 Fovant Hut
Facilities; Two pubs in Bishopstone (the White Hart on the main
road, and the Three Horseshoes in the village)
Nearest rail station; Tisbury 5 km or Salisbury 10 km

Background

Salisbury is at the meeting point of five river valleys, and the
chalky ridgeways separating these were once important lines of communication. This ride follows two of the best-preserved of these
ancient routes, the Shaston Drove and the Ox Drove. Nowadays the
main roads follow the valleys, leaving the old routes as enjoyable
traffic-free byways commanding glorious views over the surrounding countryside as they stride along the high ground. Both offer
relatively straightforward riding, much of it (particularly the Shaston
Drove, which you'll follow from White Sheet Hill over Fovant Down
and Compton Down on the way back) on hard tracks. The Ox Drove
is rather rutted in parts, but not difficult – the main thing to watch
out for is the puddles, which after wet weather can cover the whole

of the track, making parts of the ride a bit like fording a series of miniature lakes!

Shaston Drove was once the main route between Salisbury and Shaftesbury, and has had a colourful history. Over the years it has been used by Saxon soldiers, mediaeval pilgrims on their way to Shaftesbury to pay homage at the shrine of King Edward the Martyr, and in the eighteenth century it became a turnpike and coach road – complete with it's highwayman, 'Cunning Dick', who would waylay unsuspecting travellers on their way over the high ground. In the seventeenth and eighteenth centuries it was even used for horse racing, by Lord Pembroke who planted trees as mile markers between White Sheet Hill and Harnham Down (where Salisbury racecourse still is today). The Ox Drove has had a rather quieter history. It never became a turnpike, and remained a secondary route popular with the drovers, who not surprisingly preferred to avoid the tolls that would have been payable on the busier route!

These days there are few habitations along the ridgeways, and you'll have to wait until you're back in Bishopstone for your pint and pub lunch. It wasn't always like this however, and in the days when passing trade amounted to more than the occasional mountain biker and horse rider there were 'huts' at intervals along the road where travellers could buy food and drink. Although you can't see any signs of these now (worse luck!) the names have survived in one or two places, such as Fovant Hut on the Shaston Drove and Hut and Lodge Farm which you'll pass on the Ox Drove.

### Route Description

Bishopstone to Win Green, along the Ox Drove

Park in Bishopstone (**A**) (no particularly good spot, but easiest near the main road), and take the minor road next to the 'White Hart' sp. Croucheston Mill and Bishopstone village. Follow the road as it bends R, past the 'Three Horseshoes', and then L again over the river (look out for the watercress beds next to the bridge). Ignore the next right turn to Croucheston Mill, and instead go straight ahead into the stony track that heads towards the Downs. Follow the track as it winds up a long, steep-sided coombe (don't be tempted by the grassy track that forks to the right by a barn), becoming increasingly steep and rutted as it nears the ridge. At the far end there's a short but very steep climb that will test your hill-climbing abilities to the full, before levelling out and reaching the Ox Drove (**B**).

The Ox Drove here is a rutted byway running between high hedges. Turn R and follow this for 500 metres, then at the TJ turn R and immediately L to continue along the ridge on a wider, more open and better-surfaced track. Navigation along the Ox Drove from here is easy – you can switch on to autopilot for the next 12 km, almost to Win Green, following the track as it heads straight on along the ridge, and ignoring all turns off to right or left. Some parts are hard gravel track, some fairly long stretches are deeply rutted by farm traffic and 4WD vehicles, and there's a 2 km section of tarmac above Woodminton Down.

You'll need to start thinking about navigation again when you reach a second tarmac section (**C**), where a signpost points to the right (downhill) to Berwick St. John. Don't turn off here, but continue straight ahead on the tarmac for 1 km, looking for a track forking L just before the tarmac road bends right and starts to drop steeply downhill. Fork L onto the track and you'll immediately come to a track junction (**D**). Ignore the left turns signposted to Tollard Royal and Ashcombe Farm (the latter a private road), and go straight ahead, still following the ridge, along the byway towards Win Green.

Win Green itself is another 1·5 km further on – the byway skirts to the right of the hill, but having come this far it's worth it to push your bike up the grassy footpath to the top and rest for a while by the circular wood and orientation table that crown the summit.

Win Green to White Sheet Hill

Leave Win Green by passing the carpark below the hill to rejoin the byway. Just past the big gate by the car park entrance there's a small metal gate  in the fence on the R, marked with a bridleway arrow. Go through this and let it rip down the side of the bumpy grassy field, following the fence and then bearing left at the bottom to pick up an old sunken track, past a clump of hawthorn bushes to a stile/gate leading back onto the road (for a more sedate but less interesting descent, follow the byway out of the car park to the road and turn R downhill).

Follow the road downhill, and take the first turn R (sp. Ferne and Salisbury). Go straight on for 2 km, then at the TJ turn L, then immediately R again onto the main A30 road. Follow this for 1 km, past a right turn to Berwick St. John, to reach a big white house opposite the turn into Sands Lane (**E**). Turn R past the house into a stony byway, and brace yourself for a long steep climb back onto the chalk ridge.

White Sheet Hill to Bishopstone along the Shaston Drove

The track climbs all the way to the trig. point on top of White Sheet Hill, at 242 m not quite as high as Win Green, although it certainly feels as though it is! From here navigation is easy again – straight on along the ridgeway road (Shaston Drove) for all of 14 km until it's time to drop down to Bishopstone and the finish. Most of the way it's easy going on a hard stony surface, although there's a more rutted section past the woods on Compton Down.

There are only two places where you'll need to jerk yourself out of autopilot mode – first, after the rutted section on Compton Down (about 10 km after White Sheet Hill) the way is joined by a gravelled farm track coming in from the right, which it follows for 400 metres. Watch out when the gravelled track bends to the left and begins to drop downhill (**F**) – don't be tempted to follow it, but instead go straight ahead keeping to the byway along the ridge.

The second place to watch out carefully for is the junction where you turn off to Bishopstone. In the middle of a straight section of the track about 2·5 km after the fork you'll come to an X-tracks with a field gate to the left, and a double metal gate to the R (**G**). Turn R through the gap at the end of the double gate (there's a blue bridleway waymark on the far side of the gatepost), and follow the concrete-surfaced bridleway down into the woods. Continue on the concrete track through another gate, past farm buildings and a pond, and follow it all the way down to the valley bottom. Hold tight towards the end as the gradient steepens, then turn L at the road back to the 'White Hart' in Bishopstone.

*On the ranges, near Larkhill*

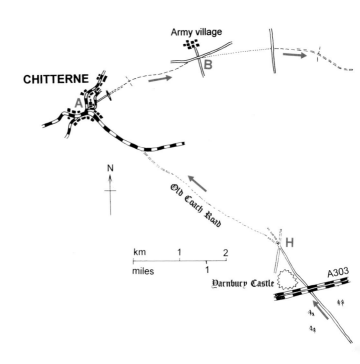

## 18

Army village

**CHITTERNE**

A

B

N

Old Coach Road

km 1 2
miles 1

H

Darnbury Castle

A303

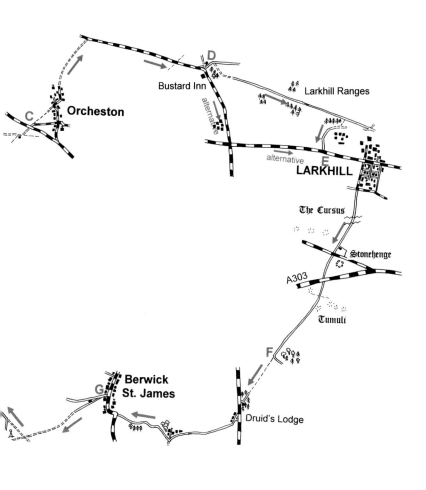

C

Orcheston

Bustard Inn

D

alternative

Larkhill Ranges

alternative

E

LARKHILL

The Cursus

Stonehenge

A303

Tumuli

F

Berwick
St. James

G

Druid's Lodge

## 18) CHITTERNE, ORCHESTON AND STONEHENGE

Grade; Moderate. The first bit, from Chitterne to Orcheston, is on grass and needs careful navigation but after this much of the route is on good quality tracks. Part of the route runs through the Army's Larkhill firing range (**see page 20 for information on access**), but there's a straightforward road alternative.

Length; 38 km (23·5 miles)

Terrain; 14 km hard/stony track

            13 km grassy track/field bridleway

            11 km tarmac

Map; OS Landranger 184 Salisbury & The Plain

Ref Points; GR 992441 Chitterne Church (start and finish)

                058453 Orcheston

                125443 Larkhill

                120424 track/road crossing near Stonehenge

                071393 Berwick St. James

                037404 track by Yarnbury Castle

Facilities; Pubs in Chitterne, Orcheston, Larkhill & Berwick St. James, & also at the Bustard Inn at GR 091460 (next to the Army Ranges checkpoint) – with so many opportunities this ride could turn into a pub crawl! Also shops & a cafe in Larkhill – go straight ahead into the village instead of turning R into Willoughby Rd.

Nearest rail station; Warminster 12 km, or Salisbury 12 km

Background

Chitterne, by itself in the middle of Salisbury Plain, has a distinctly isolated feel, emphasised on days when the lark song is interrupted by the frequent loud crashes of heavy artillery. It's a pleasant village though, with flint and stone cottages clustered around the church, also built of flint and stone giving it a distinctive marbled look.

Leaving Chitterne, the route climbs onto the Plain, crossing part of the army training area (not a live firing range) on the way to Orcheston. It's grassy and open and rather bleak in winter – one of the benefits of the Army's presence has been to preserve large tracts of downland from the plough, and on a grey misty day you can imagine what it must have been like to be a traveller in past centuries, watching out in fear of the highwayman as you crossed the Plain on the turnpike from Salisbury to Bath. On a more practical note, there are several new tracks built by the Army that don't figure on the OS Map, so care is needed with navigation. Don't be surprised by the sudden appearance of a full-scale East European village (again not shown on older OS Maps) rising like a mirage from the Plain – it's to give soldiers the opportunity to practice guerrilla warfare in realistic surroundings before being sent abroad to wherever trouble is brewing.

On the way into Orcheston look out for a row of whitewashed cottages bearing a large black metal plaque. This tells of the great flood of 1841, which destroyed many houses and left many people homeless both in Orcheston and in the neighbouring villages of Tilshead and Shrewton. The cottages were built to rehouse some of the victims. It may seem strange to think of floods devastating a village in the dry interior of Salisbury Plain, but I was less surprised after riding this route in the middle of a wet winter and finding the bridleway out of Orcheston under six inches of running water for nearly a mile after leaving the village!

After crossing a corner of the Larkhill Artillery Ranges (if the red flags aren't flying!) and passing through the edge of the unprepossessing military village of Larkhill, it's not far to Stonehenge, Wiltshire's most famous historic attraction. Unfortunately, as far as I'm concerned the reality doesn't live up to the expectation – the stone circle seems diminished by the unattractive carpark and visitor centre, the barrier fences and the crowds of tourists. Nevertheless, it's an awe-inspiring thought to contemplate the Neolithic builders dragging the huge sarsens all the way overland from the Marlborough Downs, and transporting the smaller Bluestones even further, from the Preseli Mountains in Pembrokeshire. The whole area around Stonehenge is littered with Neolithic remains – as well as the Cursus, which you'll cross on your way from Larkhill, there are countless tumuli – obviously this was the place to be buried in Neolithic times!

Another slightly less ancient monument that you'll pass further on your way is Yarnbury Castle, a huge Iron Age hillfort covering some 28 acres and with good views in all directions. Near the crossing point of two important routes (the track you'll be following is the old Coach Road from Salisbury to Bristol – look out for the ancient milestones that can still be seen alongside the track), the site has in more recent times been used to hold regular sheep fairs that attracted farmers and travellers from a wide area. The grassy ramparts of the hillfort are now silent, except for the hum of passing traffic on what is now the A303.

### Route Description

Chitterne to Orcheston

Park in the centre of the village (**A**), near the church and Village Hall on the small road which runs towards Tilshead. Cycle back towards the main road through the village, but just before you reach it turn L into Back Lane. This curves back to run behind the church – when you're about level with the church, turn R into a track sp. 'Byway – Imber Ranges Path'. Keep straight on across a tarmac farm lane (again following the sp. 'Imber Ranges Path') into a grassy/

stony track which climbs up towards the Plain.

This leads onto open grassland – keep straight on, following the wheel tracks that mark the line of the bridleway, and ignoring all turns R or L. Just as you seem to be heading into the depths of the Plain the strange sight of a deserted and rather foreign-looking village looms up ahead – this is the Army's practice area for guerrilla warfare, so keep out! The bridleway keeps to the R of the 'village', joining for a short distance a hard Army track which passes it by. At the X-rds (not far from the village entrance) (**B**), leave the hard surface and bear slightly R across the rough grass, following a rather confusing pattern of wheeltracks. This section is indistinct, but press on keeping the Army road to your left and the valley to your right and you won't go far wrong. After a while you'll cross another Army road – on the far side the bridleway becomes more clearly defined, following the crest of a wide ridge in an easterly direction.

About 3 km after passing the Army 'village' you come to a small concrete building to the right of the path, and a 'byway' sign pointing left. Turn L to follow the byway to meet the main road (**C**).

At the main road, go straight across towards Orcheston. Almost immediately turn L into a signposted grassy bridleway, which drops down the side of the hill into the middle of the village, not far from the houses built for the victims of the 1841 flood (the row of white cottages above to your right when you meet the road). Turn L onto the road, and follow it past the Crown Inn to the end of the village.

Orcheston to Stonehenge

At the far end of the village the road turns into a bridleway, and follows the bottom of the valley (possibly a stream in wet weather!) alongside an Army training area. After 1 km it meets a road – turn R and continue for 2·5 km past the edge of the firing ranges to the

Army checkpoint by the Bustard Inn (**D**).

**If the red flags are flying** you'll have to stick to the road for the next 4 km to Larkhill (bear R to follow the road past the 'Bustard', straight on for 1·5 km, then turn L at the TJ towards Larkhill). If you're lucky and it's a 'no firing day' (no red flags or lights) you can get to Larkhill on the byway that runs through the Ranges. Go straight ahead past the Army checkpoint, on the road that runs to the L of the small wood. Immediately past the wood turn R off the tarmac onto a hard unsurfaced track which runs in a straight line across the plain towards Larkhill.

After about 3 km you'll come to another wood immediately to the right of the track. At the far end of the wood the buildings of Larkhill Camp are visible behind the trees. Turn R past the end of the trees to the perimeter fence, then turn R onto the track which follows the fence and after a further 750 metres meets the road (**E**). Turn L towards Larkhill village.

In Larkhill itself, turn R into Willoughby Rd. Keep straight on past the houses, and straight on at the bottom where the road turns into a hard stony track. Before long you'll see Stonehenge rising from the plain ahead, and will cross the line of the ancient Cursus – read the information board to find out more about this enigmatic antiquity. Continue along the track to meet the main A344 road behind the busy Stonehenge carpark.

Stonehenge to Chitterne

Leave your bike in the carpark if you want to visit Stonehenge. When you've had enough, cross the A344 and continue along the stony byway. After 500 metres cross the A303 as well – take great care, this is a very busy road! The hard track continues for another 2 km, past clusters of burial mounds, and then turns L through a locked gate to become a private farm road. At this point (**F**) follow the bridleway which continues straight ahead as a grassy track running across the fields towards the corner of a wood. Follow the track through the wood to reach the main road by Druid's Lodge.

Turn L onto the road, then immediately R onto the tarmac lane that runs in front of the farm offices and then bends R to climb gently towards the ridge. On reaching the large farm at the top of the hill (about 1·5 km further on), bear slightly L to keep all the farm buildings to your right, then cross the track which runs along the ridge, and bear R past the end of the trees to enjoy a steep descent down the other side of the hill towards Berwick St. James.

At the bottom of the combe, the track meets the road on the edge of Berwick St. James. Bear R into the village, past the church, then turn L opposite the bus shelter into a signposted byway. After 300 metres fork L next to a large barn (**G**), and prepare yourself for a long, stiff climb back out of the valley. Just before reaching the radio masts at the top of the hill turn R at the X-tracks onto a similar grassy, rutted track. Before long this joins a tarmac lane coming in from the left – keep straight ahead and follow the lane along the ridge until it meets the main A303 road again, next to the huge earthworks of Yarnbury Castle.

Go straight across the dual carriageway (careful!) into the stony byway which passes by the eastern edge of the hillfort. Follow the track past the ramparts, and after a further 1/2 km. bear slightly L at the X-tracks (**H**) and continue on the wide grassy track that skirts the edge of the Army lands past a military airstrip (more like a large playing field than an airfield!).

After about 3 km, the track meets the road. Turn L, over the crest of the hill, and then coast back to Chitterne – it's downhill all the way!

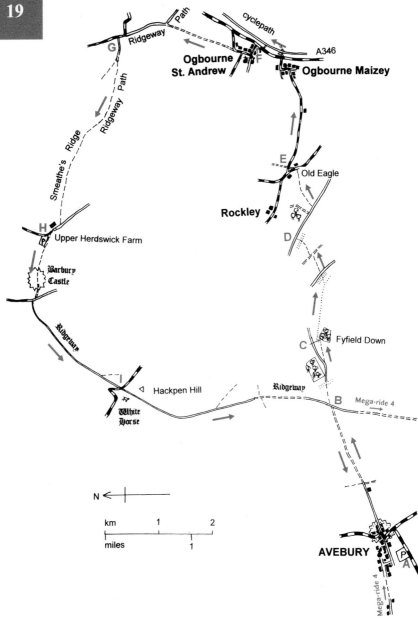

Path

cyclepath

Ridgeway

**G**

A346

**Ogbourne
St. Andrew**

**F**

**Ogbourne Maizey**

Smeathe's Ridge

Ridgeway Path

**E**

Old Eagle

**Rockley**

**H**

Upper Herdswick Farm

**D**

*Barbury
Castle*

*Ridgeway*

Fyfield Down

**C**

◁ Hackpen Hill

*Ridgeway*

**B**

Mega-ride 4

*White
Horse*

N ←

| km | 1 | 2 |

| miles | 1 |

**AVEBURY**

*P*

**A**

Mega-ride 4

## 19) AVEBURY, FYFIELD DOWN & BARBURY CASTLE

Grade; Moderate. As with most downland rides there are one or two steady climbs. Generally reasonable going, but watch out on Fyfield Down where some of the tracks are not very clearly defined.
Length; 29 km (18 miles)
Terrain; 7 km tarmac
          8 km hard/stony track
          14 km field bridleway/grassy track
Map; OS Landranger 173 Swindon and Devizes
Ref points; GR 099697 Avebury carpark (start and finish)
            140710 Fyfield Down
            168714 Old Eagle
            190724 Ogbourne St. Andrew
            149763 Barbury Castle
            129747 Hackpen Hill
            125708 Ridgeway/track junction

Facilities; Pub, shop and tourist information in Avebury – also a good vegetarian restaurant open during the tourist season. Pub in Ogbourne St. Andrew. Snacks can be bought at Upper Herdswick (near Barbury Castle) in summer.
Nearest rail station; Swindon 10 km

Background

Avebury also features in route 20 in this book (you can combine both rides in one outing if you like – see Megaride 4 on page 199), but if you haven't been here before you will probably want to spend some time after your ride wandering round the village and exploring the impressive stone circle – the largest in Europe. Although busy with tourists in the summer it's an attractive place, and as well as the stones there are a museum with displays about the rich variety of Neolithic sites in the area, a Museum of Wiltshire Rural Life (housed in the seventeenth-century Great Barn), and a sixteenth century manor and garden open to the public courtesy of the National Trust.

Fyfield Down in contrast is barely touched by the many visitors who throng Avebury, but is nonetheless a fascinating place and is now designated a Nature Reserve. The landscape is littered with sarsen stones – known as the 'Grey Wethers' because from a distance they look like grazing sheep – which are the remnants of a once much more extensive layer of hard sandstone rock. They have been quarried over the years for building stone, and many local houses (as well as the Stone Circle) are made of rough blocks of sarsen. Quarrying continued right up to the 1930's, and the graves of some of the stonecutters can be found in local churchyards. If you're interested in the history of this area, read Ken Watts' book *Exploring Historic Wiltshire*; vol.1 which has a chapter on the Central Marlborough Downs which traces the remnants of ancient field systems, relics of the Knights Templar, rabbit warreners and so on. If you're not, just enjoy the scenery and the fresh air in one of Wiltshire's most unspoilt areas.

The first part of the route follows the old coach road out of Avebury and onto Fyfield Down – before the alternative road along the valley (now the A4) became the main route, the main road from London to Bath and Bristol ran over the Downs between Avebury and Marlborough, and, being fairly remote and desolate, must have been a favourite haunt of highwaymen.

As they were less densely wooded than the neighbouring valleys, the chalk downlands of southern Britain were from ancient times important lines of communication, and today bear the traces of many old trackways and roads. At Old Eagle and again near Barbury Castle the route crosses the old Swindon to Marlborough turnpike, and from Barbury back to Avebury follows the most famous of old prehistoric trackways, the Ridgeway. The modern Long Distance Path starts near Avebury and runs north to Ivinghoe Beacon in the Chilterns, but the prehistoric track continued south across the Vale of Pewsey to Salisbury Plain, and to the north extended further along the North Downs and towards East Anglia. Today the Path is well used by walkers, and also in parts by 4WD enthusiasts and farm traffic – although mostly a good hard surface, there are some rather rutted sections to add a bit of interest!

Barbury Castle is a splendid example of an Iron Age hillfort, surrounded by impressive ramparts and ditches, and is not far from the site of the Battle of Beran Byrg, recorded in the Anglo-Saxon Chronicle as a decisive victory by the Saxons against the retreating Romano-British tribes who built the fort. A puzzle to dwell on while cycling – if the hillforts were built for defence, where did the water come from so high above the spring line?

### Route Description

Avebury to Old Eagle

The best place to start the ride is in the large National Trust carpark just south of the village (**A**). Turn L out of the gate and cycle into the village on the main road, passing the Red Lion on the corner in the village centre. As the main road bends sharply left again, instead go straight ahead into the lane which passes between the houses and then heads away towards open countryside and the Downs. This is tarmac for nearly 1 km, and then becomes a wide track that climbs steadily up to meet the Ridgeway (**B**).

Cross the Ridgeway Long Distance Path onto a wide grassy bridleway into the Fyfield Down Nature reserve, dotted with sarsen boulders, and keep straight on through two gates to cross one of the racehorse gallops. Follow the stony track straight ahead, down a steepish slope. As you race down, look out for a grassy bridleway which carries straight on where the stony track veers left at the bottom of the hill – follow the bridleway, aiming for the L corner of a small wood on the skyline (there are several lots of confusing wheel tracks among the scrub around here – don't be tempted to veer off to the left before you reach the wood).

If you have the time, look back while climbing to where the stony track bends at the bottom of the valley behind you – this is the old London to Bath coach road, and plainly visible on the opposite hill are the wheel ruts left by the coaches as they fanned out to climb the slope two hundred years ago.

By the corner of the wood, go L and then R to pass through two gates in quick succession (**C**). Ahead is a fence with another gate – don't go through this gate, but stay on the same side of the fence and follow the grassy bridleway which runs alongside it, heading due east. Where the fence ends, go through the gate into the field straight ahead, and then straight on along an indistinct path which follows the boundary of the rougher grass across the gentle slope. If you find it difficult to follow the right of way, aim for the marker post and then for the finger post visible on the skyline between two lines of trees. On reaching the finger post follow the arm sp. Rockley (half left) and cross the gallops to a gate which brings you out onto a gravel road.

Cross the road, and follow the bridleway (still sp. Rockley) down a grassy ride. After 500 metres you meet another hard-surfaced track – turn L, then immediately R to cross the track and follow straight ahead alongside the hedge on a bumpy grass bridleway. Where the hedge ends, keep straight on across another racehorse gallop and climb the slope to reach another hard track (**D**).

Turn R onto the track. Ignore the first left turn (a hard track), but after another 100 metres turn L down a narrower, bumpier but more interesting grassy bridleway that drops steeply down to the road at Old Eagle.

Old Eagle to Barbury Castle

Turn L onto the road (in case you're wondering, the name Old Eagle comes from an inn – burnt down many years ago – that used to stand here by the old turnpike road from Marlborough to Swindon, which followed what is now a quiet byway running north past Four Mile Clump, Upper Herdswick and Burderop). After 100 metres, where the road bends to the left, go straight on up the gravelly byway (the old Swindon road), but then turn immediately R (**E**) onto the minor tarmac road that leads up over the crest of the ridge and drops down (after nearly 2 km.) into the village of Ogbourne Maizey.

Follow the tarmac through the village to the main Swindon–Marlborough road. Cross straight over (mind the traffic!) into a signposted byway, and climb a short distance to the old trackbed of the disused railway. This has now been turned into an official cyclepath between Chiseldon and Marlborough, and provides flat, easy cycling. Not for today though! – turn L onto the cycleway, but after only a few hundred metres take the first turn off to the L, (just before the start of a tarmac section), and return to the main road near the Wheatsheaf pub. Turn R to pass the pub (watch that fast traffic again!), and then L into Ogbourne St. Andrew (**F**).

Follow the minor road through the village as it bends to the right – don't turn left by the church, but keep straight on to where the road bends sharply right again. Leave the road and follow the sign-posted byway straight ahead. This is slightly overgrown in places (but not usually too bad), and climbs gently for just over 1 km. until it joins the Ridgeway Long Distance Path which continues straight ahead after coming up from the right.

From here on, our route follows the LDP almost all the way back to Avebury, and is well signposted. There's a short section of road after 1 km, but very soon the Path turns off to the L (**G**) and climbs for about 3 km along Smeathe's Ridge, a delightful grassy crest with expanding views in all directions.

At the end of the ridge the path meets a tarmac lane (this is the old turnpike road to Swindon that you last saw at Old Eagle). Turn R past Upper Herdswick Farm, and then soon L again (**H**) behind the car- park for Barbury Hill, following the bridleway markers for the Ridgeway LDP (ignore the signpost for Ridgeway vehicular traffic that points straight on down the hill).

Barbury Castle to Avebury

Follow the bridleway past the carpark and after 500 metres you come to the impressive earthworks of Barbury Castle. Keep straight on through the middle of the hillfort, and then down a short, steep slope to cross a minor road (jink R then L).

The next 6 km are plain sailing, following the Ridgeway Path over Hackpen Hill (**I**) and on towards Avebury( most is on a fast, hard surface but some sections are rather more rutted). Look out for the crossroads where you met the Ridgeway near the start of the ride (**B**), and turn R to follow the track back down to Avebury [unless you're following the Megaride, in which case continue straight on along the Ridgeway].

*Cherhill White Horse*

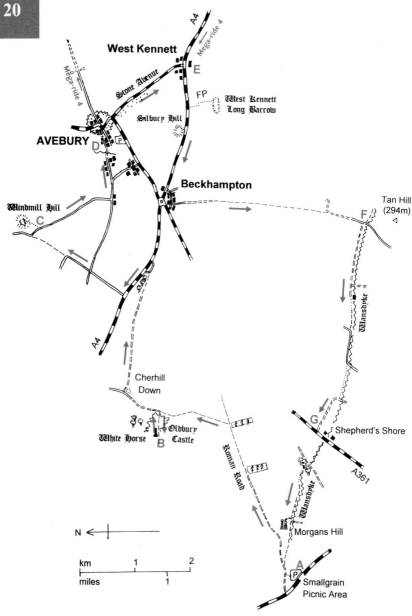

West Kennett

A4

Mega-ride 4

Stone Avenue

E

Mega-ride 4

FP West Kennett Long Barrow

Silbury Hill

AVEBURY

D

P

Beckhampton

Windmill Hill

C

Tan Hill (294m)

F

Wansdyke

Cherhill Down

G Shepherd's Shore

White Horse

Oldbury Castle

B

A361

Roman Road

Wansdyke

Morgans Hill

A

P Smallgrain Picnic Area

A4

N ←

km          1          2

miles          1

## 20) CHERHILL WHITE HORSE, WINDMILL HILL AND AVEBURY

Grade; Moderate. Generally not bad going, but likely to be muddy on one or two sections in wet weather

Length; 29 km (18 miles)

Terrain; 8 km tarmac

        8 km hard/stony track

      13 km grassy track/field bridleway

Map; OS Landranger 173 Swindon & Devizes

Ref points; GR 019671  Smallgrain picnic area (start and finish)

              047694 Cherhill monument

              087713 Windmill Hill

              101699 Avebury

              100685 Silbury Hill

              045663 Shepherds Shore Farm

Facilities; Pub and village shop at Avebury; pub at Beckhampton. Nearest rail station; Chippenham 15 km

Background

This route is steeped in history, and takes in some fine downland for good measure. Follow in the steps of the legionaries along a section of the old Roman road from Bath to London, climb to the impressive Iron Age hillfort of Oldbury Castle and the tall, pointed Lansdowne monument overlooking Cherhill and its White Horse, and pass several tumuli on the way to the neolithic causewayed camp of Windmill Hill. Next stop Avebury, with it's famous stone circle actually set amongst the houses of the village. There's a museum here with a collection of interesting local archaeological finds, and displays and booklets which explore the fascinating history of the area. Leaving Avebury, the route passes along the Stone Avenue, and past the West Kennett Long Barrow and the distinctive pyramid of Silbury Hill – even the guide books in the museum can only guess at the reason why this strange man-made mound was laboriously constructed from layers of earth and stones!

The area around Silbury Hill and Avebury is famous for crop circles – some believe that these unexplained phenomena are the result of supernatural forces or alien visitors, whilst others think the whole business is a big hoax. All that I can say is that some of the patterns are remarkably complex and perfectly symmetrical – who knows? Anyway, watch out – there may be one around somewhere near when you ride this route!

From Beckhampton the route climbs back up onto the downs, finishing with a stretch following the Wansdyke, an old defensive earthwork which crosses Wiltshire and which features in several of the rides in this book.

For a longer day out you can combine this ride with route 19 – see Megaride 4 on page 199.

### Route Description

Smallgrain to Windmill Hill

Start at the carpark at the Smallgrain picnic area (**A**) on the road between Bishops Cannings and Calne, and cross the grass between the picnic tables to join the bridleway which skirts behind through the trees. Turn R and follow the bridleway to a signpost for Morgans Hill Nature Reserve. Bear L on the rutted track which contours round the flank of the hill, with views opening up to your left of the Lansdowne Monument on Cherhill Down ahead. Straight on as the track crosses several fields – this section is the old Roman road –

until you are almost level with the Monument. To the right of the track is a line of trees, and opposite on the left is a gate. Turn L through this and head towards the flank of the Downs on the path along the edge of the field. You soon start to climb, gently at first, past a National Trust sign, and then steeply, diagonally L up the hill.

At the top go through the gate. The bridleway goes straight ahead, keeping the earthworks of Oldbury Castle hillfort on your left, until after about 200 metres you come to a chalky track coming uphill from the other side. Turn L on the track, which passes through a gap in the earthworks and heads straight for the tall column of the Lansdowne Monument (**B**).

Pause here for a few minutes to admire the view – if you want to see the White Horse carved into the flank of the hill you'll need to go just past the Monument onto one of the small hillocks, but it's only a few yards and well worth the trouble.

Suitably refreshed, it's back the way you came to where the chalky track passes through the rim of the hillfort. Keep to the track as it turns L and bounces away downhill, through two gates and past a barn. Just after passing a tumulus on the right, turn R onto a chalky bridleway which becomes a pleasant grassy track following a narrow ridge surmounted by the line of another ancient earthwork. After about 2 km the track skirts to the right of a small copse, then enters the trees and drops down to a large lay-by next to the main A4 road.

Cycle to the lay-by entrance and turn sharp L onto the A4, following the main road for about 750 metres. Turn R by a clump of trees down a track signposted 'Bridleway to Windmill Hill'. After another 1·5 km the main track turns left – ignore this and go straight on down a narrow, rutted bridleway. This bit is rather grotty, but don't worry, it doesn't last for long! Before too far the path starts to climb gently, then meets a track coming down from the right through the trees. Turn sharp R onto this track, and up a short but steep hill to pass the entrance to the Windmill Hill site (**C**).

Windmill Hill to Silbury Hill

Windmill Hill is perhaps the least impressive (and least busy!) of the Avebury monuments. Nevertheless, it is worth the effort to walk across the grass (**not** cycle - there's no right of way) to the burial mounds in the centre of the site and spend a few minutes resting and reflecting on the thousands of years that have passed since Neolithic man farmed the land round here.

Back on your bike, continue along the fast, smooth track towards Avebury. Turn L at the TJ, then approaching the village go straight on past the 'No Through Road' signs, past the thatched cottages on your left, then keep straight on again as the road turns into a narrow tarmac bridleway. Fork L to cross the stream, then jink R by a black and white half-timbered house and turn L into Avebury's attractive main street (**D**), which during the summer is likely to be busy with visitors of all nationalities.

[Megaride 4 leaves the route here]

If you haven't been to Avebury before, it's certainly worth stopping for a while – or even better, come back on another day and have a proper look around (maybe after trying route 19, which starts and finishes here). Unlike Stonehenge, you can walk right round the Stone Circle, and there is also a museum, pub and other attractions.

From Avebury, take the main road towards Devizes, but where this bends sharply to the right go straight on along the 'B' road towards West Kennett and Marlborough. This follows the line of the Stone Avenue, a row of standing stones which leads up to the Stone Circle – once there were 200 of them, now 27 remain and the positions of the rest are marked by small concrete blocks.

Where the road meets the main A4 in West Kennett (**E**), turn R – watch the traffic on this busy road! [Megaride 4 rejoins the route here]. Continue for nearly 1 km until you come to a lay-by near to the West Kennett Long Barrow. Unless you're in a hurry, it's worth leaving your bike in the lay-by and walking up to the Long Barrow – the biggest of it's kind in England – where you can go right into the mound and explore the burial chambers.

West Kennett to Smallgrain

Leaving the Long Barrow and continuing along the A4 past Silbury Hill – another enigmatic Neolithic monument – you will soon reach Beckhampton. Just before the 'Waggon & Horses' pub take the narrow L turn which leads into Beckhampton village. At the far end of the village turn L onto a signposted byway which climbs slowly but surely up towards the Downs over a distance of about 3·5 km, first as a gravel track, then turning into a field-edge bridleway and then back into a gravel track.

As you approach the bulk of Tan Hill, you will see the earthworks of the Wansdyke crossing the track ahead, and a gate. Before reaching the Dyke, turn R onto a stony track (**F**) and down the steep hill parallel to the earthworks. Keep straight on to where the track ends near a barn, and go straight ahead (keeping to the north side of the Wansdyke) across the grassy field to a gate and bridleway sign at the far end. Over the gate, straight along the field edge, and then straight on again where the bridleway meets a track.

After 750 metres the track turns sharp L to cross the Wansdyke. Ignore this, and instead keep straight on along the field edge parallel to the Dyke. Another 750 metres further, the path comes to a TJ with another track. Turn R, then follow the track as it bends immediately L. Bounce downhill, watching the ruts, to the main road (**G**).

Turn L onto the road for 300 metres to Shepherds Shore Farm.

Opposite the farm turn R onto the bridleway which follows the crest of the Wansdyke, up to the trees at the top of the hill. Go through the gate and cross straight over the track, looking for a narrow bridle path leading into the trees (difficult to spot from this side). On the other side of the trees, go through another small gate. Follow the path along the bottom of the Dyke ditch – very bumpy for 100 metres, until you come to another gate and can climb onto the bank alongside, which follows the Dyke as it winds across grassy downland towards Morgans Hill and passes to the left of the radio masts.

Keep with the Dyke as it crests the hill, then down the steep, rough descent (good technique practice here!) to rejoin your outward route not far from the carpark.

*Last leg along the Kennet & Avon Canal between All Cannings & Horton*

*Bluebell woods near East Kennett*

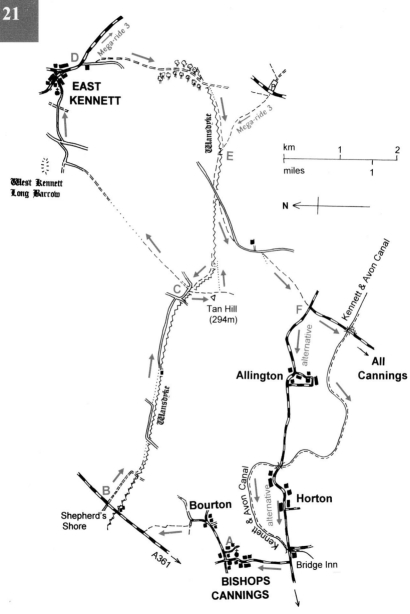

D

Mega-ride 3

EAST
KENNETT

Wansdyke

E

Mega-ride 3

West Kennett
Long Barrow

km 1 2
miles 1

N

C

Tan Hill
(294m)

F

Kennett & Avon Canal

All
Cannings

Allington

alternative

Wansdyke

B

Shepherd's
Shore

Bourton

Horton

Kennett & Avon Canal

alternative

A

A361

Bridge Inn

BISHOPS
CANNINGS

## 21) WANSDYKE AND TAN HILL

Grade; Moderate. Generally reasonably good tracks, but with some steady climbs. One or two sections may be muddy or overgrown.

Length; 29 km (18 miles) – for a long day out, this route can also be combined with route 12; see Megaride 3 on page 198.

Terrain;   5 km tarmac
           5 km stony track
        13 km grassy track/field bridleway
         6 km canal towpath

Remember you need a permit to cycle on the towpath – see page 20 for details.

Map; OS Landranger 173 Swindon & Devizes

Ref points; GR 038643 Bishops Cannings school (start & finish)
              044663  Shepherds Shore
              083646  gate near Tan Hill
              117674  East Kennett church
              118648  Wansdyke
              081629  All Cannings turn (road junction)
              039632  Bridge Inn (Horton)

Facilities; Pubs at Bishops Cannings, Horton (Bridge Inn), and also at All Cannings (just off route). Village shops at Bishops Cannings and All Cannings.

Nearest rail station; Pewsey 9 km. ('Wigglybus' minibus link possible to Alton Barnes, 3 km from All Cannings turn)

Background

This is a fine route, one of my favourites, and takes in some of the highest parts of the Wiltshire Downs. It includes some stiff climbs, bumpy descents, and fine grassy tracks giving tremendous views in all directions. Wide slopes sweep away to the north towards Avebury and the Ridgeway, and from Tan Hill the fields of the Pewsey Vale, green with wheat or bright yellow with oilseed rape, seem to lap up against the foot of the Downs like waves against a cliff.

Marching across the highest ground is the Wansdyke, an ancient defensive ditch dating from post-Roman times, which runs right across Wiltshire and beyond, from Inkpen Beacon to the Severn estuary at Portishead. This route includes some of the best-preserved sections as it crosses the high ground of the Downs.

Tan Hill and Milk Hill, at 294 m apiece, are Wiltshire's highest points. Tan Hill was formerly the site of an annual livestock fair, attracting traders and revellers from the local villages and further afield.

The last part of the route follows the Kennet & Avon canal, which we have already met on several other routes.

Back at Bishops Cannings while enjoying a drink in the Crown Inn, ponder on the local story which gave rise to the Wiltshire nickname of 'Moonraker'. In the days when brandy smuggling was commonplace, the Excisemen came to Bishops Cannings on a 'raid'. They found nothing, but doubling back at night to surprise their quarry, came across a group of men raking in the waters of the village pond with hay forks. When asked what they were doing, one thought quickly and, looking at the reflection of the moon in the pond, answered "We'm raking for that thur cheese that summun's left in the water". Chuckling to themselves at the strange habits of country yokels, the Excisemen returned to Devizes while the smugglers recovered the brandy kegs from the pond congratulating each other on how easy it was to pull the wool over the eyes of gullible 'townies'!

## Route Description

Bishops Cannings to Tan Hill

Park by the school in Bishops Cannings, on Bourton Lane(**A**). Follow the lane to the hamlet of Bourton and fork L at the 'no through road' signs. Where the tarmac ends, take the L fork, then immediately turn R following the track along the field edge climbing to the right of a narrow dry valley. After a short descent, the track jinks L then R to follow the left hand side of a hedge/earthbank to meet the main road. Turn R to Shepherds Shore Farm (750 metres) – take care, fast traffic!

200 metres past the farm turn R onto a signposted byway (**B**) and climb the hill ahead – dodging the ruts! – to the top, where it bends sharply R and passes through the earth ramparts of the Wansdyke. Don't cross the Dyke, but instead turn L onto a grassy bridleway between two wire fences. Follow this, parallel to the Dyke, along a field edge until you meet a stony track coming in from the right. Keep straight on, and follow the stony track until it bends away to the L after 750 metres; your way lies straight ahead on the bridleway following the field boundary, still parallel to the Wansdyke. Over a gate into a grassy field, then by the barn rejoin the farm track where you can see a stiff climb ahead up to the bulk of Tan Hill.

If you can spare the energy, look back when nearing the top for a view of the Wansdyke sweeping across the landscape to the radio masts on Morgan's Hill. At the top of the hill you will meet another track – turn R and immediately L to continue parallel with the Wansdyke. Within 200 metres however, fork R on a grassy track through an old wooden gate (**C**), passing through a gap in the Wansdyke onto the S side. Straight on, following the grassy track over the crest of the hill to pass 50 metres to the left of the trig. point on top of Tan Hill. Yes, after all that effort the highest point is inaccessible, in the middle of a field! Not that it matters – the best views are to be had from the gate just beyond, on the bridleway. Pause here to admire the smooth slopes of the Downs, the villages of the Pewsey Vale spread out at your feet, and Salisbury Plain beyond. It is said that on a clear day you can see the spire of Salisbury Cathedral from here, but I've never managed it! Closer to hand, the earthworks of Rybury Castle are the remains of an Iron Age hillfort.

Tan Hill to East Kennett

From the gate, a permissive bridleway runs east along the top of the slope towards Milk Hill. Turn L to follow this, keeping next to the fence, and bump down the grassy slope to a gate at the bottom. Turn left through the gate, following the green arrow, and climb back up to rejoin the Wansdyke.

Passing through the Wansdyke, turn L and follow the wide grassy bridleway back to the wooden gate that you passed through on the way to Tan Hill (**C**).

Retracing your steps through the gate, turn R onto the track and then immediately L on a rutted (and possibly muddy!) track. Take care to follow the track marked as a bridleway, following to the left of the fence as it runs away downhill – a second track to the right of the fence is a private drive to Townsend Farm.

The bridleway deteriorates as it descends, and becomes a field edge path which can be overgrown – protection against nettles is advisable in summer! Fortunately this does not last long, and riding becomes easier before the bridleway rejoins a track. Continue straight on, then follow the track as it turns R and then L. The curious mound that you can see on the crest of the hill ahead is West Kennett long barrow, a well-preserved Neolithic burial chamber. Unfortunately there are no public rights of way to the monument from this side, so you'll have to leave exploration for another day (see route 20).

Before long your track meets another descending from the Downs. Turn R and immediately sharp L onto another bridle track which crosses the brow of the hill and descends swiftly to the church in East Kennett.

East Kennett to Bishops Cannings

Past the church, turn R when the lane meets the road through the village, and then fork R just before the 'end of speed limit' signs up the track marked 'East Kennett Farm'(**D**). [Megaride 3 leaves the route here.] After 200 metres, fork L onto a grassy chalk byway which climbs across the hillside – it's a steady grind, but with expanding views over the valley and towards the Downs looming ahead. After levelling out there's a short stretch before the track enters a long thin stretch of woodland – as is often the case where a byway runs through trees, the surface is permanently wet and churned up by vehicles and horses. You're a better biker than me if you can avoid hopping off and on to avoid some of the ruts and mudbaths, but fortunately many of the worst bits can be skirted. As compensation, in spring the woods are carpeted with bluebells – a delight to the eye!

Immediately on leaving the woods be sure to turn R off the byway and rejoin the Wansdyke, on a bridleway that follows the south side of the Dyke across the fields. After about 1 km, approaching the crest of the hill, cross through a gap in the Dyke (**E**) [Megaride 3 rejoins the route here] onto the north side where a wide grassy track continues, almost seeming to form part of the fortifications. This is one of the most impressive parts of the Wansdyke, with sweeping views over the Kennett Valley – imagine you're a Romano-British soldier defending your kingdom against the Saxon invaders!

Turn L onto the farm road which crosses the ridge, and then almost immediately R. through a gate onto a bridleway which descends parallel to the road, forming a sunken track before it joins it again after another gate where the slope levels out. The bridleway gets rather bumpy at the bottom – the road would be a much faster (if less interesting!) descent, but is technically not a right of way.

Stay on the road only for a couple of hundred metres, forking R (almost straight ahead) onto a grassy bridleway where the road bends away to the left (be careful not to take the wrong route here – a higher, less distinct, track climbs slightly over the brow of the hill before petering out in a field). After a while the bridleway becomes narrower as it drops down towards the valley ahead – the horses' hooves have churned this bit up again, and it's liable to be rough in summer and muddy in winter.

Soon however the path comes out on the Devizes road, opposite the turn for All Cannings (**F**). At this point there's a choice of route. If you've bought your Kennet & Avon Canal cycle permit, whizz straight ahead downhill to join the canal towpath. If you want to miss out the canal, follow the alternative route below.

To use the canal, turn sharp L after the bridge to join the towpath, then L again under the bridge. Then enjoy the long, fast spin back to Bishops Cannings along the grassy towpath. Leave the canal by the 'Bridge Inn', taking the road towards Devizes, and then almost immediately turn R along the road into Bishops Cannings. Pass the 'Crown' (take your pick in which establishment to recover after the ride!), then turn R into Bourton Lane to where you started.

Alternative route avoiding the Canal

Turn right along the Devizes road, continue past Allington and through Horton, rejoining the main route at the 'Bridge Inn'.

*Milepost, Old Marlborough Road (Ride 5)*

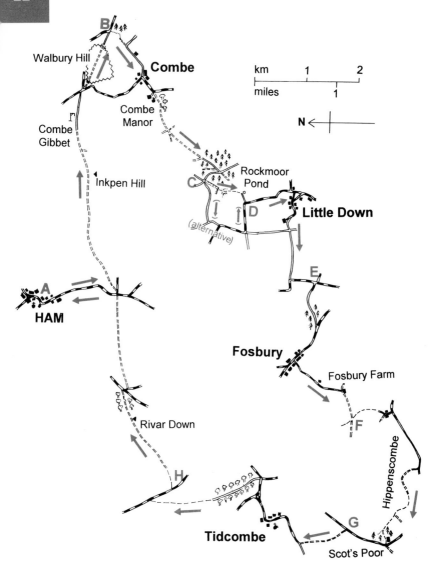

km 1 2
miles 1

N ←

**B**

Walbury Hill

**Combe**

Combe Manor

Combe Gibbet

Inkpen Hill

Rockmoor Pond

**C**

**D**

**Little Down**

(alternative)

**E**

Fosbury

Fosbury Farm

**A**

**HAM**

**F**

Hippenscombe

Rivar Down

**H**

**G**

**Tidcombe**

Scot's Poor

## 22) INKPEN HILL, TIDCOMBE AND FOSBURY

Grade; Moderate/hard. Generally good tracks, but a fair distance and some good climbs so you will know you've been out!
Length; 35 km (22 miles)
Terrain; 11 km tarmac
          10 km stony track
          14 km field bridleway/grassy track
Map; OS Landranger 174 Newbury and Wantage
Ref points; GR 331631 Ham village green start and finish
                  380616 track / road junction E. of Walbury Hill
                  369608 Combe Manor Farm
                  350590 Rockmoor Pond
                  350581 Little Down
                  320580 Fosbury village
                  311561 Hippenscombe Farm
                  291583 Tidcombe church
                  307610 Rivar Down
Facilities; Pub at Ham (Crown & Anchor). The pub at Little Down (GR351580) marked on old OS maps no longer exists!
Nearest rail station; Bedwyn 5 km

Background

I enjoyed surveying this route, as it took me into an area of the county with which I was not familiar (and into neighbouring Berkshire and Hampshire too!), and offers a good variety of scenery – a section of ancient ridgeway, secluded combes, pretty villages and hamlets, and wooded byways, to name but a few. There are some good descents and climbs into and out of the steep-sided valleys, and in contrast some fine views from the exposed tracks along the crest of Inkpen Hill and Rivar Down. The tracks are generally of good quality, although some of the byways can get rather rutted where they have been used by vehicles.

The highest point on the route at Walbury Hill (297 m) is the site of a large Iron Age hillfort, commanding spectacular views over the valley of the River Kennett. Just before the hillfort, at Combe Gibbet, a wooden scaffold marks the site of the execution in 1676 of a local man and woman for the murder of the man's son. Also on the crest of the ridge are more signs of our old friend the Wansdyke, the ancient defensive ditch which crosses Wiltshire from west to east and which we have followed on several other rides in this book.

Ham itself is an attractive little village of thatched cottages, clustered around the village green where the Crown & Anchor serves food and drinks, and provides an excellent starting and finishing point for an enjoyable ride.

### Route Description

Ham to Little Down

Start in the middle of Ham Village (**A**), near the Crown & Anchor (parking in the village is limited – if you get stuck, or simply want to miss out the first climb out of the village, there is some space for parking where the ridgeway track crosses the road at the top of the hill – GR333614).

Follow the road up the steep hill south of the village, turning L at the top into the road signposted Buttermere, then immediately L again onto the byway following the crest of the ridge. Follow the byway for a couple of miles over Inkpen Hill. Admire the airy views to the north, but watch your feet as well, or the ruts from 4WD vehicles will eat your pedals! Near Combe Gibbet the track becomes stony and fast, and drops down to cross a minor road before climbing onto the flat summit of Walbury Hill (the track here goes straight on between the fork of two minor roads, climbing slightly to the right of the interpretative signboard for the Iron Age hillfort).

Follow the track straight on across the flat grassy summit, through the earthworks at the far end of the hillfort, and then down to meet another minor road (**B**). Turn R through a small gate by the bridleway sign, go straight on for 100 metres keeping the fence and wood to your left, then bear R and hang off the back of the saddle as you plunge straight down the very steep grassy slope, following a ditch and earthbank to a line of trees which surround a sunken track. Follow the track until it meets a stony lane, then straight on down past a farm to the hamlet of Combe.

At the junction with the road, turn L. After about 750 metres you will reach the gates of Combe Manor. Leave the road and take the signposted bridleway which climbs straight ahead, past the entrance to the tiny twelfth-century St. Swithins Church. The bridleway becomes a grassy track, then crosses a farm track, then becomes stony again before a long  freewheel down through the woods to a byway crossroads at the bottom of a delightful secluded valley.

Turn R onto the byway, and follow the valley for a few hundred metres to a three-way fork (**C**). Be careful here – turn L through the gate, but immediately leave the track (which bends off again to the right along the valley bottom) and follow an indistinct bridleway which climbs over the grass along the left edge of the field, following the forest fence to a small gate at the top left corner of the field. Here the bridleway enters the trees, and continues to climb steeply. [This section could be muddy in wet weather – a longer but gentler alternative is to keep to the track after turning left through the gate, then turn L and L again on meeting the road at the top of the hill to rejoin the main route at point (**D**) near Rockmoor Pond]. At the top of the hill is a path junction – bear slightly L past an enclosure, then keep to the left along a grassy field edge to a gate at the far end of the field. Turn R onto the track past Rockmoor Pond (hidden in the trees to your left) to meet the road (**D**). Turn L for the 750 metres spin along to Little Down.

Little Down to Tidcombe

Turn R at the signpost for Little Down, and follow the road through the hamlet to Winterside Farm. Bear L as the road turns into a track. Straight on over the 'cross-tracks', then continue for another 1 km to the junction with the road. Turn L, then after 750 metres turn R into a tarmac lane (**E**). You soon pass a farm on your left, and the tarmac gives way to a stony track. There's a nice fast descent through woods (getting bumpier as the track gets steeper!) until the track meets the road again by the 'Wiltshire' boundary sign. Bear R to Fosbury, which is a quiet and attractive hamlet of flint houses.

Near the far end of the hamlet turn L at the bridleway sign into Tunbull Lane. This is tarmac as far as Fosbury Farm, at the top of a fairly stiff climb! Turn R at the TJ in front of the farm onto a stony track. As the view over the valley opens out to your left, you come to an X-tracks (**F**). Turn sharp L to drop steeply back down to Hippenscombe on a grassy track.

At the bottom, pass the farm buildings to reach a TJ on the far side of the valley bottom, and turn R to follow the bridleway up the valley – tarmac for the first few yards, then a stony track, and turning further up the valley into a field bridleway. Hippenscombe is one of the deepest of the many dry valleys ('combes') that cut into the downs in this area, and there's a feeling of remoteness as you follow the twists and turns of the valley bottom for nearly 3 km, which becomes narrower and more enclosed as it climbs to its head. Watch out for a R fork after nearly a mile, where the valley bends sharply to the right; then simply follow the valley bottom. Nearing the head of the valley, go straight ahead through a small gate to follow a path into the woods. Before long this curves to the left and starts to climb steeply – follow it up to join the road by the house at Scot's Poor.

Turn R along the road, which runs gently down through the trees for a short way. Just as the road starts to climb again, turn L (**G**) onto a grassy bridleway cutting across the flank of the hill and after 750 metres reaching a crest. At the crest we're back on the north-facing slope of the downs, and efforts are rewarded with another fine view over the valley below. (Look out for Wilton Windmill 4 km or so to the north.) Bear R on a metalled byway and speed down-hill to Tidcombe and its tiny church, tucked at the foot of the scarp.

Tidcombe to Ham

Continue on the road past the church, bearing R at the fork, then R again at the trailing junction with the 'main' road. After 300 me-tres turn L at a small X-rds onto a shady byway surrounded by a line of bushes and trees, and follow this for about a mile until it emerges back into the open with more good views over the Kennett Valley. Keep straight on to where the track descends to meet the road.

Turn sharp R uphill, following the road for about 500 metres past the head of a small combe. Turn L under the overhead power lines (**H**) onto the byway which follows the crest of the ridge.

Keep straight on along the ridgeway. After nearly 2 km cross the Shalbourne road by turning R, then L (signposted Fosbury), then immediately L again back onto the byway which, after a further mile and a half, brings you out on the road at the top of Ham Hill. Turn L and freewheel all the way back to the village – it's a lot easier in this direction!

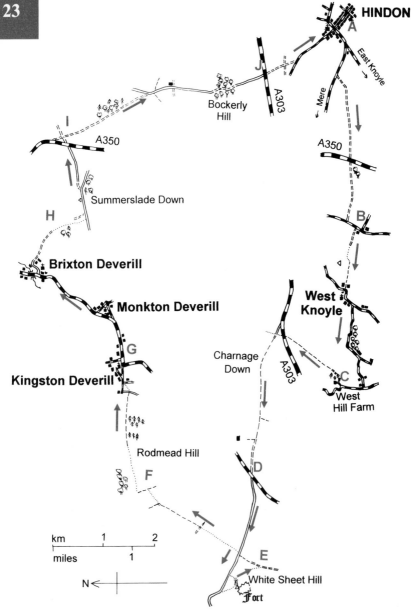

HINDON

A

East Knoyle

J

A303

Mere

A350

Bockerly
Hill

I

A350

B

Summerslade Down

H

West
Knoyle

Brixton Deverill

Charnage
Down

Monkton Deverill

A303

C

West
Hill Farm

G

Kingston Deverill

Rodmead Hill

F

D

E

White Sheet Hill

Fort

km      1      2

miles      1

N ←

## 23) WHITE SHEET HILL AND THE DEVERILLS

Grade; Moderate/hard. A fairly long ride, quite a lot on grass, and
several stiff climbs.
Length;  33 km (20·5 miles)
Terrain;  18 km grassy track/field bridleway
        7 km hard/stony track
        8 km tarmac
Maps; OS Landranger 183 Yeovil & Frome and 184 Salisbury &
The Plain
Ref Points; GR912328 Hindon (start and finish)
             859327 West Knoyle Church
             844343 Charnage Down
             807348 White Sheet Hill (bridleway nr summit)
             845371 Kingston Deverill
             864388 Brixton Deverill
             888383 A350/byway junction
Facilities; Pubs and shop in Hindon.
Nearest rail station; Tisbury 5 km

Background

This route takes in some of the best downland in south-west Wiltshire, offering good riding and wide, airy views from the broad ridge
that runs west of Hindon to White Sheet Hill and then turns north
towards the valley of the Deverills.

Hindon, where the ride starts and finishes, is an attractive village
of well-built stone houses and tree-lined streets, which once had
pretensions to a higher status than you would judge from today's
sleepy appearance. Planned as a town at the same time that Salisbury was built, it was granted the right to hold fairs and a market,

but although larger than its neighbour Tisbury until the coming of the railway it never grew particularly large. Much of the town was destroyed by a disastrous fire in 1752, and although rebuilt it never fully recovered from this blow.

The first section of the ride runs along bridleways and green lanes through pleasant farmland, followed by a scenic and rather more technical descent to West Knoyle. From here there's a steady climb onto Charnage Down, to pick up the wide grassy ridge towards White Sheet Hill. This enjoyable track follows the route of the old London Drove Road, formerly used by herds of cattle and sheep making their way on foot from the farms of the Somerset Levels to market in the big city. It is still marked at intervals by old mileposts showing the distance from London and Sarum (Salisbury) – watch out for the 100 mile marker, in the middle of the track just before White Sheet Hill.

White Sheet Hill is marked at its summit by a trig. point surmounting the ramparts of an Iron Age hillfort. Unfortunately the summit itself is half-hidden behind a large radio mast surrounded by a security fence, and is not on a bridleway. You can approach on foot by crossing a stile from the main track, but the view is almost as good from the bridleway followed in the route description which turns off the track short of the stile. From here you can see across the valley to the woodlands around Stourhead and Zeals, and further afield into neighbouring Somerset and Dorset.

Around White Sheet Hill, and on the first part of the next section towards Rodmead Hill, the land is owned by the National Trust. Contrast the short-cropped grassy carpet, speckled with downland flowers in spring, with the 'improved' lands all around, and imagine the days perhaps a century ago when all of the surrounding hills would have been like this, grazed by large flocks of sheep tended by shepherds from the isolated villages in the valley. Don't be too depressed though – it still makes a fine landscape to ride through! The section from Rodmead Hill to Kingston Deverill is particularly scenic, contouring round the steep side of the hill with great views across to the massive bulk of Brimsdown Hill and the odd narrow ridge of Long Knoll. Ahead unfolds the pastoral valley of the Deverills – from here you can see why it was given it's name 'dwfrial' ('river in fertile uplands') by the early Welsh-speaking settlers. Today the valley is home to a string of attractive small villages and hamlets clustered along the upper reaches of the River Wylye, and despite being on the road to Mere still retains a sense of remoteness.

Don't think the hard work is all over once you've made the steep ascent from Brixton Deverill to Summerslade Down – the last section has a couple of stings in its tail as it crosses the grain of the land on its way back to Hindon. There's nothing too serious, but just enough to make you know you've been out and about when you finish speeding down the final descent into the village!

### Route Description

Hindon to White Sheet Hill

Start in Hindon's main street (**A**), and take the road towards Mere. Pass the turn signposted East Knoyle on the edge of the village, and continue for 500 metres to a dip in the road. Turn L into a bumpy track which climbs onto a low ridge and then bends R to follow the ridge. Continue along the wide 'green lane' for 1·5 km, and cross the busy A350 (careful – fast traffic is hidden by a blind summit!).

Keep straight on for another 1·5 km to a TJ with a minor road. Turn L downhill to the farmhouses at the bottom. Before the first house on the right, turn R into a bridleway track (**B**) which climbs past the hedge to the right of the farm, not along the farm drive itself.

500 metres further on, the track ends in a field. Keep straight on along the R side of the field, and at the top follow the field edge round to the L across the head of a steep combe. Bear R through a small gate and along a narrow ridge to the left of the combe. Then enjoy the steep, bumpy and scenic descent down to West Knoyle Church!

Passing through a farmyard at the bottom, bear L into the road and pass the church. Shortly after, take the first R turn (sp. Charnage). Follow this lane for 2 km, ignoring a left fork marked with 'No Through Road' signs, to a TJ. Turn R towards Mere.

After 500 metres the road bends round to the left – turn R instead into the drive leading to West Hill Farm (**C**). Before the farm buildings turn R into a muddy track which bends round behind the trees and then climbs steadily up the ridge towards Charnage Down. Although it's hard work following the bumpy grass bridleway along the edge of the fields, spare a glance behind you as you near the top for the panorama unfolding across the vale towards Gillingham and the Downs beyond Shaftesbury.

Ahead you will see the A303 climbing onto Charnage Down. Where the track meets the main road at the top of the hill, cross straight over but take extreme care – it's a horrendously fast and busy road, and you may have to wait several minutes for a safe gap in the traffic. On the far side of the main road, go through the metal gate and straight across the grass to an X-tracks with a hard stony track (the bit on the grass is a footpath not a bridleway, so you'll have to push for about 50 metres until you reach the track). Turn L onto the track, which becomes a wide grassy road sweeping along the crest of the Downs, with superb open views. This is the old Drove Road – watch out for the milepost telling the distance from London and Salisbury!

Follow the Drove Road for about 2·5 km to the X rds with the road to Mere (**D**). Cross straight over, and into the hard unsurfaced track opposite – this is still the Drove Road, which continues along the high ground towards White Sheet Hill, 2 km further on. Follow it.

White Sheet Hill to Brixton Deverill

When you reach a point level with the radio mast by the summit, turn L through a gate marked with a blue bridleway marker (if you want to go to the summit itself, you need to stay on the Drove Road for about 200 metres further, then watch out for the stile on the left marking the permissive footpath to the trig. point – walk, don't ride!). Cross the field to the fence surrounding the mast, and turn L again to follow the fence to the end of the compound. Continue following the field fence along the crest of the hill – if you look back you can see the earthworks on White Sheet Hill as it juts out to dominate the valley. When you meet a track coming up the ridge from the right (**E**), turn sharp L and follow the track back over the crest of the hill to meet the Drove Road again.

Cross straight over the Drove Road, through the gate opposite and bump along over the grass following the bridlepath towards Rodmead Hill. Cross a farm track, and continue straight on along the field bridleway opposite. At the far end, the track bends left around the end of the field – ignore this, and instead go straight ahead through the gate (marked with a blue bridleway waymark), and across a grassy field to another gate on the far side (**F**). Go through the gate and turn L on a grassy track along the side of the airfield (used by gliders). Drop down to pass through a small gate, and turn immediately R to follow the bridleway over bumpy grass behind the fence, along the crest of the hill.

Follow this path all the way along the edge of the valley, passing to the L of two woods after about 1 km. Next to the second wood go through a gate and continue along the bridleway as it begins to descend, then swoop down the bumpy ridge towards Kingston Deverill village. At the bottom cross a track, go through the small gate marked with a bridleway arrow, and diagonally across a field to the gate which leads into the lane into the village.

Head along the lane towards the church, where you join the 'main' road from Mere at a right-angle bend (**G**). Keep straight on and follow the road out of the village, past Monkton Deverill and to Brixton Deverill (3 km).

## Brixton Deverill to Hindon

In Brixton Deverill, turn R (just before the river bridge) into a lane which passes the church, bends L then R, and then turns into a track which climbs steadily (and steeply!) back onto the Downs. Halfway uphill, the track ends at a gate (**H**); go straight ahead, climbing across the grassy field, passing to the left of the distinctive clump of trees. Keep straight on over the brow of the hill, then bear L to a gate next to some gorse scrub and a rather incongruous wooden totem pole!

Turn L onto the tarmac track, past the trig. point on the top of Summerslade Down, and at the track junction (by the corner of a wood) fork L onto a stony track which after 1 km meets the main A350 road.

Cross the main road into the byway opposite, then immediately turn R into another bumpy bridleway (**I**). Follow this past the RH side of a wood (this section of about 1 km is muddy and rather heavy going after wet weather, but then improves when the way joins a hard track). Keep going on the hard track past a barn, then steeply downhill and equally steeply back up to the wood on Bockerly Hill. At the top, bear L to stay just inside the wood (another short muddy section) before dropping steeply down to cross the A303 (**J**).

Watch out again when crossing the busy road, straight over into the bridleway that climbs steeply up the other side of the valley. After 750 metres you'll come to a TJ with a minor road – turn L and fly down the hill all the way back to Hindon!

*Dropping down to West Knoyle*

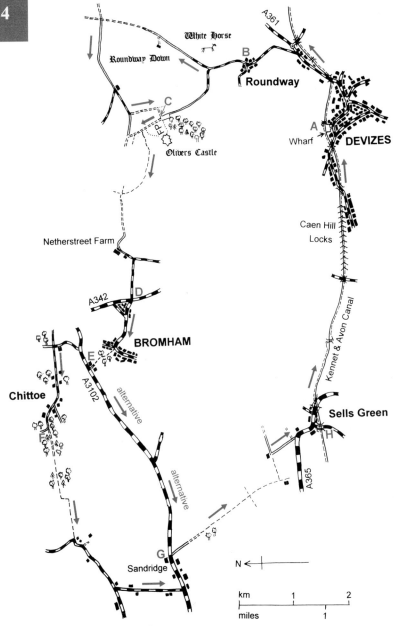

White Horse

A361

Roundway Down

B

Roundway

C

FP

Olivers Castle

A

Wharf

DEVIZES

Caen Hill
Locks

Netherstreet Farm

A342

D

BROMHAM

E

Chittoe

A3102

alternative

Kennet & Avon Canal

F

Sells Green

H

alternative

A365

G

Sandridge

N

km          1          2

miles          1

## 24) DEVIZES, ROUNDWAY DOWN AND CHITTOE

Grade; Hard. Not very hilly, but lots of churned-up bridleways that are pigs when wet.

Length;   30 km (19 miles)

Terrain;   10 km tarmac

7 km canal towpath

3 km stony/hard track

10 km field bridleway/muddy track

Don't forget – to cycle along the canal you need a towpath permit – see page 20

Map; OS Landranger 173 Swindon & Devizes

Reference points; GR  005618 Devizes wharf (start and finish)

020650 Roundway Down

002647 Oliver's Castle

982654 Netherstreet Farm

955668 Chittoe

925645 Sandridge

951620 Sells Green

Facilities; Pubs in Bromham (The Greyhound, off-route in the village centre), Sells Green (Three Magpies), and past the top of Caen Hill locks (Black Horse). Pubs, shops, eating places and all town facilities in Devizes.

Nearest rail stations; Trowbridge 12 km (along the canal); Chippenham 10 km; Melksham 4 km (limited service)

Background

I recce'd this route after wet weather and regretted it. There's nothing more frustrating than huge balls of sticky clay jamming up around your brake blocks and completely stopping all chance of forward motion, leaving you no alternative but to pick up your bike and carry it, complete with what feels like a significant part of the Wiltshire countryside adhering to the wheels. Having said that, after a dry spell it should be much more rideable, although still rough where horses and cattle have churned up some of the bridleways.

The route starts and finishes at the Wharf in Devizes, where there is a visitor centre and exhibition about the Kennet and Avon Canal. The first and last sections of the route follow the canal, including the famous flight of 29 locks at Caen Hill. These are now fully restored and are a fine sight, but until recently lay derelict. A tremendous amount of work has been put in by the Kennet & Avon Canal Trust and British Waterways, both here and elsewhere, to reopen the canal for its full length from Bath to Newbury. The canal was engineered by John Rennie and opened in 1810, carrying coal, grain, stone and other commodities from Bristol and the West Country to London before declining after the opening of the railways.

Up on Roundway Down, the route passes the site of the Civil War battle of 1643, a victory for the Royalist troops under Lord Wilmot. Every now and then the battle is re-enacted by the Sealed Knot – you may be surprised by a Roundhead or Cavalier in full battle dress! Oliver's Castle is of course named after Oliver Cromwell, even though he was not at the battle himself. The earthworks are another Iron Age hillfort, and a good place for a picnic or rest stop, with extensive views over the whole of West Wiltshire. The steep slopes are popular with hang gliders, giving an added interest.

### Route Description

Devizes to Oliver's Castle

Start from the Wharf Carpark in Devizes (**A**) (signposted from

New Park St., on the main route through the town from Trowbridge to Swindon). Cycle to the bottom corner of the carpark, by the canal visitor centre, and underneath the canal bridge heading east. Follow the canal towpath, go under the main road bridge, under a second bridge, and then leave the canal after about 2 km at the third bridge (a new brick one, with a coat of arms and a plaque identifying it as 'Coate Bridge 1990'). Turn L onto the road. At the roundabout turn L again onto the main road, then almost immediately turn sharp R signposted 'Roundway Industrial Estate'.

Continue 1 km to Roundway village, then fork R by the telephone box sp. 'No Through Road' (**B**). Halfway uphill fork R again – on your right you'll see Wiltshire's newest White Horse, carved in 1999 to celebrate the Millenium. Carry straight on where the tarmac ends, into a wide stony lane. This soon becomes an equally wide but grassy lane, unfortunately rather rutted and muddy (and very slippery in wet weather!). Look out for the tumuli up here on Roundway Down – they are supposedly haunted by the ghost of a black dog.

At the X-tracks (about 2 km after the fork) turn L onto a stony lane, and continue to the farmhouse about 1 km further on. Here fork L onto a tarmac lane – avoid the R fork which leads away downhill. After 500 metres turn L onto a rutted and muddy byway, which after yet another 500 metres or so bends sharply R and very soon comes to a small car parking area by the entrance to a wood. (**C**) (If you want to visit Oliver's Castle, leave your bike here and follow the footpath straight ahead to the earthworks at the end of the hill.)

Oliver's Castle to Sandridge

Take the signposted field bridleway running NW from the corner of the carpark (i.e. turn R from the direction from which you arrived). Just after the footpath from Oliver's Castle rejoins the bridleway (where the bridleway meets the steep slope that marks the edge of the hill), turn L onto a grassy track which plunges down a steep-sided gully – good fun, but the chalk makes it slippery and rather technical in the wet! Half way down, the path bears R under the scarp and becomes less steep. Eventually it turns L again (can be very sticky again around here) and crosses the fields to Netherstreet Farm.

At the farm, go past the white farmhouse and into the lane. Turn R at the junction and in 750 metres meet the main road (**D**). Straight across, heading into Bromham village.

After another 500 metres, where the road bends to the left, pass the junction with Greystones on the right and turn immediately R into a narrow footpath marked 'Bridleway, Stoney Lane'. (Slowly, please – and remember to give way to pedestrians.) The path drops down to cross a small stream, then climbs again to join a lane and finally comes out on the main Calne–Melksham road (**E**).

Turn R onto the road, then soon take the first L, following the minor road signposted to Chittoe. After 500 metres turn L at the small crossroads, towards Chittoe village. Keep straight on past the church, and past Silver Street Lane. Descending through the trees, the road bends away to the right – don't follow it, but go straight on along the signposted bridleway (**F**). This starts out with a hard surface made up of bits of red brick, but soon deteriorates and becomes extremely muddy and well churned up. You'll almost certainly have to carry the bike for good chunks of this section – you have been warned! [An alternative wet weather route is to omit the Chittoe section altogether by turning L on the main road at the end of Stoney Lane at point (**E**), and rejoining the main route in Sandridge at point (**G**) – see below].

After a while the bridleway bends L then R, and after a further 750 metres comes out onto a minor road. Turn L, and then 1 km further on turn L again into New Road. At the far end, turn L at the TJ onto the main road into the hamlet of Sandridge.

## Sandridge to Devizes

Just past Sandridge School the main road bends to the right. Immediately after the bend (next to a small lay-by) turn R through a gate into a stony track. (**G**) (If you have missed out Chittoe, you will be coming along the main road in the opposite direction and will need to turn L into the track just before reaching the school).

Before long, the track deteriorates into a wide, grassy green lane (named Praters Lane on the 1:25000 maps). This looks quite easy to cycle on, but don't be deceived – cows graze here and it's very bumpy under that nice grassy surface (and again, particularly heavy going after a wet spell). Persevere for about 2 km, keeping straight on through several gates as the lane gets gradually less wide. After crossing a small stream you can see a farm ahead. Keep going until you're nearly there, but 100 or so metres short of the farm turn L into a similarly rough and bumpy wide green lane (this turn is easily missed, and will probably mean negotiating a moveable wire fence). After 500 metres you will reach Broad Lane Farm. Turn R onto the farm access road and spin along to the TJ with the main road.

Turn L onto the main road towards Sells Green, and then at the 'Three Magpies' turn R onto the minor road to Seend. At the canal bridge turn L onto the towpath (**H**), and it's plain sailing all the way back to Devizes.

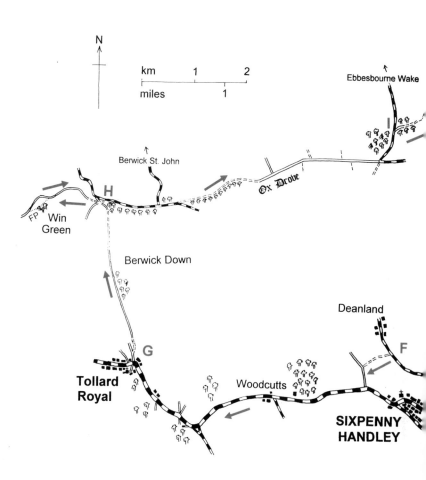

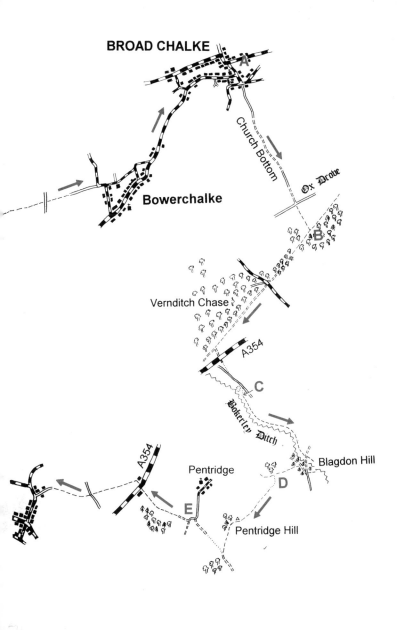

**BROAD CHALKE**

A

Church Bottom

Ox Drove

B

Bowerchalke

Vernditch Chase

A354

C

Dowterley Ditch

Blagdon Hill

A354

Pentridge

D

E

Pentridge Hill

## 25) MARTIN DOWN, TOLLARD ROYAL & WIN GREEN

Grade; Hard. A fairly long ride, with several stiff climbs.
Length; 43 km (26·5 miles)
Terrain; 20 km grassy track/field bridleway
          10 km hard/stony track
          13 km tarmac
Map; OS Landranger 184 Salisbury & the Plain
Ref Points; GR 041253 Broad Chalke Church (start and finish)
                  043193  Martin Down
                  040171  Pentridge Hill
                  944179  Tollard Royal
                  925207  Win Green
                  960210  Ox Drove Ridgeway
Facilities; Pub and P.O./shop at Broad Chalke. Garage selling drinks and sweets/crisps etc. where the route crosses the A354 after Pentridge Hill (GR 022177). Pub and shop in Sixpenny Handley, 500 metres off route. Pub in Tollard Royal (King John Inn, at the top end of the village 400 metres past where the route turns off the road).
Nearest rail station; Salisbury 13 km or Tisbury 10 km

Background

There's fine scenery and plenty of interest on this route, with open chalk downland, pretty villages, the woodlands of Cranborne Chase and Vernditch Chase, and sweeping views from Pentridge Hill, Win Green and the Ox Drove Ridgeway. Although fairly long and hilly and with a relatively high proportion of grassy tracks, it's generally quite rideable – I've ridden it in the middle of a wet winter and apart from a couple of muddy sections had no problems.

The route starts in Broad Chalke, an attractive village of thatched cottages nestling in the valley of the river Ebble. The crystal-clear chalk streams nearby feed beds of watercress, some of which you will see on the way back into the village at the end of the ride.

There's a good climb out of Broad Chalke onto the Downs up the lovely combe of Church Bottom, and after crossing the Ox Drove you follow the line of the old Roman Road from Salisbury, still visible as an earthbank lined with trees. The Roman Road passes along the edge of Vernditch Chase – surprisingly, the delightful beech woods were only planted fairly recently, and before 1920 the area was all bare chalk downland.

Martin Down is still open downland, with good views unfolding as you climb steadily towards Blagdon Hill along the Bokerley Ditch. This is another of those enigmatic earthworks, like the Wansdyke on the Pewsey Downs, which are believed to date from the Saxon invasion but which are still shrouded in mystery. The countryside around here has enough ancient remains to keep any archaeologist happy – look at the OS map, and as well as the Bokerley Ditch and the Roman Road you'll see Grim's Ditch, Soldier's Ring Hillfort, ancient field systems and the Cursus, as well as countless long barrows and tumuli. In more recent times, this area was the setting for W.H. Hudson's *A Shepherd's Life* – an account of life on the remote downs in the last century, in the days before much of the smooth grassland was ploughed to make way for crops.

After the splendid views from Pentridge Hill there's a road section to Tollard Royal – unfortunately there are no convenient bridlways through the woods and parkland of Cranborne Chase. Cranborne was once owned by King John, whose name is now borne by the village pub in Tollard Royal. The hunting rights to the Chase have caused trouble over the centuries, with conflicts between landowners who have tried to reassert their traditional rights of free access for hunting and deer grazing, and the farmers who wanted to enclose and cultivate the land. In the seventeenth and eighteenth centuries this led to 'poaching wars' with occasional pitched battles between poachers and gamekeepers, and even a couple of murders after feelings ran high.

Just outside Tollard Royal are the Larmer Tree Pleasure Gardens, a relic of a more enlightened owner of the estate who opened the gardens in 1880 for 'the recreation of the people of the neighbouring towns and villages'. They are still open to the public on certain days of the year, with ornamental gardens and exotic buildings to admire – worth noting for a more relaxing visit on another day!

After Tollard Royal there's a steep climb onto Berwick Down and then Win Green – at 277 m the highest point in south Wiltshire, and reputedly with views as far as the Isle of Wight on a clear day. The final section of the route follows the Ox Drove Ridgeway, which as the name suggests was one of the old droving roads that were used to move cattle and other animals to market before the coming of the railways, before leaving the downs and dropping back into the valley to Broad Chalke.

### Route Description

Broad Chalke to Pentridge Hill

Park near Broad Chalke Church (**A**), and take the small road south sp. Martin. At the TJ (still in the village) go straight ahead into the bridleway which climbs steadily uphill towards the downs, along the wide combe known as Church Bottom. Further up, the track becomes more rutted and then climbs steeply up the back of the combe to meet the Ox Drove which runs along the crest of the ridge. Go straight over, into a narrower bridleway which drops gently down towards Knighton Wood.

On reaching the woods (**B**), turn R into a wider bridleway which follows the edge of the wood. Keep straight on at the end of Knighton Wood along a row of trees that mark the line of the Roman Road. After 750 metres the path drops down to cross a minor road – on the far side take the bridleway (the smaller track running uphill slightly to the L), and **not** the larger Forestry track. Follow this through the edge of the pleasant beechwoods of Vernditch Chase, and then out into the open continuing straight on along the forest fence. Go through a small gate and turn L into the track which leads to the main road.

Cross over into the small carpark and go straight ahead into a grassy bridleway (not very well-defined) that runs through the scrubby bushes. After about 300 metres this meets a hard track coming in at an oblique angle from the right. Bear L on this track to pass to the left of the large man-made mound (part of an old rifle range) clearly visible ahead. Immediately past this (**C**), turn R to cross the grass directly behind the mound to reach the long earthbank of Bokerley Ditch, which can be seen winding across the landscape like a prehistoric railway embankment. Turn L onto the grassy bridleway which follows the Ditch.

Stay on the bridleway by the Ditch for 2 km, crossing a wide valley and winding up towards Blagdon Hill which looms ahead. **Before** the final part of the climb however, turn R onto a white chalky track that crosses the Ditch and runs through a narrow belt of trees. Turn sharp R again at the far edge of the wood into a waymarked bridleway, and then very soon L through a small gate into a narrower bridleway which begins to climb again towards Pentridge Hill (this is narrow, muddy and well churned by horses – you'll be lucky to avoid carrying in places, but fortunately it doesn't last long!).

At the top of the hill follow the field edge towards a small wood straight ahead. By the wood is a bridleway sign pointing L across the field (**D**) – follow this, and at the far side of the field bear R into a small copse, through a small gate and onto the grassy ridge of Pentridge Hill. Enjoy the views, which make all the effort of the climb worthwhile!

Pentridge Hill to Win Green

The summit of Pentridge Hill is at the far end of the ridge, crowned by a small wood. Follow the bridleway track, which passes to the L of the wood and follows the fence as it bears away to the L following the crest of the ridge downhill. After 500 metres you come to a gate – **don't** go through, but instead turn sharp R and follow the fence down off the ridge. Let it fly down the steep grassy slope, joining a rutted track near the bottom, and bounce down to meet a farm track in the valley (**E**).

Turn L onto the track, and follow as it bends to the R and becomes a field edge bridleway. After the bend, continue straight on, following the barbed wire fence over a low ridge (keep the wood well to your left), and descending to cross the main road next to a petrol station.

Go straight across the road into the signposted bridleway opposite, which drops into a gentle dip and bears L to follow the hedge as a wide, grassy field edge track. Continue straight ahead for 1 km and cross a farm road. Keep following the bridleway, which runs over the fields as a grassy path, bearing gradually R down towards a white house. This eventually joins a track which runs past the houses to a road near the edge of Sixpenny Handley village.

Turn R at the road (away from the village), then soon turn L past 'No Through Road' signs towards Newtown and Deanland. After 1 km, just before Deanland, turn L into a tree-lined byway (**F**), which runs for about 750 metres to a TJ with a tarmac lane. Turn L and before long you'll reach the main road from Sixpenny Handley to Tollard Royal.

Turn R for 5 km of tarmac, past the fringes of Cranborne Chase and the Rushmore Park estate, until you reach the pretty cottages of Tollard Royal nestling among the trees in the bottom of the valley. Just as you enter the village, there's a pond on your R (**G**). Turn past this into a track that runs up into the trees, and follow the R fork (sp. 'Byway to Win Green') to climb steeply through the woods. The gradient eases off after the first climb, but it's a steady haul nevertheless all the way over Berwick Down and up to the main ridge.

On reaching the ridge you'll come to a track/road junction (**H**). Ignore the tarmac roads dropping down off the ridge to the right and left (the latter is a private road to Ashcombe Farm), and instead go straight ahead on the byway following the crest of the ridge towards Win Green. Win Green – the highest point on the ridge – is about 1·5 km from the junction. The byway skirts to the R of the summit, but having come this far it's definitely worth pushing your bike the short distance to the top and spending a few minutes resting and admiring the view!

Win Green to Broad Chalke

Suitably refreshed, rejoin the byway and retrace your steps the 1·5 km to the junction (**H**) with the bridleway back to Tollard Royal. At the junction, go to the L of the trees and join the minor road running east along the ridge. Pass the left turn to Berwick St. John, and where (about 400 m further on) the road bends right, go straight ahead into the track marked 'Byway, Ox Drove'.

Follow this rutted track along the ridge for another 4 km, ignoring all turns off to right or left, until you meet a tarmac minor road. Turn L and coast downhill, passing through the edge of East Combe Wood.

*Win Green*

Near the end of the wood, about 1 km after the junction, turn R through a gate into a waymarked bridleway (**I**).

Follow the wide but muddy track down through the trees, and then out into a field. Continue to follow the line of the bridleway, and go through a small gate on the L which leads to a narrow path following a line of trees. Go through another gate into a field, and follow the bridleway along the RH fence. Cross a private farm track onto another field edge path, straight ahead.

Eventually the bridleway meets a track – follow this to the road on the edge of Bowerchalke village. Keep straight ahead, past the 'Bowerchalke' sign, and go straight on again into the minor lane which bypasses the main village street. At the far end bear L, and then L again, to rejoin the 'main' road to Broad Chalke, which is 3 km further along the valley.

## MEGARIDES

If you think the rides in the rest of the book are too easy, here are five suggestions for a more challenging day out! Strictly for fit and experienced bikers, I've linked together pairs of routes to give rides of between 45 and 75 km in length. Expect to be in the saddle for most of the day, and plan a short cut back to the start if you find you've bitten off more than you can chew.

### MEGARIDE 1 – GREAT RIDGE GRIND
Combines routes 14 and 8
Length; 48 km (30 miles)

Start from Tytherington and follow route 14 as far as the TJ with the Chilmark road, where it leaves the Western Drove Road just before Down Farm. Instead of turning left onto the road, cross straight over into the metalled byway opposite. Soon cross straight over another minor road, and continue to follow the byway for about 2 km ignoring all turns to right or left. After passing Juniper House the track enters trees and bends L. Just round the bend turn R into a signposted byway which runs along the edge of the wood to the junction with a road. Cross straight over into the tarmac byway opposite. You're now on route 8.

Follow the second half of route 8 along the old Drove Road (south of Grovely Wood), to the wide avenue of beech trees just before the final descent to Wilton. At the big track junction by the farm buildings turn sharp L to join the first part of route 8 near the start, and follow the route back through Grovely Wood to where you joined it at the road/ track junction at the far end of the wood.

Retrace your outward journey along the metalled byway to where you left route 14, and follow the rest of route 14 back to Tytherington.

## MEGARIDE 2 – ALONG THE RIDGEWAY
Combines routes 10 and 13
Length; 45 km (28 miles)

Start in Aldbourne and follow route 10 past Liddington Hill to the junction with the main road (**F**). Turn L onto the main road for 400 metres, then turn R sp. Little Hinton (the Ridgeway Path also follows the road for this section). Cross the M4, and at the Foxhill X-rds (by the Shepherds' Rest pub) go straight ahead. At the top of the hill turn R where the Ridgeway Path leaves the road.

Follow the Ridgeway Path for the last few km of ride 13, but instead of turning downhill into Bishopstone continue straight along the Path, past Ridgeway Farm, to join the start of route 13 on it's way to Uffington Castle. Follow ride 13 round past Uffington, as far as the bridge over the M4 motorway at Peak's Downs (**C**).

Instead of turning onto the bridleway to Foxhill, carry on over the motorway bridge and turn L at the TJ. Near the top of the hill turn R into a signposted byway through the trees, and follow it over the crest of the hill and then all the way down into the valley bottom. At the bottom, cross over the road and continue along the stony byway for the last 1 km into Aldbourne.

## MEGARIDE 3 – PEWSEY DOWNS EXPLORER
Combines routes 21 and 12
Length; 45 km (28 miles)

Begin in Bishops Cannings and follow ride 21 past Tan Hill and down to East Kennett. Leaving East Kennett, continue on the road instead of turning onto the track to East Kennett Farm. Climb the hill and drop down into the valley on the other side, to a TJ with the Lockeridge–Alton Barnes road. Turn L, then immediately turn R into the rutted byway climbing out of the valley towards a radio mast on the hill.

You're now on route 12. Follow it all the way to the end at Knap Hill carpark. Cross straight over the road, through a gate and into the grassy bridleway that climbs straight ahead towards the ridge, following the fence. The bridleway keeps to the R of the shallow combe, climbing to reach the Wansdyke. Cross through the gap in the Dyke, and turn L to rejoin route 21 at point (**E**). Follow route 21 along the Wansdyke for a short distance, then down to the canal and back to Bishops Cannings.

## MEGARIDE 4 – KENNETT KILLER
Combines routes 20 and 19
Length; 56 km (35 miles)

Start off on route 20 from Smallgrain Picnic Area, past Cherhill monument and Windmill Hill to Avebury. By the Red Lion in the centre of the village, pick up route 19 and follow the track up to the Ridgeway.

Follow ride 19 to Ogbourne, then past Barbury Castle and back along the Ridgeway. At the end, instead of turning R at point (**B**) to drop back down to Avebury keep straight on along the Ridgeway until it meets the main A4 road by The Sanctuary. Turn R onto the main road to West Kennett, where you rejoin route 20 at point (**E**). Continue along the A4 past Silbury Hill, and follow ride 20 back to Smallgrain.

## MEGARIDE 5 – FOLLOWING THE NORTHERN PERIMETER
Combines routes 9 and 11
Length; 70 or 74 km (43 or 46 miles)

Start at Enford and follow ride 9 through Netheravon, and across the Larkhill and Westdown Ranges to Redhorn Hill (**E**). This is the starting point for ride 11 – do the complete ride (with or without the diversions, depending on how masochistic you're feeling!). Then pick up route 9 again for a final spin along the ridgeway track back to Enford. Sounds easy, doesn't it? – but it's a long way!

*Happy bikers*

For further information about our series of mountain bike guides, see our web site – **www.ernest-press.co.uk**

# Walks in the Country
# CHESHIRE

## David H. Pill

COUNTRYSIDE BOOKS
NEWBURY, BERKSHIRE

First published 1998
© David H. Pill 1998
Revised and Updated 2006
Reprinted 2007

COUNTRYSIDE BOOKS
3 Catherine Road
Newbury, Berkshire

ISBN 1 85306 509 9
EAN 978 1 85306 509 5

*For Tony Beaman,
my companion on these walks,
and his wife Mary, in appreciation of many kindnesses.*

Designed by Graham Whiteman

Photographs by the author
Maps and illustrations by Trevor Yorke

Produced through MRM Associates Ltd., Reading
Printed by Cambridge University Press

# Contents

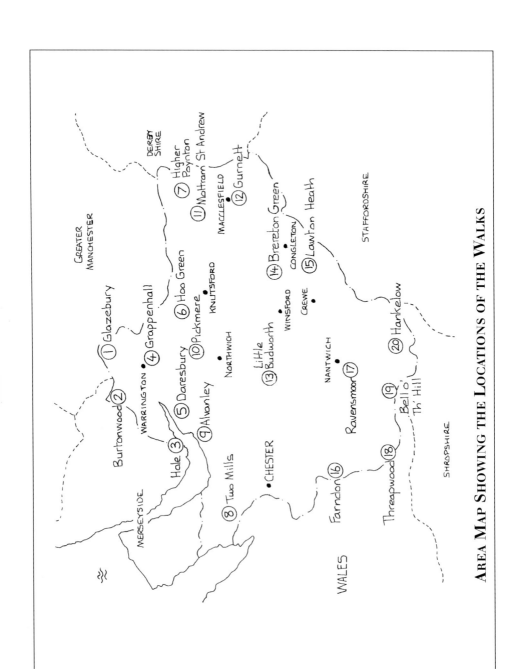

**Area Map Showing the Locations of the Walks**

WALK

## Publisher's Note

We hope that you obtain considerable enjoyment from this book; great care has been taken in its preparation. Although at the time of publication all routes followed public rights of way or permitted paths, diversion orders can be made and permissions withdrawn.

We cannot of course be held responsible for such diversion orders and any inaccuracies in the text which result from these or any other changes to the routes nor any damage which might result from walkers trespassing on private property. We are anxious though that all details covering the walks are kept up to date and would therefore welcome information from readers which would be relevant to future editions.

# Introduction

The walks in this book range across Cheshire from her most northerly village to her most southerly town, from the Welsh border to the Peak District National Park. They will take you into the mosslands of the north, to the forgotten shoreline of the Wirral peninsula, across the rolling Cheshire plain, into the sandstone hills which are the county's backbone and onto the high gritstone moors of the Pennine chain.

You can visit picture postcard villages and ancient churches, walk along canal towpaths and abandoned railway tracks, see windmills, watermills, a lighthouse, a dovecote and a Victorian hearse-house. Discover an Iron Age hill fort, a border castle and a barn which was the great hall of a medieval manor house. Picnic on village greens and find refreshment in Cheshire's oldest inn, a pub which was once a railway booking office and a café that was a medieval vicarage.

And along the way be prepared to meet friendly donkeys and inquisitive ostriches, lots of sheep, cows, and the original Cheshire cat. There is even a maze, and you may meet a ghost or two. In fact, something for everyone – young and old.

Some of the walks are even more enjoyable at a particular time of the year: spring when daffodils illuminate the greens and verges, summer when the wildflowers lend their colour to your path, autumn when you can go blackberrying, search for conkers amongst the fallen leaves or pick mushrooms for breakfast, or winter when a warm bowl of soup by a roaring pub fire makes a fitting end to a tramp through crisp snow. So do read about a walk before you set out.

Not only are places to eat listed and sampled dishes recommended but places to visit are suggested where you can extend your knowledge of the natural history of the area in which you have walked. Please check on the opening times of these and of the pubs and restaurants before you leave home; because they do change. And please do not park in a pub car park unless you are going to eat or drink there. Alternative parking spots are suggested.

It is a myth encouraged by sports shop proprietors and magazines dependent on advertising that you need to be expensively kitted out to go walking. Perhaps you need special equipment to walk the Pennine Way, but for these walks I wore sports coat and flannels and, in inclement weather, a cap and old-fashioned raincoat. So just wear anything in which you feel comfortable, making sure you will not get too hot in summer and that you keep warm and dry in winter. I wore ordinary but well-made shoes with non-slip soles, but boots can be an advantage when it is wet or muddy underfoot. Remember to change them if you are going to eat in a pub.

Where there are problems with excessively muddy footpaths or waterlogged fields or where unfriendly farmers have ploughed up rights of way, I have tried to provide an alternative route. I have also given some indication where there are gates or fences to climb. A simple sketch map accompanies each walk but I strongly recommend you arm yourself with the relevant OS Landranger map and the appropriate map number is given. I have frequently gone back to check the routes, but I feel there may be places where, following the line on the map, I have missed a stile or open gate. So do look around you carefully before you resort to climbing a fence and, of course, do avoid trampling on crops. The crops mentioned, by the way, were those being grown at the time of writing, and of course these may change. It is a fairly safe assumption, however, that arable will remain arable, and pasture, pasture.

Some of the routes are entirely suitable for children and for walking the dog, so you could turn a walk into a family outing and take a picnic. I carried my camera, maps, notebook, etc around in an ordinary carrier bag, but a rucksack can be more convenient when you are carrying thermos and sandwiches or when you need to cross a stile, take a picture or use your binoculars. Do take your binoculars with you because you are going to see some superb views on these walks and of course there will be birds, rabbits and squirrels to watch. Simple spotters' guides to birds, trees and flowers would be useful too, although I have described some of the local flora and fauna you are likely to encounter.

Please take the time to look around you as you walk Cheshire's lanes and pathways. Then you will, I hope, enjoy them as much as I did.

*David H. Pill*

# Walk 1
# OVER THE CARRS AT GLAZEBURY
### Length : 3 ½ miles

*The Chat Moss Hotel at the start of the walk.*

**GETTING THERE**: Glazebury is on the A574 Leigh to Warrington road, 1 mile south of its junction with the A580 and 4½ miles from junction 11 on the M62. It can be reached from the M6, junction 22 via Croft and Culcheth.

**PARKING**: The road through Glazebury village is busy and on-road parking is not advisable. However, if due consideration is given to residents and farm traffic, there may be space in Hurst Lane on the left of the A574 about 200 yards north of the

Chat Moss Hotel. There is parking for customers both at the hotel, our starting point, and at the George and Dragon Inn.

**MAP**: OS Landranger – Manchester 109 (GR 673968).

G lazebury is the most northerly village in Cheshire. Until the 19th century it was just a scattering of farms and cottages amongst the mosslands. The relative inaccessibility of the area is reflected in its history. Celtic culture seems to have survived well into Anglo-Saxon times:

the names of the neighbouring villages of Kenyon and Culcheth and of the local river, the Glaze, are Old Welsh in origin. Later the district was to be a stronghold of the Roman Catholic religion in times of religious persecution.

In the 18th and 19th centuries cotton and silk weaving was carried on in the cottages and a textile mill was built alongside the Liverpool-Manchester railway, which arrived in 1830. The great railway engineer George Stephenson had to float the line on the Moss on hurdles of birch branches covered with cotton waste. The silver birch is the native tree of the mosslands, but here and there are islands of sandstone whose soils support a variety of deciduous trees, notably beech and horse chestnut, which both grow to a great height.

Peat is still cut on the mosses to the east of the village. Though some may have been used for fuel for cottage fires, in the past it was usually shredded to provide bedding for farm animals; now it is sold to gardeners. Most of the mossland has been drained, however, and is devoted to market gardening, particularly lettuce growing, and to grazing sheep, while the sandier soils support grain, potatoes and other arable crops. Your walk takes you mainly through the woods and fields of these sandy acres, but also across a section of the old wetlands. In such varied habitats there are many different butterflies, birds and plants to spot as you walk. The return route offers a splendid view of the distant cotton mills, great relics of the

**FOOD and DRINK**

The Chat Moss Hotel (tel: 01925 762128) serves bar meals and Burtonwood ales, which can be enjoyed in its pleasant garden on the banks of the Glaze. Just down the road, opposite Glazebury's handsome Methodist chapel, is the timbered George and Dragon (tel: 01925 763296), which serves good value meals lunchtimes and evenings. Main courses include cheese and asparagus tart, gammon, and steak and ale pie. Should you want morning coffee or afternoon tea, try Bent's Garden Centre on the northern edge of the village (tel: 01942 262066).

past, and the chance to see a barn that was the great hall of a medieval manor house. It is level, easy walking suitable for all ages, but there is a short woodland stretch which can be muddy.

**THE WALK**

**1** Carefully cross the road from the Chat Moss Hotel and follow the narrow path between the railway embankment and a ploughed field. Turn left alongside a hawthorn hedge. The new houses ahead stand on the site of Glazebury Mill, where corn was ground for well over 200 years.

**2** About 200 yards after passing a splendid solitary beech tree and before you reach a small wooded area, take the path to the right across the open field to a bridge over a stream. After crossing the bridge, immediately turn right over a stile and follow the stream to the next stile. Climb it to enter Hitchfield Wood. The path can be

*The Methodist church in Glazebury.*

muddy in places, even in hot weather, but the muddy sections can be avoided if you take care. The wood is delightful and is composed of a variety of deciduous trees, including oak, hawthorn, sycamore, willow, beech and horse chestnut. See how many varieties you can spot, and look out for tree creepers and for dragonflies around the stream.

**3** Where the path forks, bear left to emerge from the wood into a meadow. In these more open spots you are likely to see skylarks and wagtails, while the nettles at the wood's edge attract tortoiseshell, hedge brown and large white butterflies. Skirt the wood for about 100 yards until you meet a more clearly defined path, and there turn right over a stile. Proceed along the path with, at first, the wood on your right and a cornfield to your left. When you reach a hawthorn hedge, keep straight ahead but with the hedge on your left-hand side.

**4** At the end of the path turn right onto a somewhat overgrown farm track. Pass some tall chestnut trees on your left and go under a railway bridge onto Culcheth Carrs. The word carr means an area of mossland or marsh overgrown with brushwood. At the fork in the path pass over the stile, keeping to the right of an odd-looking group of mounds. These are a former munitions store.

**5** When you are level with the

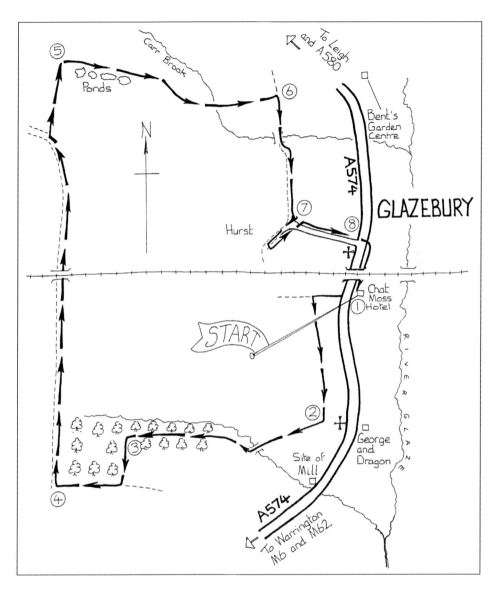

mounds, turn right. There will be an arable field to your left and an interesting chain of ponds to your right. Fringed with willows, these may be old withens or osier beds, some of which are known to have existed in the area in the early 19th century. The willows were cultivated for basket weaving and hurdle making, often in marl pits from which clay had been extracted to enrich and increase the moisture-holding capacity of the sandy soil.

Cross the footbridge over the Carr brook into an open field. Slightly to the left and in the distance is a splendid group of cotton mills, the palatial relics of the last great days of the industry early this century. At the fork in the path bear right and then left, noting a remaining area of wetland to your right.

**6** A number of paths meet at the old hedgerow ahead. Here turn right, keeping the barbed wire fence to your left. Recross the brook and the path becomes a farm track and then a metalled road.

**7** The group of buildings to your right form the hamlet of Hurst. Here you can make a slight detour to see the splendid timber roof of a barn which was once the great hall of a medieval manor house. Retracing your steps, bear right past the village cricket field out onto the main road.

**8** Turn right to pass Glazebury's neat little Victorian parish church and return to the Chat Moss Hotel. The small industrial complex on the left called Albion Park is on the site of Glazebury's cotton mill. And the hotel, which has Stephenson's *Rocket* on its sign, once housed the booking office of the village's long-gone station.

> ### PLACES of INTEREST
>
> Some original mossland is conserved at **Risley Moss Nature Park**, just off the A574, about 3½ miles south of Glazebury. Here, in the viewing tower, you find an excellent explanation of how the moss was formed. From the tower you can watch grey herons, goshawks, marsh harriers and buzzards, while hides amongst birches and alders provide views of woodland birds like the greater spotted woodpecker. Adjacent to the park, which is open every day but Friday, is **Birchwood Forest Park**, a recently created area of over 500 acres of wood and glade with a walled garden. Nearer to Glazebury, and also on the A574, is **Culcheth Linear Park**. A former railway cutting, it is now an attractive wooded, streamside walk with picnic areas. The haunt of jays and bank voles, it is also host to a remarkable number of different butterflies, and rangers are on hand to help you recognize them.

# Walk 2
# IN THE VALLEY OF THE SACRED STREAM
### Length : 3 miles

*The St Helens Canal.*

**GETTING THERE:** Burtonwood is signposted from the A49, ½ mile north of junction 9 on the M62 and 1½ miles from junction 22 on the M6. The starting point, the Fiddle I' Th' Bag Inn, is on the right after 1¼ miles.

**PARKING:** There is parking for patrons at the Fiddle and room for one or two cars by the public footpath sign 100 yards down Hall Lane on the right.

**MAP:** OS Landranger – Liverpool 108 (GR 585929).

Part of Cheshire's northern boundary lies along the Sankey valley, now a linear park. Sankey means 'sacred stream', and the river is just one of the many interesting features of a fascinating walk in the parish of Burtonwood.

The name Burtonwood was first recorded in the 13th century. It means 'the wood attached to the fortified house'. Most of the woodland has been rooted up for agriculture; so, sadly, have many of the hedgerows. However, there are still several moated manor houses in the area. One of them, Bradlegh Old Hall is on your route.

Burtonwood is still very much a farming community, with old farmhouses scattered amongst the fields which surround the village. Some of the fields sustain beef cattle, others grow corn and vegetables. Work is also provided by the local brewery, founded in 1867. The brewery's owners planted the attractive lime avenues along the lanes leading into Burtonwood from the west. Although the village itself is not on your route, it is worth a brief visit. It has a neat Georgian church and is particularly attractive in springtime when daffodils colour its greens and verges.

The area is full of interest, both for the naturalist and the industrial archaeologist. Indeed, there is much for everyone to enjoy on this walk. Wildflowers, birdlife, some surviving woodland, an historic canal and important relics of the earliest days of steam railways will all enhance your pleasure on this excursion to the valley of the sacred stream. It is a fairly short one, suitable for quite young children, so take it slowly and savour its delights.

## THE WALK

**1** From the Fiddle Inn turn right onto the main road and then right again into Hall Lane. This is a very pleasant lane, particularly in May when it is scented by the flowers of both pink and white hawthorn. Look out for red campion in the verges. Although there is little traffic on this road you may prefer

### FOOD and DRINK

The Fiddle I'Th Bag derives its curious name from a device for sowing grain. It is a nice, unspoilt country inn which provides food lunchtimes and evenings. You will find its excellent home-made soup particularly welcome if you do this walk in winter (tel: 01925 225442). The Fiddle serves Theakston's ales. If you want to sample the local Burtonwood beers you should try the Elm Tree or the Bridge Inn in Burtonwood village. The latter serves good value bar lunches.

to walk through Gypsy Wood, which fringes the lane on the right. You reach its footpath about 250 yards after the second farmhouse.

**2** At the end of the wood and of the lane turn right through the gate-posts. For a glimpse of Bradlegh Old Hall and its lovely garden turn almost immediately left. In the 1480s the Hall was visited by King Richard III, and it does not take too much imagination to see Shakespeare's villain riding across the moat and through the gatehouse to be greeted by his host, Sir Piers Legh.

**3** Retrace your steps and turn left through a gate onto a rough track. This is a good spot for blackberrying. Looking slightly to your left you will see the Sankey viaduct. Known locally as the Nine Arches, this is one of the world's oldest railway viaducts. It was built in 1830 to carry George Stephenson's Liverpool-Manchester railway across the Sankey valley.

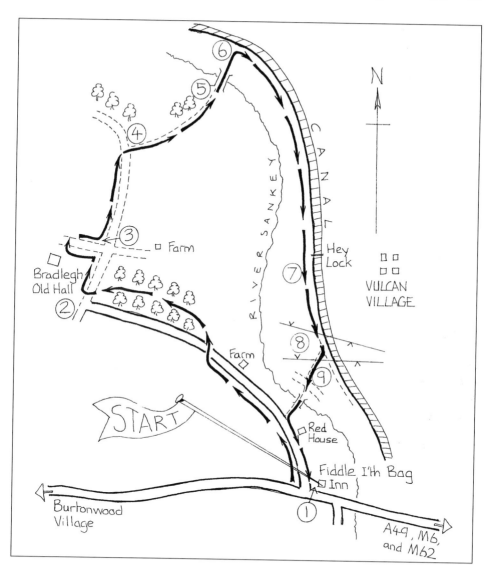

**4** At a fork in the path, to your left you will see a wood (called Park Brow Plantation from Bradlegh's vanished deer-park) which is carpeted with bluebells in early summer. However, unless you wish to explore it, you should take the right fork and drop down into the valley. There is another small area of deciduous woodland on the left, largely oak, elm and sycamore, but buttercups rather than bluebells are the predominant flower here.

**5** At the footbridge over the river Sankey the sharp-eyed may catch sight of a kingfisher. Having crossed the bridge, go ahead through the gate onto the towpath of the St Helens Canal. The picturesque rock formation on the opposite bank is actually waste from a long-gone chemical works!

**6** Turn right along the towpath to enjoy one of the most attractive sections of the canal. Known also as the Sankey Navigation, this is the oldest of the canals of the Industrial Revolution. It was opened in 1757 to supply Liverpool with coal from the Lancashire coalfield. No longer navigable so far upstream, its quiet waters are popular with anglers. In them grow flag irises, water lilies and bulrushes, while the towpath is fringed with nettle-beds and cow parsley, and overhung with oak, willow, birch and hazel.

**7** You may like to rest awhile at the site of Hey Lock, where there is a picnic area. There is also a plaque which tells the history of the canal and its surroundings. As you walk on you will see, across the field to the left, the cottages of picturesque Vulcan Village, built to house workers at a locomotive factory owned by George Stephenson's son, Robert.

## PLACES of INTEREST

It is unlikely that any of the original 'Burton Wood' survives, but there is oak woodland of long standing in Gypsy Wood and Park Brow Plantation. There is more mixed deciduous woodland in **Burtonwood Nature Park**, which is accessible from Chapel Lane, the village's main street, via Green Jones Brow. The park has a wildflower meadow and picnic area. Just 2½ miles south-east, off the A574, is **Bewsey Old Hall**, another moated manor house. In the adjacent part of the **Sankey Valley Park** (Old Hall car park) you will find a wetland reserve which is an important breeding ground for waterfowl such as mute swans, coots and moorhens. There is also a garden specially planted to attract butterflies and a maze that will delight children.

**8** Leave the towpath at the first footpath on the right after passing under the first of two rows of pylons, and cross the field in the direction of the farmhouse on the left. This is Red House Farm, but although it has a lovely old red brick barn, the house itself, despite its red sandstone footings, has a curious but not unattractive timbered appearance.

**9** Pass over the footbridge to regain Hall Lane, where, unless you have left your car here, you should turn left and retrace the first hundred yards or so of the walk back to the Fiddle Inn.

# Walk 3
# HALE AND THE RIVER MERSEY
## Length : 4¼ miles

*The war memorial on Hale green.*

**GETTING THERE:** Hale is 4 miles south-west of Widnes and 2 miles east of Speke, and easily reached by minor roads from the A561 and A562 Widnes to Liverpool roads or from junctions 6 and 7 on the M62.

**PARKING:** There is parking for customers at the Wellington Inn and on-street parking in its vicinity. Otherwise use the car park in Dungeon Lane and start the walk at point 5.

**MAP:** OS Landranger – Liverpool 108 (GR The Wellington 468826, Dungeon Lane 449821).

Celebrated in verse by Poet Laureate Sir John Betjeman, Hale was once regarded as the prettiest village in Lancashire and in 1968 it won that county's best-kept village award. Since 1974 it has been firmly in Cheshire but it is still a place of rare charm.

Hale's name means either a piece of flat alluvial land by the side of a river or the place at the bend of a river, and it is situated at the widest point of the

Mersey estuary. It has a lighthouse, a manor house and numerous lovely old cottages, some of them thatched. Indeed, they were still building houses with thatched roofs in Hale in the inter-war years.

A notable former inhabitant was the Childe of Hale, John Middleton, a 17th century son of the village who was 9 feet 3 inches tall. The bodyguard of Sir Gilbert Ireland of Hale Hall, he went with him to London, where he wrestled and defeated King James I's champion and was rewarded with the king's purse of £20.

The walk alongside the river offers views in all directions, from the road and rail bridges that link Widnes with Runcorn to the distant hills of North Wales. Do take binoculars if you can, and enjoy the sighting of birdlife along the estuary – and of planes taking off from nearby Liverpool Airport! Something in which to collect elderberries and blackberries in their season might be useful too! Apart from climbing a few steps, this is easy walking for all the family.

## THE WALK

**1** From the Wellington car park turn right into Town Lane to pass a parade of shops. Soon you will arrive at the first of Hale's two small greens, where a handsome Georgian house overlooks the War Memorial cross. In medieval times when Hale was a market town this was probably the market place.

**2** Turn left into Church End, noting the sign of the Childe of Hale pub on your right. John Middleton's cottage is the thatched one at right-angles to the road, and it is said that when he was in bed his feet protruded through the two windows in the gable end!

Across the second of the two greens from the long row of thatched cottages is the Manor House. It was originally the parsonage, and if you look at it from the side you will see that its elaborate 18th century façade hides an older, somewhat meaner building.

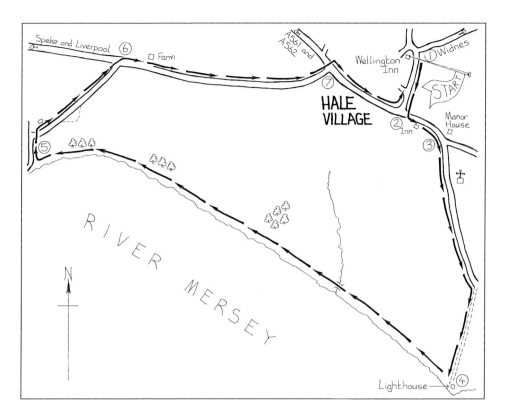

**3** At the fork bear right towards the church, another building which is not all it seems. It was gutted by arsonists in 1977 and has been reconstructed within its old walls, the tower dating from the 14th century. You will find the Childe of Hale's grave in the churchyard, and opposite is his image carved from a dead beech tree. The details on the figure's surface represent aspects of the village's life and history.

As you leave the houses behind, look over to the left and you will see the road and rail bridges which link the towns of Widnes and Runcorn across the Mersey and the Manchester Ship Canal. The power station is at Fiddler's Ferry. The other one coming into view to the right is at Ince near Ellesmere Port. Pass through the gate and head for the lighthouse. Now part of a private house, it was built in 1906 to replace one from the 1830s and decommissioned in 1958.

**4** On reaching the lighthouse turn right, through the gate, and pause to read the information boards about the history of the river crossing and the wildlife of the estuary. As you proceed along the low sandstone cliffs look out for widgeon, sandpiper, shelduck, mallard and heron and listen for the distinctive piping cry of the oyster catcher. Across the estuary are the oil storage depots around Eastham docks on the Wirral, and beyond, in the distance, the Clwydian Hills of North Wales.

The path is fringed with the black marram grass which is a feature of our northern shores, with yellow ragwort and white mayweed, while twisting amongst the other plants are both pink and white varieties of convolvulus. Cross the wooden bridge over the stream and carry on along the path between shore and cornfield. Do not be tempted to turn right into the wood (called Ice House Plantation from the underground storage place for ice for the kitchens of Hale Hall in pre-refrigeration days), but continue straight ahead. At the trees you have the choice of carrying on along the same footpath or dropping down onto the shore. Take the upper path. The trees are largely sycamore and grey poplar, whose leaves show their grey undersides in the breeze, while the tall plant with prickly leaves and dandelion-like flowers is the prickly sow-thistle.

Shortly the path becomes more open and the trees give way to blackberry and elderberry bushes. At the meeting of tracks bear left. Near the house go down some steps through a small wood, across a bridge and up some more steps to an open area. Go down the slope to where once stood the Dungeon Salt Works and up the steps to the car park in Dungeon Lane.

**5** Turn right up the lane. On the left is the airport's boundary fence. For a glimpse of the runway go past the road junction and look through the gate. Otherwise turn right onto Bailey's Lane. Alongside it are the airport's landing lights. They are even on the roof of Overton House, which looks across the estuary to the Overton Hills above Frodsham and Helsby. Continue along the lane, pausing to chat to the ponies, till you meet Hale Road.

**6** Turn right, noticing on the left the old farmhouse dated 1726 and the probably older timber-framed barn. On the right of the road are some thatched houses of the 1930s and on the left thatched cottages of an earlier age.

**7** Bear right onto the High Street and look out for the old school-house of 1739 with its cupola topped with a weather-vane in the form of a schooner. It is somewhat hidden behind trees and hedges. Further along is the timber-framed and thatched Shepherd's Cottage, dated 1665, and then on both sides of the road pretty cottages built by the Ireland Blackburnes of Hale Hall for their estate workers. The Hall itself has gone and part of its park is a recreation ground, but you can see one of its lodges a little hidden on the right before you reach the war memorial once again. Here turn left and head back to the Wellington.

# Walk 4
# UNDER THE GAZE OF THE CHESHIRE CAT
### Length : 4¼ miles (or 2¾ miles)

*St Wilfrid's church seen from the canal bridge.*

**GETTING THERE**: Grappenhall village is just south of the junction of the A50 with the A56, 1¼ miles north-west of junction 20 on the M6 and 1½ miles from junction 9 on the M56.

**PARKING**: There is parking for customers at the Parr Arms and the Ram's Head on the village street (Church Lane). Alternatively, park on Glebe Avenue on the other side of the

canal bridge.

**MAP**: OS Landranger – Manchester 109 (GR 639863).

Grappenhall is a place of contrasts. North of the A56 it is very much a suburb of Warrington, Cheshire's largest town. South of that road it is a picturesque, unspoilt village with the open countryside on its doorstep. Its quiet cobbled street is lit by quaint iron lanterns and overlooked by an old sandstone church, St Wilfrid's. Within its 16th century walls the church contains relics of much earlier times – 14th century glass, the

## FOOD and DRINK

Grappenhall has two delightful inns and it is a pleasure to sit outside them in the sunshine with a pint of Marston's ale and enjoy this tranquil village. The Ram's Head (tel: 01925 226162) is stone-built and has colourful tubs of flowers on its forecourt; the Parr Arms (tel: 01925 267393) is colourwashed and has equally colourful hanging baskets. In the Ram's panelled rooms hung with pictures of old Grappenhall, you can enjoy Lamb Henry or chicken stroganoff, while cheaper meals include chicken tikka masala. In the Parr Arms, with its lace tablecloths, brasses and pictures of bulldogs (one is kennelled in the yard), meals range from a hot beef bun, through chicken Kiev to the mixed grill, price corresponding to size. Vegetarian meals are also available.

tomb of a 13th century knight, and a font and parish chest which may be Norman or even Saxon in origin. And outside, high up on the west face of the tower, is a carving of a cat which is said to have been Lewis Carroll's inspiration for the Cheshire Cat of *Alice's Adventures in Wonderland*.

The walk takes you from the village onto the Cheshire Plain with its corn-fields and dairy farms. The Plain is not flat, as is sometimes thought, but rolling countryside, and attractive because the old hedgerows remain. The route also includes a stretch along the Bridgewater Canal. Its earliest section was constructed in the late 1750s to carry coal from the Duke of Bridgewater's mines to Manchester. This is an extension, cut to link that city with the port of Liverpool, and was completed in 1776.

Opinions differ locally as to why nearby Australia Lane was so called. Some say it is where emigrants used to embark on the first stage of their journey, others that, along with a now vanished New Zealand Lane, it was named in commemoration of the ANZAC forces of the First World War.

There is a long, gradual pull uphill in the first part of the walk, and later a more difficult section where the path has been ploughed over. However, an alternative shorter route is provided. This can easily be managed by quite young children, who, in April or May, may be lucky enough to hear their first cuckoo.

## THE WALK

**1** Start by the village stocks at the church gate. Turn left along the churchyard wall, noticing the handsome early 19th century Rectory on the right and the Old Rectory, which paradoxically is newer, on the left. Before the bridge, turn right along Canalside.

**2** At the junction with Australia Lane turn up a farm track on the left-hand side of the hawthorn hedge, and keep left at the oak tree. There is a meadow on your left and a very interesting old hedge on your right. In addition to oak and hawthorn it contains elderberry, holly and even broom, which all appear to grow out of a ditch. This may be the ditch which gave Grappenhall its name, for it means the quiet or remote place by a ditch or drain. Soon the meadow gives way to cornfields and views over the Cheshire Plain.

*The Ram's Head pub.*

Where the track veers to the right, keep straight ahead through the kissing gate into rough pasture filled with buttercups. Keep the woodland (Park Wood) on your right. Cross a stream and eventually, after passing a pond, enter a field with holly bushes and a patch of foxgloves to the right initially and then an old hawthorn hedge. Its dead sections give one some idea of how the hedge was originally layered. On nearing a house, pass through a gate and walk along a narrow path between the hedge and a fence. At the house, turn left and then right onto a path between two gardens.

**3** Turn right onto Cartridge Lane and look out for the hybrid campion at the footpath's side. At the end of the lane on the right is Reddish Hall Farm. See if you can spot the line of the moat of the original hall. Its richer grass seems to attract the cattle.

**4** Turn right here if you are taking the easier route and go down the lane to just beyond Whitehouse Farm to rejoin the walk at point 8. Otherwise turn left and go straight ahead at the roundabout. This section of road can be busy so please walk on the right-hand verge. Turn right at the next junction. On the open land here you may see wagtails and lapwings (recognizable from their call 'peewit', which gives them their alternative name), and kestrels hovering overhead.

**5** There is a large lay-by on the left, where you may get some refreshment, and then at the end of a hedge on the right a footpath sign is hidden in the bushes. Turn right here along a narrow path past a split oak tree. This is the difficult part of your journey. Keep to the right-hand edge of the field but be careful not to slip into the ditch! Eventually, having passed a pond on your right, bear left at a footpath sign and then immediately right, finding oaks on your left hand.

**6** Go ahead, keeping a wire fence to your left. On reaching a made-up path turn right and head for the left-hand end of a wood. The wood is actually covert, planted to provide a breeding ground for foxes and game birds. The rhododendrons are not there simply to add colour to the scene but to enable pheasants to raise their chicks in shelter and comparative safety. Cross the ditch at the end of the wood. Turn right, cross a stile and walk on with the wood to your right until you reach a ladder stile at the bottom of the field.

**7** Cross the stile and bear left through some recently planted woodland. At its end turn right onto a green lane. Where the track divides go ahead through a kissing gate to turn right onto Broad Lane. Across the field to the left is Grappenhall Hall, now a school but once the home of the Greenall brewing family.

**8** Just before the barns of Whitehouse Farm, go left through a kissing gate into Grappenhall Wood, which was planted to commemorate the Millennium. Read about it on the interpretation board and then carry on along the track ahead. At the second fork bear left and follow the overhead wires. Got through a metal gate and walk along a narrow path with the school grounds on your left and a beech hedge on your right. You will soon be back on Canalside, from where you can retrace your steps to the church.

---

**PLACES of INTEREST**

Some 2½ miles west of Grappenhall on the A56 at **Walton Lea** (tel: 01925 860143) is the walled garden of a vanished house which has been rescued from dereliction and provides employment for people with learning difficulties. They organically cultivate and sell heritage varieties of fruit and vegetables and old cottage garden type plants. Nearer to the centre of Warrington, in Loushers Lane (B5156), just off the A50, is **Black Bear Park**. Once part of the route of an 8 mile canal built in 1804 to avoid an awkward tidal stretch of the Mersey, it now contains both woodland and meadow and picnic areas. Further up the A50, at the junction of Kingsway North and Farrell Street, is **The Twiggeries**, a willow coppice which once supported a thriving basket-making industry. Now it is a dense wood which, together with adjacent areas of wetland, scrub and grassland, supports a variety of wildlife.

# Walk 5
# IN LEWIS CARROLL COUNTRY
### Length : 3½ miles

*The 16th century tower of Daresbury church.*

**GETTING THERE:** Daresbury is just off the A56 Warrington-Chester road, about a mile north of junction 11 on the M56 and 5¾ miles west of junction 20 on the M6.

**PARKING:** There is parking for patrons at the Ring O' Bells. Alternatively use the church car park just across the road in Daresbury Lane or find a quiet on-street spot.

**MAP:** OS Landranger – Liverpool 108 (GR 579828).

The name Daresbury means the fort of Deore, an Anglo-Saxon landowner. There is no trace of a fort today, but the village has its place in history. It is known throughout Cheshire and beyond as the birthplace of Charles Lutwidge Dodgson, otherwise Lewis Carroll, the author of *Alice's Adventures in Wonderland*. His father was the local vicar. Sadly, the vicarage where the writer was born has been demolished, but there is a window to his memory in the church which depicts a number of his characters, including the Mad Hatter and the March Hare, the White Rabbit, the Duchess and the Mock Turtle. The church is open every afternoon except Wednesday, and you can visit it at the end of the walk.

Daresbury is a small, pleasant village, much more like it was in Carroll's day since it was by-passed by the A56, but it does not languish in the past. It is home to one of the Science Research Council's biggest laboratories, providing the academic community with research facilities which are too large, too complex or too expensive for an individual university to support. The laboratory also provides important services to industry.

For all that, Daresbury remains a rural community and this walk takes you through mixed woodland and across fields. Some of it is along the towpath of the Bridgewater Canal and it is all easy walking, suitable for all the family and even for quite elderly dogs – just the thing to give you an appetite for or to help you digest an excellent Sunday lunch at the Ring O' Bells! And, although it involves little climbing, it is a walk with quite splendid views.

## THE WALK

**1** From the Ring O' Bells car park turn right across the front of the pub. The building next door, which has recently been incorporated into the pub, is the former magistrates court. Pass the group of attractive whitewashed

---

### FOOD and DRINK

The Ring O' Bells (tel: 01925 740256) is a large inn with a pleasant garden. It serves traditional pub food, including fish and chips, beef and ale pie, ham and eggs, sausage and mash and an excellent steak and kidney pudding. The desserts menu includes tarte au citron and hot chocolate truffle pudding as well as the expected sponge puddings. The beers available are Courage Directors, Theakston's Best and John Smith's Smooth, plus two guest beers.

---

cottages known as The Square, and continue along the main street until you reach the Village Farm. Notice the Cheshire Cat on the newer of the two barns and contemplate the antiquity of the other.

**2** Opposite the farm turn right along a cart-track. Near a lovely big oak tree this swings towards the right to a kissing gate. Here you must take care with children and animals as you cross the busy main road to some steps which lead to another kissing gate. Now your way smells sweetly of clover.

**3** Beyond a further kissing gate it is worth taking a brief detour to the left at the sign indicating a viewpoint. The view is of Cheshire's sandstone ridge and of the Clwydian Hills of North Wales beyond. Prominent in the near distance are the water tower at Norton and Halton Castle, the former stronghold of the earls and dukes of Lancaster. To the right are the Runcorn-Widnes bridge and the power

*The Sessions House now part of the Ring O' Bells*

station at an earlier crossing of the Mersey, Fiddler's Ferry.

Returning to the main path the smell is of bracken and pine as you follow the sign to the canal and pass through a mixed woodland of pines, birch and young oaks. Crossing a broad walk the wood becomes darker. It is called Daresbury Firs, though the trees are actually Corsican, lodgepole and Scots pines. On emerging from the wood, go along the edge of the field, bearing left and then right onto a lane.

**4** Beyond the canal bridge turn right onto the towpath. Reflected in the water is a splendid display of marguerites which must have escaped from someone's garden. The tall white tower is the research laboratory's nuclear accelerator. On the laboratory's well-cut lawn you may be lucky enough to see a heron waiting for a catch, while swallows swoop low for their meal of insects. At the water's edge are a number of interesting sedges.

Pass under the old Keckwith Bridge and the newer bridge which carries the Daresbury Expressway. Just before the next bridge you will see a crane which is a relic of the days when the canal was an industrial waterway. Now pleasure boats are tied up in the cool, tree-sheltered stretch as you approach the village of Moore.

**5** Here leave the towpath and turn right over the bridge into Hobb Lane. The beeches and sycamores thrive on

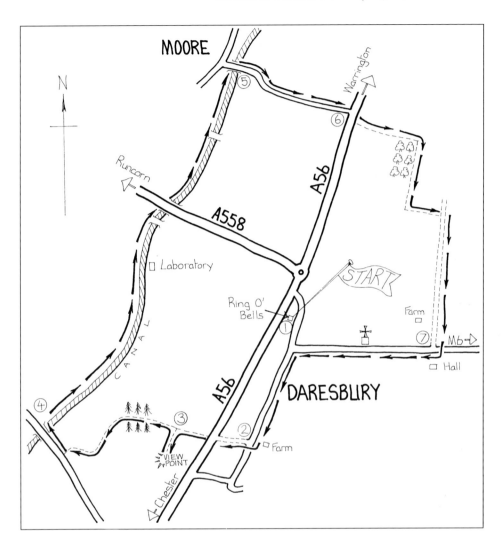

the sandy soil here and grow to a great height. Soon you pass into the parish of Walton, whose name reminds us that a British or Welsh (*Wealas*) community survived here after the Anglo-Saxon invasions. Towards the end of the lane there are wide views to the left. The nearer spire is of Walton church; the further, at 281 feet the tallest in the county, crowns the big, partly medieval parish church at Warrington. The distant hill is Winter Hill (otherwise Rivington Pike) in the Lancashire Pennines.

**6** At the main road, again take care as

you cross towards the right to a footpath which takes you over a stile onto a farm track between two fields. At the time of writing they were growing corn and lilac-flowered potatoes. As you approach the woodland, turn round for another fine view. The prominent grey tower is a gas holder at St Helens and beyond that and slightly to the right is Billinge Hill, a place to visit for some more splendid views.

Pass along the left-hand side of the wood and turn right, following a narrow track between the wood and a cornfield. Through the kissing gate bear left across the field to a farm gate and a further kissing gate. Here you will pass onto a farm track which becomes a metalled road at Hall Lane Farm. This is the home of Lord Daresbury, the chairman of the Grand National. You will see some of his racehorses in the paddocks, and his handsome roosters may accompany you down the lane.

**7** At the end of the lane you will see 18th century Daresbury Hall. Here turn right and head towards the 16th century tower of Daresbury church. If the church is open do go inside. Not only will you see the Lewis Carroll window but also a 17th century pulpit whose intricate carvings include a most voluptuous mermaid! One hundred yards beyond the church you are back at the Ring O' Bells.

## PLACES of INTEREST

West of Daresbury off the A558 expressway (left at the first roundabout) is **Sandymoor Wood**, a small wet wood which has been designated a Site of Biological Interest for its flora and fauna. It is one of a number of similar woods in the area which are now maintained by the Woodland Trust. Contact them on 01925 816217 and ask them to send you their woodland walks leaflet. Another place worth visiting is on Lapwing Lane north of Moore village. Here on 186 acres of former farmland between the Manchester Ship Canal and the Mersey has been created the **Moore Nature Reserve** (tel: 01925 740840), whose varied woodland, grassland and wetland habitats provide a home for many different animals, birds and plants. One and a half miles north of Daresbury, on the A56, is **Walton Hall Gardens**, part of the Mersey Forest. There is a children's zoo and a play area (tel: 01925 601617).

## Walk 6
# THE LARGEST LAKE IN CHESHIRE
### Length : 4½ miles (or 3 miles)

*Rostherne church.*

**GETTING THERE:** Hoo Green is on the A50 Warrington to Knutsford road, 3¾ miles south-east of junction 20 on the M6 and 1 mile north-west of Mere on the A556(T).

**PARKING:** There is parking for patrons at the Kilton Hotel. Otherwise park on the verge round the corner in Hulseheath Lane, preferably beyond the junction with Bucklowhill Lane,

as the first part of the lane is on a bus route and adequate passing space is essential.

**MAP:** OS Landranger – Manchester 109 (GR 719827).

H oo Green is a small hamlet of the Cheshire Plain bisected by a busy main road, but off this road are some of the county's most delightful country lanes. This walk takes you along them and across the fields to the lovely, unspoilt village of Rostherne with its lake and nature reserve. Rostherne is the estate village of Tatton Park, once the home of the Lords Egerton and now a National Trust property, and the route lies partly along the park's boundary. Do allow plenty of time if you wish to explore the park itself.

At 122 acres and a depth of 100 feet, Rostherne Mere is the largest and deepest lake in Cheshire (see Places of Interest). Partly a glacial depression and partly the result of subsidence caused by salt-mining, there is a legend that it is connected to the sea by an underground river. Sea-fish such as smelt certainly live in the mere, which suggests at least a former connection with the sea, as of course does the presence of salt in the area.

The landscape is one of woodland (mainly oak and sycamore), arable fields and dairy pasture. Cows' hooves can stir up a lot of mud, so you are advised to wear appropriate clothing and footwear. Although Hoo means the spur of a hill, this is barely discernible and the walk is largely along level ground. It is the perfect walk for a June day, when the scents of the countryside are marvellous.

## THE WALK

**1** From the Kilton turn right along the main road and then immediately right into Hulseheath Lane. At the road junction go straight ahead past a line of mature oaks and chestnuts. Over to the left Friesians graze amongst the humps and bumps of extensive earthworks. These represent the foundations, moat and fish ponds of a great medieval house which archaeologists have tentatively identified as Street Hill, the seat of the Venables family. At the road junction turn left into Chapel Lane and notice the

yellow loosestrife at the roadside.

**2** Having passed Gorse Cottage on the left, look out for a stile on the right just before a belt of trees. Cross the stile and follow the path along the edge of the wood. On reaching the second gate with its 'No right of way' sign, turn right and walk along the bottom edge of the field, following an oak-fringed stream. Cross a stile, turn left and descend the stone steps by the gate on the right. Walk past the well to cross another stile and climb the bank to a further stile.

**3** On reaching a lane turn right. In June foxgloves brighten your way and elder blossom scents the air. You may see a very colourful display of rhododendrons at Rushford Cottage, while just across the way is the delightful box-framed and thatched Denfield Cottage.

*Estate workers' cottages in Rostherne.*

**4** Take care crossing the busy main road to enter a welcomely quiet lane, complete with soothing pond and weeping willow. At the end of the lane is Denfield Hall Farm. Go to the left of the farm and through a kissing gate. The way is cobbled here, but the cobbles are likely to be covered with slurry, so take care. Even beyond the next kissing gate the going is hard, but eventually you pass through a hedge into a drier field. Aim for the church tower to cross a stile in the shade of a sycamore and descend some steps through a wood. Ahead is Rostherne Mere.

**5** Emerging onto a lane, you have a good view of the 18th century tower of Rostherne church to your right. The rest of the church is much older. It is open on Sunday afternoons from 2 pm till 4 pm. Head up the lane towards the church, crossing a bridge and turning left towards the lychgate. The actual gate is 17th century and very unusual, swivelling as it does on a central post. Pass through it into the churchyard and go round to the left of the tower to sit for a while and enjoy the view over the mere, watch the graceful flight of the swallows and listen to the chattering of the house martins.

Continue round the east end of the church and turn left onto the churchyard path. To the right are the quite modest graves of the more recent Egertons of Tatton; their ancestors have grander tombs in the church

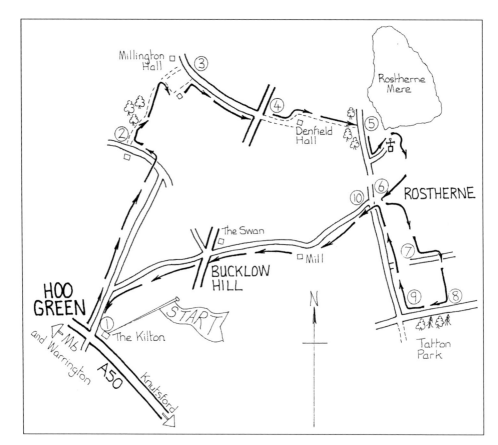

itself. Beyond the graves is the thatched roof of one of the most picturesque of Rostherne's many pretty cottages. Follow a sandstone wall out onto a lane between the village cricket pitch and the former village school.

**6** You may, if you wish, shorten your walk at this point by going straight ahead into New Road (point 10). Otherwise turn left along the cobbled pavement of the village street. By a plaque commemorating Rostherne's being named as Cheshire's best-kept

village and opposite Willow Cottage, turn left onto a farm track. Cross the stile ahead into a field where daisy-like chamomile or scented mayweed grows amongst the corn. The path here is what all field paths should be – well-defined and dry.

**7** Arriving at another stile, cross it and turn left into a lane. You will pass a farmhouse on the right. Thirty yards further on, turn right over a stile into a meadow. If you are lucky you may find it newly mown and be able to enjoy its scent. Where four hedges and several tracks meet, keep straight ahead along a path with a hedge to the right and a solitary tree on the left.

**8** On reaching a lane, turn right, taking care because cars are driven at speed along this straight run. The woodland beyond the wall to the left is in Tatton Park. It is more arboretum than simple woodland since tall pines can be seen amongst the deciduous trees.

**9** At the end of the wall is a handsome Classical lodge. Unless you want to explore the park with its herds of red and fallow deer (and entrance is free to people on foot), turn right here along a lane hedged with holly and with giant hogweed in its verges. This will take you briefly back to Rostherne village, passing some estate workers' cottages attractively set around a green on the right.

**10** Take the first lane on the left. Its name, New Road, is deceptive, for this is one of the quietest and loveliest lanes in Cheshire. Take your time and enjoy its beauty and variety. At its entrance are the village pump and pretty Widows' Cottages. Further along on the left is handsome Cicely Mill with the date 1650 on its timbered façade, its peaceful mill pond a quiet haven for anglers. And there are verges

> **PLACES of INTEREST**
>
> **Rostherne Mere** is a National Nature Reserve administered by English Nature. It is home to a wide variety of water fowl. It is also visited by thousands of gulls, whose peace is sometimes disturbed by birds of prey such as the peregrine and the sparrowhawk. There is an observatory with a powerful telescope in the woodland on the lake's shores. For a permit to use it you should get in touch in advance with the Site Manager's Office, The Rowans, Rostherne, Knutsford WA16 6RY (tel: 01565 830226). **Tatton Park** and its adventure playground are freely accessible (tel: 01565 750250).

where the red and blue flowers of the Russian comfrey bloom, hedges of oak and hawthorn, woods where the larch, identifiable from its neat female cones, grows amongst the oaks and sycamores, and pleasant streamside glades. At the lane's end at Bucklow Hill is the Swan, a 17th century coaching inn.

**11** Across the main road from the inn are two lanes. Take the one on the left, where the sign says 'Hoo Green 1 mile'. Here your way in summer is scented by the honeysuckle which grows profusely in the hedgerows. At the end of the lane bear left to return to the Kilton.

# Walk 7
# LYME PARK AND THE MIDDLEWOOD WAY
### Length : 4½ miles

*The pub at the start of the walk.*

**GETTING THERE:** Poynton lies at the junction of the A5149 and A5102 roads to Cheadle and Wilmslow with the A523 Hazelgrove to Macclesfield road, 2 miles south of the latter's junction with the A6.

From the town centre the Boar's Head, your starting point, is reached via Park Lane and Anson Road.

**PARKING:** There is parking for patrons at the Boar's Head, and free public parking off Lyme Road, just across the way.

**MAP:** OS Landranger – Manchester 109 (GR 943834).

Poynton's name harks back to the days of the Anglo-Saxon settlers, meaning the place of the tribe or family group called the Puningas. More recently it was a mining village; now it is a smart commuter town on the southern fringe of the Greater Manchester conurbation.

The public car park from which you may start your walk is on the site of a colliery, and the nearby Boar's Head has an oddly urban appearance in what is now very much a rural landscape. It looks in fact like what it was – a small railway hotel, for just across the road is the platform of the former Higher Poynton station, which must have seen the comings and goings of many miners. But even in the heyday of the local pits early this century ramblers would have alighted here to explore the Middlewood valley and the moors beyond and to find refreshment at the farmhouses and tea rooms which catered for them.

You may be fortunate enough to catch a glimpse of Lyme Park's famous herd of red deer (note the warning not to enter the Park between dawn and 8 am in the shooting season, when a cull of the deer takes place). Lyme Hall is probably Cheshire's grandest stately home and although it lies off our route, you can make a short detour to see the house which was Mr Darcy's Pemberley in the acclaimed television production of *Pride and Prejudice*. For 600 years the home of the Legh family, the Barons Newton, it is now owned by the National Trust.

The return route is along the Middlewood Way. When the railway closed in 1970 nature quickly reclaimed the embankments and cuttings, which became a tangle of birch and hawthorn. With the creation of the Middlewood Way this natural vegetation was thinned and young oaks, wild roses and other fruit-bearing shrubs were planted to provide food for animals and birds. Ponds and ditches

> **FOOD and DRINK**
>
> The Boar's Head (tel: 01625 876676) serves bar meals between 11.30 am and 2.45 pm. These include lamb chunks in red wine and plum sauce, home-made cheese and onion pie and an 'all-day' breakfast and can be washed down with a pint of 'Boddies'. The Miners' Arms (tel: 01625 872731) serves meals from an extensive menu evenings as well as lunchtimes. There are basic meals available at the Coffee Tavern, including take-away chips which can be eaten in the picnic area over the road.

were created alongside the new path and planted with iris and other water-loving flora.

This walk is one of great variety, embracing sweeping views, the physical relics of the mining era, the canal and railway which served the pits, farmland, parkland and woodland. Although there is some gradual climbing to do initially, there is just one (unploughed) field to cross and on the whole surfaces are good, so it is a pleasant walk for the whole family. Do keep the dog on a leash though when there are cows or sheep about. The views are marvellous, so bring your binoculars.

**THE WALK**

**1** On leaving the Boar's Head car park pause for a moment to look at the pub's neighbour, the Original Coffee Tavern. Established in 1877 when the temperance movement was seeking to sway the miners away from the demon drink, it has given good service to hikers too over the years. Notice the

*Another refreshment stop at the beginning of the walk.*

metal Brooke Bond tea advert on its gable.

Now cross into Lyme Road, where from the first bridge there is a good view of what is left of the station and from the second of the Macclesfield Canal (see Walk 12). Keep straight ahead at the cattle grid, where a track goes off to the left. There is gorse to the left of the path as you make your way over what looks like a cross between moorland and parkland and is a foretaste of things to come, as indeed are the mature oaks which line the track as they would a drive. The lumps in the ground are old colliery spoil heaps.

Cross another cattle grid by a pleasant wooded stream. Here you may be lucky enough to see newly born calves if you come in September. Carry on uphill past the typical Pennine stone farmhouse which is now Haresteads Cattery. Pass through the gate and the track becomes stony. Here you might like to stop for a breather. Turn round and you have a magnificent view of the Cheshire Plain and, looking right, across Greater Manchester to Rivington Pike.

By the house aptly called Windgather, for the wind can be strong up here, you will pass through a kissing gate into Lyme Park (and, incidentally, into the Peak District National Park). Go straight ahead at the first junction. If you want to see Lyme Hall, bear left at the second junction.

**2** At this second junction the walk route turns right. Pass through a gate, leaving the open moorland for a sheltered dell. This with its pines and rhododendrons as well as its oaks and chestnuts, is a fine example of Victorian landscaping. The stream which runs through it enters a gorge and you leave the park at the lodge at West Parkgate.

**3** Turning left, enter the small hamlet of Green Close with its Methodist church of 1861 and attractive miners' cottages. Go straight ahead on reaching the lane, which is edged with dry-stone walls, put together without the aid of cement or mortar.

**4** Take the first turning on the right onto a farm track. Beyond the first house you get a view of the fine old buildings of Redacre Hall Farm. Before you reach the farm, look for a stile on the left and cross the meadow, going more or less straight ahead and bearing right where there appears to be a fork. Just before the house which has now come into view go right over a stile. Cross a further stile and proceed down the lane away from the house, which is a stud farm. This path is like a heathland lane with its bracken and what appear to be thistles but are actually knapweed.

**5** At the canal bridge you have the choice of either taking the towpath back to your starting point or following the former railway track. The walk route takes the latter option. Before

> **PLACES of INTEREST**
>
> **Poynton Coppice**, which can be reached from the Middlewood Way via the Shrigley Road car park or from the Boar's Head via Shrigley Road North and Coppice Road, is an ancient semi-natural woodland which has never been ploughed up or used for any purpose other than timber production. Only a fifth of our woodland comes into this category. It was felled every seven years and its alder wood used in the local clog-making industry. It was last coppiced in 1945 and has been undisturbed ever since, providing a habitat for flowers like the stately yellow archangel and the white bell-like wood sorrel, for jays and blue-tits, for orange-tip butterflies and garden swift moths.

you do so, you might like to refresh yourself with a pint at the Miners' Arms at the end of the lane. Although with its extensions it looks quite new, the pub is a 400 year old former farmhouse where the farmer had a sideline selling beer to the miners.

Having crossed the canal and railway bridges descend the steps on the right into the cutting. The 11 miles of the old Macclesfield to Marple railway (opened in 1869) are now the Middlwood Way. It takes you past a conifer plantation onto an embankment, where, from a seat inscribed 'Fred Woodhead, His Second Home', you can contemplate, as he must have done, the horses in their paddock and the view of Lyme Park beyond. Cross the car park which gives access to Poynton Coppice (see Places of Interest) and take the path on the left just before reaching the road. If you have children

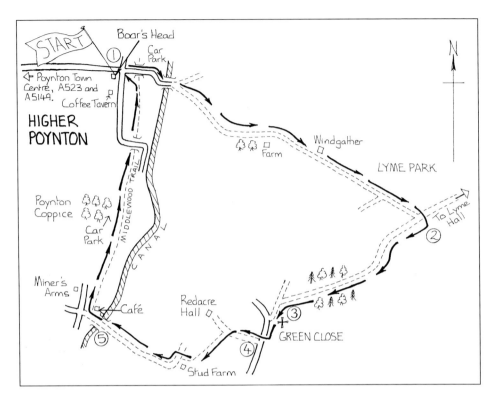

with you, you may wish to go up the steps beside the next bridge and spend ten minutes in the well-equipped playground. Otherwise carry on past montbretia and yellow loosestrife to Higher Poynton station. Here you will see a plaque commemorating the opening of the Way by the well-known naturalist David Bellamy in 1985. Having enjoyed the scent of the dianthus in the station's beds, climb the steps back to the Boar's Head.

# Walk 8
# WHERE SHIPS ONCE SAILED
### Length : 5½ miles (or 5 miles)

*The path near Heath Farm.*

**GETTING THERE:** The Tudor Rose is at the intersection of the A550(T) Eastham to Queensferry and A540 Hoylake to Chester roads, 3 miles south-west of junction 5 on the M53 and 2½ miles north-west of the western end of the M56.

**PARKING:** The main roads are so busy that the only safe place to park is the car park of the Tudor Rose but please ask permission first. Alternatively, drive to Puddington village, park by the green and start the walk at point 4.

**MAP:** OS Landranger – Chester 117 (GR 348742).

Two Mills is little more than a busy crossroads on the Wirral peninsula. In a document of 1668 the district is described as 'Two Milnes on the Heath'. The mills are thought to have been water-mills on the Shotwick Brook but they disappeared long ago. There is, however, an 18th century windmill a couple of miles down the road. This is Gibbet Mill, so called because two murderers were hanged from a nearby ash tree in 1750.

## FOOD and DRINK

The Tudor Rose (tel: 0151 339 2399) is part of the Brewer's Fayre chain and serves both Boddington's and Tetley's bitter. It offers a bargain two-course lunch from 12 noon to 6 pm Monday to Saturday with main courses such as gammon and pineapple, highland cottage pie, liver and bacon and scampi. A good ploughman's lunch is also available. The pub is well-known for its strawberries and cream in the summer, but the desserts menu also includes giant apple pie, exotic fruit salad and ice cream, and heavenly toffee cake.

The walk takes you away from the incessant traffic to the peace of two delightful villages, Puddington and Shotwick.

Puddington's green is in two parts – one a pleasant place to rest awhile in the shelter of a tree, the other a place to pasture both sheep and geese. A house on the green is dated 1710, but down a lane diagonally opposite it is the much older Old Hall with its *columbarium* or dove-cot. Pigeons were once kept here to provide food in winter.

Strange as it may seem, Shotwick was once an important Deeside port, and ships tied up against the churchyard wall. However, the estuary began to silt up and in the 18th century a new deep channel was cut 2 miles away. What had once been an arm of the sea became farmland.

Both villages are places in which to linger, so as this is one of the longer walks you could make a day of it, picnicking on the village green at Puddington as well as taking refreshment in Two Mills. Unless you go in very wet weather the walking is easy and can be enjoyed by all the family, but do take care where you have to cross the main roads.

## THE WALK

**1** From the Tudor Rose turn right and walk to the crossroads. Having crossed the road you could turn right again and walk along the pavement of the A550, but the traffic is so noisy and moves so quickly that it is quite unpleasant. You may prefer, therefore, to go straight on, past the shack called Eureka the Cyclists' Cafe. This, with the house which was its predecessor, has been a rallying point for cycling enthusiasts for something like a century. Turn right down Walden Drive, a track which eventually becomes a short footpath.

**2** Now cross the A550 again and pass through a kissing gate and over a stile. Follow the oak trees on the left-hand side of the field, then cross a stream, the Shotwick Brook. Pass through a gate to enter a large field traversed by a power line. There is a clear path to the right to a stile. Having crossed this follow the right-hand field edge and skirt the woodland to reach a lane.

**3** Turn left along what is, if you do not mind the smell of pigs, a very pleasant lane! Notice the interesting signs at the farm gates and look out for fungi in the well-kept verges. There are the field mushrooms which add such flavour to an English breakfast and the wavy

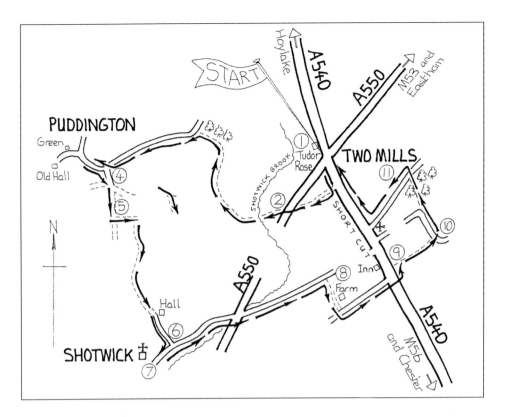

edged funnel caps.

At the fork in the road (4), it is worth taking a detour right into Puddington village.

**4** Having retraced your steps out of the village turn right at the gates of the present Puddington Hall down Chapel House Lane towards Home Farm. There are sheep in the fields and woods, but sadly the pigs are kept in the sheds to the left and ahead of us.

**5** At the second road junction do not go along the avenue of trees ahead. Instead turn right and then go left at a footpath sign opposite a farm building onto a green lane edged with poppies. Take the path going diagonally right across an arable field. Follow this path past a pond to pass through two gates. You can just make out a track ahead of you through the meadow, close to its right-hand edge. This is another place where you will find mushrooms, perhaps in a fairy ring.

Pass through a gate onto a track, where one hedge is well-kept, the other rather wild. Eventually you will reach a concreted section. Here on the left is Shotwick Hall, a mid 17th century building with impressive gate-posts.

*An 18th century house on the green at Puddington.*

**6** At the end of the lane, turn right to explore Shotwick village. Notice the iron-framed Gothic windows of the sandstone cottages as you head towards the churchyard. Have a good look at the church porch. The grooves are said to have been made by our ancestors sharpening their arrows for archery practice, which was compulsory after the Sunday service. Inside you will find box pews over 300 years old, and on the floor, a bell of 1664, now cracked and out of tune.

**7** Retrace your steps, but go straight ahead at the junction. The road is a sunken lane, well below field level, because it was well-trod by our ancestors over the centuries. It is hard to believe that the lovely valley to your right was once a tidal creek. Cross the main road, where the valley, now called Shotwick Dale, shifts to your left.

**8** There is an echo of long ago in the name of a bungalow on the right after about ½ mile, Sea Ridge. Turn along the path between it and its neighbour and cross a stile. Bear right, following the fence on your left to another stile. Go ahead onto the drive and at its end turn left onto a lane.

**9** At the end of the lane, cross the road and turn left along the pavement. Soon you will reach the entrance to a footpath. This will take you into a field which can be very waterlogged. You may prefer to continue back to the Tudor Rose along the pavement. This is the least busy stretch of main road in these parts and passes some interesting buildings, including the Yacht Inn, said to have been the haunt of sailors in Shotwick's seaport days.

Look out for the interesting collection of animals in the paddock at the first junction on the right. There are ostriches, miniature ponies and pigmy and angora goats.

If you decide to take the footpath, which is entered by a stile at the side of a gate, walk on to another stile at the side of a gateway and enter a large field. Keeping a hedgerow on your right, aim for a stile at the side of a large tree across the field. Cross the stile, a concrete plank bridge and then another stile. Follow a footpath along the left-hand edge of the next field to cross a stile at the field corner and emerge onto a lane.

**10** Turn left to walk along the lane, where you are likely to find sheep grazing on the left and cattle and ponies in the fields behind the copse which lines the lane on the right. Where the road swings to the left, cross the stile by the sign for Ledsham. You are now on a green way marked as a road on 19th century maps. If you look through the gate on your right you will see rabbits darting amongst the ridge and furrow of ancient ploughing. Here the path becomes wooded and can be over-

## PLACES of INTEREST

What is now farmland was once part of the Wirral Forest, one of Cheshire's four royal forests. A remnant of it remains in **Stanney Woods**, which can be reached by going south along the A540 and turning left onto the A5117. Now a country park, it is an area of wet woodland which existed at least as long ago as 1296. Largely oak and birch with hazel understorey, the standard oaks were once cut down on maturity for shipbuilding and their bark used to tan leather, while the hazel was coppiced, ie trimmed to make baskets and hurdles for fencing. Today the quiet woodland is home to grey squirrels, horseshoe bats, foxes, jays, greater spotted woodpeckers and tree creepers.

grown. At the end of the wooded section there is a stile and then a plank bridge, a further plank bridge with a stile at either end and a final stile onto a road.

**11** Turn left and then right by the tiny Bethesda Chapel and walk the last ½ mile along the main road.

# *Walk 9*
# THE OLD MAN AND THE ROYAL FOREST
### Length : 3 miles

*Alvanley church.*

**GETTING THERE:** Alvanley is on the B5393 about 2½ miles south-west of Frodsham on the A56(T) and 5 miles north of Tarvin on the A54(T). It is easily reached from junction 14 of the M56 via the A5117.

**PARKING:** The lanes around Alvanley are narrow and busy. If you do not intend to patronize the White Lion, which has a large car park, the safest place to park is probably in Ardern Lea, a small housing estate off

Frodsham Road, just around the corner from the pub.

**MAP:** OS Landranger – Chester 117 (GR 497740).

Alvanley means 'Aelfwald's clearing'. It was an area of land cleared for agriculture by our Anglo-Saxon ancestors in the forest of Mondrum. This, together with the forest of Mara on the other side of the

ancient highway which is now the A49, was after the Norman Conquest to become the great royal hunting forest of Delamere. There were no towns or large villages in the forest, but arable and pasture land were allowed subject

**FOOD and DRINK**

The White Lion (tel: 01928 722949) is a Chef and Brewer pub which serves food all day. Starters include peppered mushrooms with Stilton on toast and goat's cheese and tomato tart with rocket salad, while among the main courses are baked Moroccan lamb, Whitby breaded scampi, grilled whole sea bass and honey-glazed duck breast. The beers available include Theakston's and John Smith's.

to strict regulations. The deer and boar could not be harmed even if they damaged crops, and there were punishments for letting your grazing domestic animals damage the forest vegetation.

Since there were no large settlements, there are no ancient parish churches. They all date from after 1812 when the land was disafforested. A curate was appointed to serve the needs of the people of Alvanley as early as the 17th century, but the church, although it is in the style of about 1300, was not built until 1861. Up to that time Alvanley was more a scattering of farmhouses than a village.

The walk takes you down the lane from church and pub to the Iron Age hill fort on Helsby Hill at the northern end of the chain of sandstone hills which form Cheshire's backbone, and back through woods and fields. From the hill (known as the Old Man because it appears to have the shape of a man's face when seen from below) there are some stunning views, so take your binoculars. The walk is a short and easy one which can be tackled by

all, but do take care to keep away from the hill's precipitous edge. You may encounter some mud in the woods, so boots will be an asset after rain.

## THE WALK

**1** From the White Lion car park turn left and walk past the village school, keeping left at the first road junction. There are some lovely old farmhouses along this lane. One on the left has an interesting sign of a terrier dog and donkeys or mules in its paddock, while to the right is a venerable sandstone barn. At the next junction, where you go straight ahead, notice the interesting gable of Poplar Tree Farm with the date 1684, initials and a heart.

Oaks form part of the hedgerow now and there are views of the power station on Ince marshes. Go ahead at

**PLACES of INTEREST**

If you have time do take a closer look at **Helsby Quarry Woodland Park**. Sandstone was quarried here from the 1820s to the 1920s, but after the quarry's closure it was colonized by self-seeded woodland that now provides a home for many species of fauna. To learn more about **Delamere Forest**, travel south along the B5393 to Mouldsworth. Here turn left along a road through the heart of the remaining forest. There are forest trails here, while south of Hatchmere, near Delamere station, you will find a visitor centre (tel: 01606 882167), run by the Forestry Commission. To see the rare and endangered species being nurtured at the **Foxhill Arboretum** (tel: 01928 739192) take the B5393 in the opposite direction, towards Frodsham. It is open on Saturday and Sunday from 10 am till 6 pm.

the crossroads. The lane is now somewhat suburbanized but there are still a few old houses. Look out for the Spillers advertisement on the gable of the stone cottage on the left, and notice how the trees beyond have been colonized by ivy. They form part of the Helsby Quarry Woodland Park (see Places of Interest).

**2** Having passed the park's picnic area, turn right into Hill Road South. The road becomes a footpath at the National Trust sign. The woodland ahead is the natural vegetation of Cheshire's sandstone country – oak and birch with undergrowth of brambles and bracken. Take the higher and left-hand of two parallel paths. (The lower one is sunken and soon bends to the right.) You begin to climb and there is bare stone underfoot. Fine views over the Mersey open up to the left as you make your way through the gorse. Soon you are looking down on Helsby village and the M56.

The path is now a sandstone pavement. The line of bracken to the right marks the ramparts of an Iron Age hill fort. Climb up to the triangulation point to get a good view of it. You are 464 feet above sea level, but the sheer drop makes the hill seem higher.

**3** Now keep to the higher and right-hand of two paths, passing between oak trees rather than along the cliff edge. There is a fine view across to neighbouring Frodsham Hill just before the path swings to the right. Frodsham Hill was once a place of resort with a helter-skelter (see Walk 10). There are Scots pines and rhododendrons along the way now, a reminder that this too was a Victorian pleasure ground. Keep right along the main path, descend a small flight of steps to the left and then turn right onto a broader track.

**4** Cross the stile ahead and walk along a narrow path where you may have grey squirrels for company. Beyond the next stile you are on a wider track which soon becomes a made-up road. Turn left at the junction along a lane with privet and holly hedges. Ahead of you is a farmhouse in an unusual 'Dutch' style. On reaching it turn right. The lane now takes you through a pleasant pastoral landscape with dairy herds, both mixed and Friesian, grazing in fields which have kept their traditional hedgerows. The big house on the hillside is Foxhill, the Chester diocesan conference centre; part of its grounds is an arboretum (see Places of Interest).

**5** At the end of the lane turn right. After 20 to 30 yards go left through a gate into a field and walk along its right-hand edge to a kissing gate by a large oak. Pass through it and head across the field to a footpath marker post by a clump of trees. You will find a stile in the bramble hedge to its left. Cross it and walk ahead along the right-hand side of the field with a dry valley to your left. Notice the gazebo on the wooded hillside beyond it.

**6** On reaching a lane, turn left and

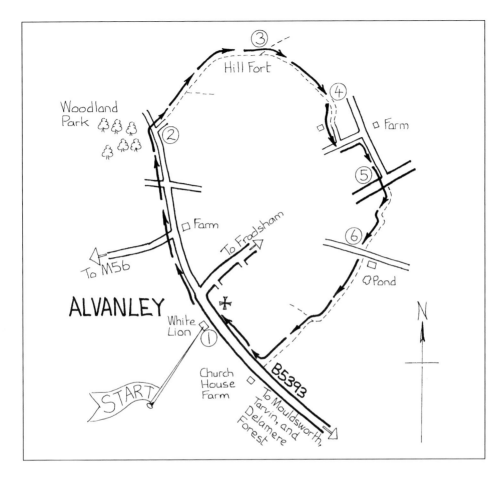

then right through the gate just before the bungalow. Walk ahead past the pond to cross a plank bridge and pass through a kissing gate. You are likely to encounter sheep in this field so it is important you put your dog on its lead. Keep right, walking alongside the hawthorn hedge and passing through another kissing gate, where you will find foxgloves growing. Carry on along the hedge and go through yet another gate on your right. Now keep left along the edge of the arable field on the better defined of two paths.

You arrive back at Alvanley opposite the handsome Georgian Church House Farm. Here turn right to the church and pub. Have a look at the war memorial and the church lychgate. It used to be the custom to 'rope' newly wed couples here, not allowing them out of the churchyard until they had paid a forfeit which was spent on drinking their health in the White Lion.

# Walk 10
# PICKMERE'S PLEASURE GROUNDS
### Length : 5¼ miles

*Church Street, Great Budworth.*

**GETTING THERE:** Pickmere village is on the B5391 about 2¼ miles from the M6's junction (19) with the A556(T) Altrincham to Chester road.

**PARKING:** There is parking for patrons at the Red Lion Inn in Pickmere village. Otherwise use the car park by the lake and start the walk at point 2.

**MAP:** OS Landranger – Stoke-on-Trent 118 (GR 693771).

Pickmere village was once a scattering of cottages and very lively. Now it is suburban in appearance and quite quiet. It was lively because on the shore of its lake was one of the last of the pleasure grounds to which working people went by waggonette or charabanc when many could not afford to holiday at the seaside, let alone travel abroad. Now the ghost train and the helter-skelter have gone and the amusement arcade has been stripped of its machines. No rowing-boats line up at the landing stage, and

## FOOD and DRINK

The Red Lion (tel: 01565 733247) is an old-fashioned country pub. It serves Tetley bitter and, lunchtimes and evenings, has a menu of genuine home-cooked food. Main meals include beer battered cod and chips, steak and ale pie and ham and eggs. There are also some far from run-of-the-mill vegetarian dishes. On your walk you may care to call at New Westage Farm (tel: 01606 891211) and enjoy the home-made ice cream. It opens from April to October from 12 noon till 6 pm and has a picnic area.

the lake is a peaceful haven for coots and the occasional heron. If you visit Pickmere in June you may be lucky enough to see the coots with their chicks. Do take some bread.

The walk takes you along the shores of the lake (first recorded in the 13th century as 'the pike mere') and over the fields of a gently undulating landscape to the village of Great Budworth, whose name means the dwelling by the water. You may have visited this most picturesque of villages before, since it rightly appears in most books of Cheshire walks. If not, do spare ten minutes to explore its ancient church with its splendid early 16th century oak roof, pre-Reformation stone altar and two old chests – a medieval one with five locks and a richly carved 17th century one. Notice too the much mutilated but still impressive effigy of an armoured Elizabethan knight – Sir John Warburton of Arley Hall.

You make your way back to Pickmere along country lanes with thatched cottages and across rich grain fields, and all in all the walk is a delightful one. Do, however, make sure you are suitably clothed and well-shod, for along the lakeside, where many a family once strayed away from the fairground in search of a suitable spot for a picnic, the path is muddy in places.

## THE WALK

**1** From the Red Lion car park turn left along a lane which retains a few old cottages, such as that which houses the post office and village store. One notable survivor of old Pickmere is the tall and handsome house of 1772 on the left which now serves as a guest house. Turn left into Mere Lane. Just beyond the new housing estate on the right you will see a footpath sign. Turn right here and walk through the ornamental gates into the car park. There is a café, which opens on Sunday afternoons only, on the left and a picnic area.

**2** Go through the wooden gate ahead and turn left onto the lakeside path with its fine stand of weeping willows. Pass through a metal kissing gate onto a rougher track at the edge of a sloping meadow. Cross a small stream on a stepping stone and go through another kissing gate and over a footbridge into a wood. Here your walk may be accompanied by the song of the sedge warbler. Cross a further footbridge onto a duck-board. At its end, head up the bank away from the lake until you are level with a house on your right. Now follow a footpath which heads

*An attractive cottage in the High Street at Great Budworth.*

slightly to the right of the house. This will lead to a footbridge. Here go forward along the right-hand edge of a big field to a kissing gate. Ignore the permissive path sign and follow the path at the bottom of the bank, taking care to avoid the marshy ground. You have left the lake behind now and have good views of the open countryside. Watch and listen to the skylarks as you head for a metal gate. Here turn right into Hield Lane.

**3** Climb uphill until you reach the beginning of a holly hedge on the left. Here climb some steps and go ahead along a path between a hedge and a wire fence. When the path becomes a broader track beyond the farm build-

ings, turn right into a meadow. You will get a good view not just of the grand early 16th century tower of Great Budworth church but also of 21st century Northwich and its chemical works. Cross the field towards a long line of trees, passing a solitary tree on your right.

**4** On reaching the line of trees, you find it is a magnificent lime avenue. Go left along it till you come to a meeting of paths by a hockey field. If you do not wish to explore Great Budworth village turn right here to regain the route at point 6. Otherwise go straight ahead.

**5** The path becomes a cobbled street with lovely old timber and brick cot-

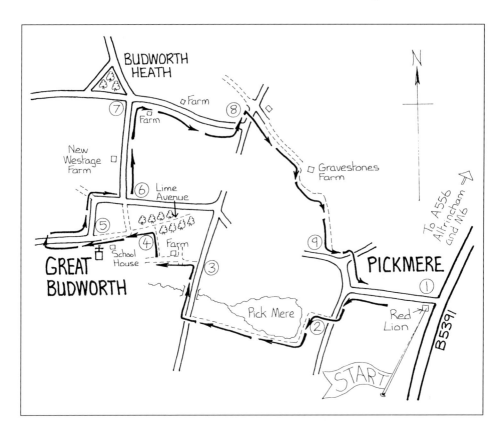

tages on the right and the churchyard
with its picturesque school-house of
1600 on the left. When you have had a
look at the church and the old houses
down the High Street, take the road
(Church Street) at right-angles to the
one you have just come along. Turn
right by the Old Smithy at the end of
the street, and follow the beech hedge
by the laneside until you come to a
road junction by a delightful example
of the thatcher's art. Here turn left onto
Heath Lane.

**6** This is a pleasant sunken lane, its

verges covered with a white carpet of
mayweed in early summer. Soon you
pass New Westage Farm, one of a
growing number of Cheshire farms
which use the milk from their dairy
herds to produce ice cream, though
some still make the traditional
Cheshire cheese.

**7** Now you are on Budworth Heath,
though it does not seem much like
heathland today. At the end of the lane
there is a triangle of oak woodland
which may give some idea of what the
land was like before it was turned into

arable and pasture but it seems too dense to be true heath. Here turn right into Knutsford Road, passing Heath Farm with its splendid barn. There is another wonderful old barn at Hilltop Farm, further along on the left. Between the two there are wide views of fields and woods and, over to the left, of Arley Hall and its park. Although you may be troubled by one or two speeding cars, this is a lane to be enjoyed, with its cool wayside ponds and, if you are lucky, two very friendly donkeys in a field on the right.

**8** At the road junction turn left and then right opposite one of the drives to Arley Hall. The hall is an early 19th century Jacobean-style building on much earlier foundations and has a notable garden which is well worth visiting while you are in the area. There is the perfect birthday card cottage garden to delight you at the beginning of the lane. Pause for a moment to enjoy it.

The lane becomes a farm track and at Gravestones Farm bear right to follow a hawthorn hedge, enjoying here the tiny blue flowers of the field

> **PLACES of INTEREST**
>
> Some 3 miles to the west of Pickmere and reached via Great Budworth and Comberbach is **Budworth Mere**, the home in their season of goldeneye, great crested grebe, and greylag geese. Marsh marigolds grow beside the lakeside paths, and willow warblers, chiff chaffs and blackcaps nest in the woods along the lake's shores. These form part of **Marbury Country Park** (tel: 01606 77741), where you will find a bird-watcher's hide and picnic areas.

forget-me-not. By a dead tree turn left along the field bottom, taking care not to slip into the deep ditch to your right. Eventually pass over a plank bridge and a stile into another field. Look with care for the path amongst the crop, heading just to the right of a large clump of trees.

**9** You emerge onto a lane, where you turn left, bearing right at the first junction and left at the second to return to the Red Lion. If you have parked by the lake turn right at the second junction. Note the interesting Gothic windows of Wayside Cottages on the right between the two junctions.

# Walk 11
# HALLS AND HORSES
### Length : 3½ miles (or 3 miles)

*Mottram Hall.*

**GETTING THERE:** Mottram St Andrew is on the A538 Altrincham – Macclesfield road, 1½ miles north of Prestbury and 2 miles

south of Wilmslow.

**PARKING:** There is parking for customers at the Bull's Head. Otherwise find a quiet spot

round the corner in Priest Lane.

**MAP:** OS Landranger – Stoke-on-Trent 118 (GR 881785).

In a place with a name like Mottram St Andrew one would expect to find an ancient church dedicated to the patron saint of Scotland. There is no church however; just a Methodist chapel. There is a tradition that one stood close to Mottram Hall, though,

and that its successor is the chapel in the hall itself.

Mottram is a place for lovers of halls and horses. You will pass at least four handsome old houses on your route, as well as a stud farm and another farm which is a refuge for hor-

## FOOD and DRINK

The Bull's Head (tel: 01625 828694) is a 16th/17th-century inn which has recently undergone some structural modification but still has lots of character. Open all day, it offers a variety of main meals including Stilton and walnut salad, local pork and leek sausages, a homemade burger and really excellent haddock, chips and mushy peas. Each is accompanied by a board with a choice of breads. There are also sandwiches and ploughman's lunches, which can be washed down with a pint of Greene King IPA or Jennings' Crag Rat.

ses and ponies of all shapes and sizes. The name Mottram, however, is derived from an ancient British or Old Welsh word for a pig farm!

Magnificent Mottram Hall, built in 1753 for the Wright family, is now an hotel. Nearby is the 17th century Old Hall. Georgian Mill House, and Legh Hall, a picturesque and complex group of buildings dating in part from Elizabeth I's time, are also encountered on the walk.

The walk takes you through gently undulating countryside and is pretty easy going as well as full of interest. If you want to introduce a friend to the joys of walking in Cheshire, this is the walk to take him or her on. It is suitable for children too.

## THE WALK

**1** From the Bull's Head turn left and left again into Priest Lane. Shaded with sycamores and oaks, it has exceptionally trim verges and it is no surprise, having passed the village school, to come across a best-kept village sign.

**2** Almost opposite the Methodist church turn right to pass the plant nursery and village hall. The slightly odd looking tree on the left with the large holly-like leaves and yellow catkins is a sweet chestnut.

**3** Having reached Higher House Farm (the Mottram stud farm) on the left, look for a metal gate on the right-hand side of the road. Here cross a stile and follow the right field edge until you come to another stile. Cross it and head for the trees, crossing a plank bridge over a stream. Now walk parallel to the stream to a stile which gives access to the main road.

The road is extremely busy so cross

## PLACES of INTEREST

Just 3½ miles to the south-west of Mottram on the B5087 Prestbury to Alderley Edge town road is the main car park and visitor centre of **Alderley Edge Country Park**. Now supervised by the National Trust, this prominent ridge, the product of millions of years of folding and faulting, was progressively cleared of its native oaks and birches by our distant ancestors to create agricultural land and provide both building material and charcoal for smelting the copper and lead found in its rocks. In time it became a desolate heath, but in the 18th century first Scots pine and then birch was planted, an enclosure act stopped casual grazing, and natural regeneration took place. As a result the Edge is now the home of a variety of birds and small mammals, including woodcock, sparrowhawks, field voles and long-tailed wood mice.

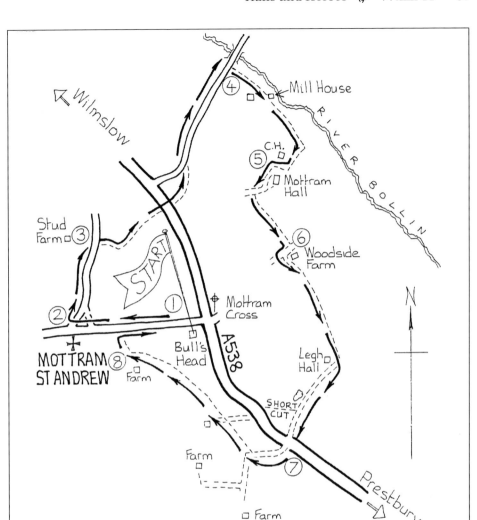

it with care, bearing slightly to the right to cross two stiles in close succession. Now walk along the left-hand edge of a field of ragwort and (if you are lucky) Highland cattle. Pass over another stile, cross a track, and climb a ladder stile out onto a lane.

Turn right along the park wall. This is a pleasant lane, scented with yarrow and giving views of the very handsome Georgian Mill House across the fields to the right.

**4** Just before the bridge over the river Bollin, turn right onto the Bollin Valley Way. Head for a gap between the Mill

House farm buildings and a smaller house to the left. Cross two stiles and follow the path between a barbed wire fence and a hedge, eventually passing through a kissing gate into a clover-filled meadow. At a left-hand bend in the river take the stile onto the golf course. Keep to the edge of the course, passing nettles which sustain a large number of butterflies and keeping in the shade of the horse chestnuts. Then turn right towards the club house, still following the edge of the course.

**5** At the club house follow the right-hand footpath sign past the magnificent west front of Mottram Hall. Turn right onto the main drive and then left near a sleeping police-man onto a footpath through a meadow. As you walk uphill to cross two stiles, you may notice another house to your right. This is the 17th century Old Hall. Emerging once again onto a golf course, keep straight ahead across the fairway, aiming for some farm buildings and eventually crossing two more stiles.

**6** At the barn of what is in fact Wood-side Farm turn right along the farm track and then left past the farm's garden. Now you are very much in horsy territory. Having passed the sta-bles go left over a stile through the hawthorn hedge and then right along the side of the hedge amongst the horses and ponies. Cross another stile, and head towards Legh Hall.

Through the kissing gate pass between two walls to turn right past the splendid Georgian south front of the house. From the sweet chestnut on the right after the pond, there is a short cut to the Black Bull if you have had enough, but do take care on the busy main road. Otherwise go ahead under the beeches to cross the road towards the left and enter a farm track.

**7** Before the track bends to the left, turn right to walk along the right-hand edge of a sloping meadow. Go forward to a stile and cross a track leading to a thatched house. Cross another stile and head diagonally left through a small orchard to a stile by a damson tree. Go ahead, keeping the apple trees to your right, and then descend a bank to a further stile. Walk to the left of a large ash tree to a wooden bridge over a stream and head up the bank. Cross a stile onto a narrow path along the edge of a copse. At its end, cross a stile onto a long green which is an exten-sion of the garden of the farmhouse on the left. There is a clump of meadow-sweet growing on it and willowherb and ragwort at its edge.

**8** Go right onto the house drive to emerge on Priest Lane, where you will turn right to head back to the Bull's Head. At the end of the lane look across the road into the woodland to see the partly medieval Mottram Cross. Its purpose is unknown. There may have been a market here in times past or it could simply have been been a way-marker.

# Walk 12
# AT THE FOOT OF THE PENNINES
### Length : 3½ miles

*The Macclesfield Canal at Gurnett.*

**GETTING THERE:** Half a mile south of Macclesfield town centre on the A523(T) Leek road, turn left into Byron's Lane (signposted to Langley and Wincle). The starting point, the

Old King's Head at Gurnett, is ½ mile further along on the left.

**PARKING:** There is parking for patrons at the Old King's Head. Otherwise park in the lay-by by

the canal bridge in Bullocks Lane, which is almost opposite the pub.

**MAP:** OS Landranger – Stoke-on-Trent 118 (GR 924719).

Gurnett is a pleasant hamlet on the banks of the river Bollin just to the south of Macclesfield. The origin of its name, which is that of a rather ugly fish, is something of a mystery. It may mean a muddy piece of ground or valley. However, in a document of 1849 the place is called Garnett, which can mean a small granary or barn. Upstream rise the gritstone hills of the Pennines, their lower slopes given over to sheep pasture, their higher ones to forestry.

The Old King's Head, where the walk begins, is a former coaching house dating from 1695. The right-hand part of the building was once a smithy. There is another former smithy attached to Plough House on the other side of the canal aqueduct. This was where, from 1733 to 1740, the great canal engineer James Brindley was apprenticed to the millwright and wheelwright Abraham Bennett.

Another interesting pub is the Fool's Nook Inn. The pub was officially the Royal Oak until 1962, although it had for a long time been known by its Fool's Nook nickname. Several expla-nations are given for the name, none of them very satisfactory. One tale popu-lar locally is that the pub was the favourite drinking place of one Mag-goty Johnson, England's last professional jester, who entertained the squire at nearby Gawsworth Hall. However, he died in 1773 and the pub was not built until 1829. It is possible, though, that Maggoty and his friends met amongst the trees which grew where the pub now stands, half-way round your route.

The first part of the walk is along the towpath of the Macclesfield canal. It was built as a link between the Peak Forest canal at Marple and the Trent and Mersey at Hall Green, Church Lawton. Not opened until 1831, it was such a late-comer to the canal network that it was considered covering the 26 miles with a railway instead. It is par-ticularly noted for the fine masonry and indeed beauty of its bridges.

---

**FOOD and DRINK**

The Old King's Head (tel: 01625 423890) serves meals lunchtimes and evenings The imaginative main courses include pan-fried steak with apple and calvados, homemade Cajun fishcake, chicken au poivre, and sautéed mushrooms with Stilton cream sauce. Bar meals can also be obtained at Sutton Hall (tel: 01260 253211) and at the Fool's Nook (tel: 01260 252254). The beer on draught at the Old King's Head is Banks's of Dudley; at the Fool's Nook it is Boddington's.

---

From the canal you venture briefly into the Pennine foothills, with a ramble along quiet lanes before drop-ping back into the Bollin valley by lane and field path. It is a good walk to do on a crisp winter morning when ducks play in the pools they have pecked out of the ice on the canal's surface, the vegetation along its bank is Christmas card white with hoar frost, and the higher peaks are carpeted with snow. And, being short and easy, it makes a good introduction to the joys of walk-ing for the younger members of the family. There are birds to watch, ani-mals with which to make friends, and any number of fascinating features of canal life, not least the colourful narrow boats which tie up for the winter by Royal Oak Bridge.

### THE WALK

**1** Walk up the steps at the right-hand side of the pub, and turn right onto the aqueduct. From the lay-by, simply turn right onto the towpath of the Maccles-field canal.

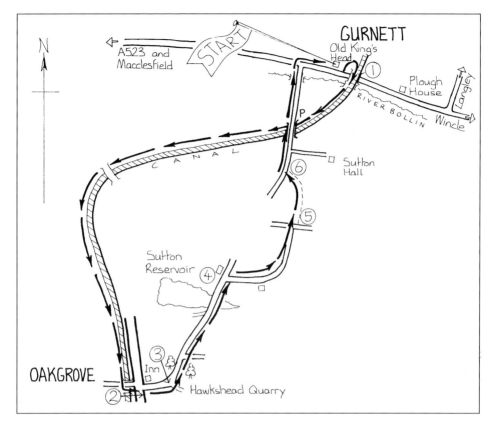

As you pass a magnificent beech tree you may see lapwings with the sheep in the field to the right, and beyond the bridge carrying the main road look out for one of the canal's milestones. You eventually have the main Manchester to London railway as a companion on your right. A farm on the other bank has its own swing bridge, which you may find is closed against intruders. There is a copse to the right now, and in frosty weather you can clearly see that the field opposite was once ploughed in the medieval ridge and furrow style. The hilltop ahead with the mast is Sutton Common, where the villagers of Sutton had their common grazing, quarrying and peat digging rights.

Notice the attractive, sandstone Canal Cottage with its own footbridge over the waterway. Beyond it is a sluice which allows an overflow of water from the canal into a tributary of the river Dane. As you approach the Royal Oak swing bridge you may be able to spot a tumulus or prehistoric burial mound on the hillside to the right. Turn left and cross the bridge to enter the hamlet of Oakgrove.

**2** Here is the Fool's Nook Inn with its colourful sign of fools or jesters at play. Go ahead up the side of the pub into Radcliffe Road. This is a most pleasant road with a view of gently rounded hills to the left and the sound of a stream rippling amongst the oaks to the right. At the top of the rise is the road to Hawkshead Quarry, where millstone grit was extracted from the hillside. A type of sandstone, it was not only made into millstones, but was and is an excellent building stone.

**3** Turn left into Leek Old Road, a quiet remnant of what was the main road before the present one which passes the Fool's Nook was constructed. Holly bushes grow on the banks beneath the trees and in December are bright with berries. You emerge from the trees onto more open sheep pasture, going straight ahead to cross Sutton Reservoir. It was constructed in 1831 as a compensation reservoir to supply water to the canal when drought caused it to run low. Known locally as the Turk's Head reservoir from its shape, today it provides a home for mallard and Canada geese.

**4** At Turk's Head Cottage turn right to enter Parvey Lane. Take time to enjoy the lovely pastoral landscape and watch the blue-tits in the hedgerows. The cottage called Gosling Green has a fine collection of pines in its garden.

---

**PLACES of INTEREST**

If you are tempted to wander further into the Pennines, and you have the energy left for a good climb, take the first road on the left after the aqueduct and drive to Langley. There turn left down Holehouse Lane to the **Tegg's Nose Country Park** (tel: 01625 614279). It is a peaceful place with marvellous views over the Bollin valley. For some less strenuous activity, drive a little further along the road to the present-day **Macclesfield Forest** – not the hunting ground of old, which was more open moorland than wood, but a Forestry Commission plantation. Planted with larch and spruce, it provides woodland walks and the opportunity to watch the birds on Trentabank reservoir.

---

**5** At the road junction, cross slightly to the right to a stile. This will take you into a field where you will probably find sheep grazing, so please keep your dog on its leash. There is a good view of the hills of the Macclesfield Forest to your right with the village of Sutton nestling beneath them. There is a stream to your left. Cross it towards the bottom of the field, where it runs through a pipe, and aim for the stile by a field gate in front of a group of houses.

**6** Turn right into the lane and pass the entrance to the partly 17th-century Sutton Hall's drive. Then continue down the lane to return to your starting point.

# Walk 13
# LITTLE BUDWORTH AND ITS COUNTRY PARK
### Length : 3¾ miles

*The war memorial at Little Budworth.*

**GETTING THERE:** The Shrewsbury Arms at Little Budworth (Common Side) is on the A54, 1¼ miles east of its junction with the A49 and 4 miles west of Winsford.

**PARKING:** There is parking for customers at the Shrewsbury Arms. Alternatively park in the main car park of the Little Budworth Common Country Park just to the west of the village centre and start the walk at point 5.

**MAP:** OS Landranger – Chester 117 (GR 596668).

L ittle Budworth is a delightfully peaceful village, though crowds were once attracted to a race-course on the common behind the Shrewsbury Arms, and today its peace is sometimes broken by the sounds of a different kind of racing. Oulton Park, the site of the local 'big house', is now occupied by a well-known motor-racing circuit.

Little Budworth is so called to dis-tinguish it from Great Budworth but

## FOOD and DRINK

From at least the 1840s up to the 1930s the Shrewsbury Arms was a farmhouse which also sold beer. It became part of the Earl of Shrewsbury's estate in 1872, hence the name, and is now a Robinson's house, serving their famous Old Tom strong ale, which can be enjoyed in the large beer garden. Sandwiches and bar snacks are available and there is a separate restaurant where from Monday to Friday a bargain two-course lunch can be enjoyed. Separate menus are available for children and vegetarians. (tel: 01829 760240).

Bar and restaurant meals can be obtained lunchtime and evening at the Fox and Barrel on the A49 at Cotebrook, which, curiously, is noted for its ice cream (tel: 01829 760529).

the names have completely different origins. Great Budworth's refers to its position by the water but Little Budworth was once Budworth le Frith, meaning Bodeur's clearing in the forest. Bodeur was probably a Saxon settler and the forest was the great hunting forest of Mara and Mondrum. Today some of the area is in cultivation or provides grazing for dairy cattle, but there are still large remnants of ancient woodland and heath.

This is a walk which will be particularly enjoyed by lovers of wild flowers and is, for them, best done in July when so many of them are in full bloom. Little Budworth Common Country Park (see Nature Notes) has a great deal to offer the walker and lies at the heart of this lovely ramble.

On the whole the going is easy and an ideal family walk. There may be some muddy patches where the bridle-paths have been churned up by horses' hooves, but in the main, being sandy, the paths will be dry.

## THE WALK

**1** This walk has an unusual start in that the right of way takes you through someone's garden. Cross the road from the Shrewsbury Arms into Shop Lane and go through the gates of a house called Ross Lea. Walk alongside the hawthorn hedge and then take the path across the lawn to a stile in another hedge. There may be an electric fence across the stile so take care  and cross it where it is insulated. Cross a meadow, bearing slightly right to a gate. Pass through the gate and go left and then right along the field's edge to another stile. Here your path through the cornfield is delightfully carpeted with the tiny cream flowers of the field pansy.

**2** On emerging onto a sandy lane turn left and then right into a metalled road. At the corner notice the sweet-smelling white flowers of the yarrow. Further along the lane you will see a pink-flowered version of the same plant. The road dips down to a stream, beyond which the verges are particularly rich in wild flowers. Notice the harebell (the bluebell of Scotland) and the betony with its clusters of tiny purple flowers.

**3** At the first road junction on the left is a pinfold. Here straying animals were kept until their owner paid a fine

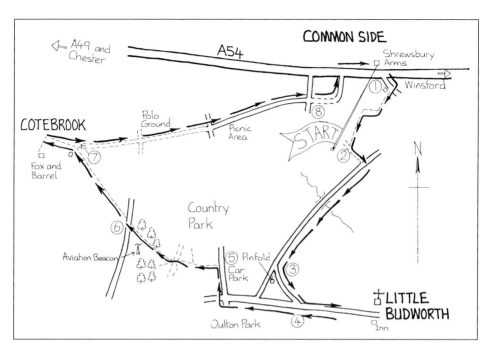

for their release. Turn left down Pinfold Lane to reach Little Budworth's war memorial, which is in the shape of a Celtic cross. There is a bench under the trees here if you feel in need of a rest and there are few pleasanter spots to take one.

**4** From Pinfold Lane turn left into Vicarage Lane if you wish to explore this lovely village. You will notice two former vicarages, one a charming little thatched cottage. The church has an ancient sandstone tower but the rest was rebuilt in Georgian times and contains good furnishings of that period. You can get the key from the post office. The village inn, the Red Lion, dates from the early 18th century and is quite unspoilt but unfortunately is

not open all day.

Retrace your steps along Vicarage Lane and continue until you reach the gates of Oulton Park on your left. The race-track can be clearly seen from here. Now turn right up the old coach road until you come to the Country Park car park. Here you will be able to pick up some literature about the park and on how the local mire and heathland were formed.

**5** From the car park, cross the coach road and a parallel bridleway onto a sandy footpath amongst the gorse and ferns so typical of heathland. Follow this path until it takes a sharp swing to the right. Here go straight across a broader track in a clearing and you will find two paths through the birch-woods which are also typical of this sort of landscape. Take the one on the right, eventually passing to the right of a small aviation communications centre.

**6** You will emerge onto a metalled road. There are so many paths through the woods you could easily have come out at the wrong point so take care. You will find two stiles on the far side of the road. One has no signpost; the other has one indicating Cotebrook. This is the one you should cross to enter an arable field. Follow a succession of stiles through meadows and cornfields, heading all the time for a grey house.

**7** If when you reach the house you feel in need of refreshment and you are within traditional pub opening hours, go more or less straight ahead along a lane fringed with purple opium poppies until you reach a ladder stile on the left. This will take you to the Fox and Barrel Inn, whose facilities include a bird hide. Otherwise turn right along the lane which is scented with honeysuckle and has the dandelion-like flowers of the smooth hawksbeard growing in its verges. On crossing a track you will see a polo ground to the left and pass under some splendid beeches. Keep going across a metalled road (the coach road again),

> **PLACES of INTEREST**
>
> **Little Budworth Common Country Park** is a marvellous place for studying not only the flora but also the fauna of both heathland and mire (ie the peat created by the remains of plants around the local ponds). There are badgers, hares and rabbits, the latter hunted by foxes and polecats, and there are rare spiders, green hairsteak butterflies, red and blue damselflies, black darter dragonflies, and green tiger beetles. Long-eared, pipistrelle and noctule bats feed in the woodlands at dusk and Daubenton's bats hunt over the ponds which are home to newts and frogs and whose banks provide a place for grass-snakes to bask in the sun. Local bird-life includes barn owls, ravens, goldcrests, pipits and warblers, and the woodcock winters here.

where you may wish to pause at the picnic area on the right. If not, carry on along Beech Road. Here the predominant colour is purple – the pinkish purple of foxglove and willow-herb.

**8** On reaching a T-junction, go straight ahead onto a cart-track. It becomes a lane, where the scent is of elder and an avenue of trees provide welcome shade. The lane swings left to meet the main road. Cross with care and turn right along the pavement to make your way back to the Shrewsbury Arms. Even here there are flowers in the hedgerow.

# Walk 14
# BRERETON GREEN AND BRERETON HEATH
## Length : 5 miles

*Brereton church.*

**GETTING THERE:** Brereton Green is on the A50 Holmes Chapel to Stoke-on-Trent road, about 1½ miles from junction 17 on the M6 via the A5022 and 3 miles from junction 18 via Holmes Chapel.

**PARKING:** There is parking for patrons at the Bear's Head. Otherwise find a quiet spot in the new housing estate off School Lane, a few hundred yards east of the hotel, but please show consideration for the residents. Or you could

park at the Country Park, signposted from the A54 Holmes Chapel-Congleton road, and start from point **4**.

**MAP:** OS Landranger – Stoke-on-Trent 118 (GR 776644). Country Park GR 795653.

Brereton is mentioned in the Domesday Book; its name means the place where the briars grow. Until comparatively recently it was a scattered rural com-munity whose life centred on its manor house, Brereton Hall the home of a family of the same name.

A twin-towered Elizabethan build-ing, the Queen herself is said have laid

---

**FOOD and DRINK**

The Bear's Head (tel: 01477 535251) is a lovely timbered house built in 1615. It was once the place where the tenant farmers paid their rents and enjoyed a game of bowls. Now it has gone upmarket and serves such dishes as baked chorizo chicken, double breasted open chicken pie, and creamy dolce latte and pear lattice pie. You can still get a decent pint, and can choose between Bass, Courage Directors and John Smith's.

---

the Hall's foundation stone and to have been a frequent visitor.

The churchyard yew trees nearby are thought to have been the source of wood for arrows for the archers which every manor had to supply in times of war. They are also a symbol of eternal life, since they live to a very great age. The church, St Oswald's, is said to have been founded in the reign of Richard the Lionheart as a thanksgiving offering by one of the Breretons who had safely returned from the Crusades. The present building is later but has a richly carved roof and a font dated 1660 which replaced one thrown out by the Roundheads in the Civil War.

Today the great house is empty and a small estate of executive housing keeps the village primary school going. This is still very much a farming area however, although it has had its brush with industry. Brereton Heath, an area of unproductive estate land, was from 1959 until 1973 mined for pure silica sand for use in the glass industry. When the mine closed the large open pit was turned into a lake which is now the nucleus of Brereton Heath Country Park.

The walk takes you past the manor house and church and through the country park, as well as across grazing land and through cornfields. There may be electric fences, but they are easily negotiated. So, if slightly longer than some of the walks, it is not a difficult one.

## THE WALK

**1** The Bear's Head is so-called because one of the Breretons from the Hall fell foul of his king and only avoided a spell in the Tower by inventing a muzzle for a bear in the royal menagerie there. From the hotel car park bear left past Smithy Cottage and turn through the impressive castellated sandstone gate-house. You will probably expect to find a drive through parkland, but what you get is a country lane with giant hogweed in its unkempt verges, honeysuckle in its hedgerows, and elderly oaks.

Keep right at the fork and soon you will reach a bridge over a stream. This is the river Croco, on whose banks you may see the white flowers of the rare insect-trapping plant, the sundew. Pause for a moment before the bridge and look left for a glimpse of the main, west front of Brereton Hall. Having passed the gates to the house, turn left into the churchyard, where you will get a close up view of its south wing.

**2** Having admired the church and the magnificent beech tree and noticed the mounting block at the church gate, turn left into more open parkland. Keep right at the junction. By the farm gate, pass over a stile onto a track where oak apples grow on young oaks and there is blue flowering vetch and bugloss at the laneside. The prominent hill over to the right is Bosley Cloud on Cheshire's Pennine fringe.

**3** Beyond the lodge cottage with its poppies and hollyhocks and Bagmere Bank Farm you emerge at a 'crossroads'. Go straight ahead into Brereton Heath Lane and turn immediately left onto a path through the oak woodland of the country park. Turn left onto a wider path, noting the different members of the thistle family growing here. On reaching the car park make for the visitor centre to learn something of the history of the Heath.

**4** Before moving on you may wish to sit for a while and enjoy the peaceful, open aspect of the lake with its mute swans. The reed at the water's edge has been introduced by the rangers as cover for breeding birds and spawning fish, while the pleasant smelling, yellow-flowered ragwort provides food and camouflage for the tiger-striped caterpillars of the cinnabar moth.

You may be tempted to take the path at the lake's edge. However, it is not continuous and will involve you in some clambering up banks and wading through undergrowth. Instead, take the broader and higher path from the visitor centre which will bring you eventually to a typical heathland landscape.

**5** As you reach the lower end of the lake, look out for a bench by a life-belt. Here turn left and immediately left again onto a narrow path amongst the holly and bracken. Turn right at the fence and follow the path until you reach a metalled road.

**6** Cross the road and follow the path along the edge of the cornfield. A welcome sight here is the corn marigold, which farmers used to hate because it starved and choked the corn but which has become a rarity since the introduction of modern herbicides. Cross a stile, then a bridge and a further stile, and bear left at the meeting of the footpaths. Here you will find both scented and scentless mayweed. Cross over two stiles, heading for the large house. A plank bridge will lead you to a further stile. Cross the meadow and another stile to emerge onto a lane to the left of a row of trees.

---

### PLACES of INTEREST

The natural vegetation of the Brereton area is heathland, of which some remains in and around the country park. A couple of miles walk from the park, but reached by road via Holmes Chapel or the outskirts of Congleton, is the tiny, picturesque village of Swettenham, where you will find **Swettenham Meadows**. This is an area of unimproved grassland managed by the Cheshire Wildlife Trust. It is rich in wildflowers, including devil's bit scabious, greater bird's-foot-trefoil and betony, as well as sedges which support the eponymous warbler. Also at Swettenham is the **Quinta Arboretum**.

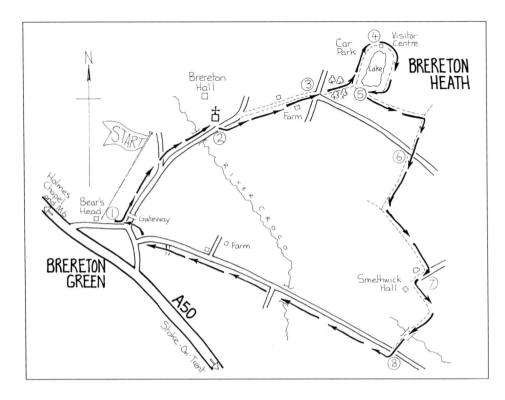

**7** Turn right to pass the gate to the large house, Smethwick Hall, and its duck pond and head towards the farm buildings. Turn left at the cobbles and go straight ahead through the gate, keeping a hawthorn hedge on your left. At the line of telegraph poles, do not pass through the gate but turn right and follow them to cross a stile and a bridge. Keeping the hedge on your right, emerge onto a metalled road.

**8** Turn right and follow the lane. Here as the giant hogweed dies back in late July, you will see its daintier relation the upright hedge parsley coming into flower. If you are a gardener you will envy the owners of Lightfoot Green Farm their perfect lawn, while Broadhey Lodge on the next corner, which has the appearance of a toll-house, has the perfect cottage garden. Continuing straight ahead, the lane will take you past the village school and back to the Bear's Head.

# Walk 15
# THE CANAL AND THE SALT LINE
### Length : 4½ miles

*The church at Church Lawton.*

**GETTING THERE:** The Horseshoe Inn at Lawton Heath is on a by-road linking the B5078 with the A50 Holmes Chapel to Stoke-on-Trent road about a mile from the centre of Alsager, which is itself about 3 miles from junction 16 on the M6.

**PARKING:** There is parking for patrons at the Horseshoe, but the road it is on, Sandbach Road, is quiet enough and wide enough for on-street parking.

**MAP:** OS Landranger – Stoke-on-Trent 118 (GR 798567).

This walk differs from the rest in this book in that it is an excursion into what might be described as 'suburban countryside'. You are but a few miles from the North Staffordshire conurbation which includes Newcastle-under-Lyme and Stoke-on-Trent, and your route takes you briefly through a housing estate on the outskirts of the small but pleasant industrial town of Alsager. However, for most of your way you could be deep in the country, and a foreign country at that, given the local farmers' predilection for growing maize.

On this fascinating walk we see something of the causes of urban growth, in the Trent and Mersey Canal and an abandoned railway – the Salt Line. The former was partially financed by the famous potter Josiah Wedgwood to enable him to get his raw material, china clay, from Liverpool, to where it had been brought up the coast from Cornwall. It would also help him ship his delicate finished goods safely to his customers. Designed by James Brindley, it was begun in 1766 and finished in 1777. Today you can enjoy watching the narrow boats in Lawton's flight of six locks.

The Salt Line, a branch of the line between Stoke and Crewe, was opened by the North Staffordshire Railway in 1852 to enable salt, an important element in earthenware glazing, to be transported from the mines around Sandbach to the Potteries. It closed in 1970.

It is a pleasant surprise, half-way round the route, to discover Lawton Hall and its church. The Hall once gave refuge to Charles II when Cromwell ruled the country, and the King stood sponsor to the squire's son at his baptism in the church. Standing on the hlaw or hill which gave Lawton its name, the body of the church was rebuilt of brick after a fire in the 1790s. The tower, however, is older, built in the time of John Bybber, who was rector in the reign of Henry VIII. You can see his initials and chalice carved into the stone. Older still according to some experts, though a 19th century fake according to others, is a Norman archway you can see if you peer through the outer door into the porch.

## THE WALK

**1** From the Horseshoe turn left and left again into Cherry Lane. The lane passes across Lawton Heath and has the characteristic vegetation of a heathland road, including bracken, foxgloves and yarrow. Pass Lawton Mere, almost hidden in the trees on the right, and drop down into a pleasant little valley before climbing back up again to the canal.

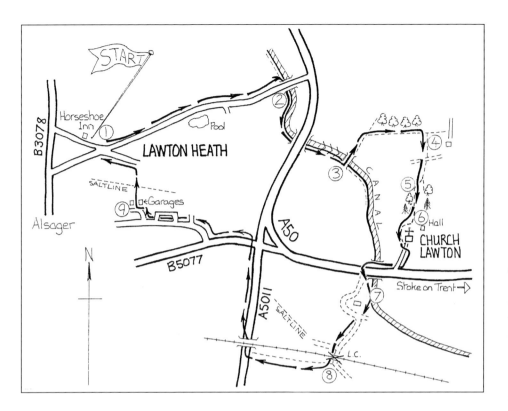

**2** Just before the bridge, turn right onto the towpath, which becomes more pleasant once you leave the roar of the traffic on the A50 behind. Amongst the variety of vegetation here, look out for the attractive purple flowers of the wild geranium, meadow cranesbill, and for red bartsia, a semi-parasitic member of the figwort family which lives on the roots of other species.

Pause a moment to appreciate the interesting curved parapet of Snape's aqueduct and to enjoy the view from it, and stop again to watch the waters of the canal overflow seeming to rush under the nearby houses. You may wish too to watch the narrow boats being manoeuvred up Lawton's flight of six locks.

**3** Turn left over the first bridge and go directly ahead across the meadow and cross the stream. Do not be tempted up what appears to be a broad track but is in fact the road to nowhere, but look for a path on the right which skirts the right-hand fringe of an area of decidu-ous woodland called Bratt's Wood.

**4** After about ½ mile just before reach-ing a lane and farm, take a path on the right along the right-hand edge of a field. As you cross a farm track, look over to the left and you will see the hill Mow Cop, crowned by what appears to be a castle. It is actually a folly built by the squire of Rode Hall to improve the view from his windows, and it became a gathering place for Primitive Methodists at the time of their breakaway from the main Methodist body.

**5** Go straight ahead to cross a stile, where you should take the right-hand of the two paths. This will take you through a pleasant woodland glade to a stile and bridge and then through thicker woodland. This is Summer House Plantation and, with its mixture of oak, sycamore and pine, seems more like an arboretum than an ordinary wood.

Emerging from it, into a field where the corn is perhaps as high as your eye, if not an elephant's, you will see a picturesque church. And over to the left, through the trees, you will see the reason for the 'arboretum' – one of Cheshire's great houses, Lawton Hall, recently restored and the centrepiece of a new development of houses in a similar style.

**6** Go right and then left around the church wall to arrive at the churchyard gate. From the churchyard steps go ahead down the drive which served both church and house, being careful not to annoy the Grey Lady who is said to haunt it. You emerge at the main road by what is now the Lawton Manor nursing home. Here, turn right across the canal bridge, then cross the road and go down steps onto the canal bank.

**7** Where the path divides at a stile, turn right, cross the cattle grid and bear left. As you approach the level crossing you will see a track which leads to the point where the Salt Line branches from the main route. You may find it interesting to see how nature has reclaimed the abandoned cutting and to count the varieties of wildflower you will find there. Do not, however, wander too far, as the going becomes difficult. Some of the line has been utilized as a part of a long-distance footpath, the South Cheshire Way, but not this section unfortunately.

**8** Cross the level crossing, turn right and walk along the right-hand edge of the field, roughly parallel to the main line. Go through the gate onto a narrow path to reach Linley Lane near the railway bridge. Turn right onto the lane, which can be busy though it does have wide footpaths. At the road junction, turn left and then right into Moorhouse Avenue and a very pleasant housing estate.

**9** Take the fourth avenue on the right, called The Rode. On the right you will see some garages. Pass between them to cross a recreation ground to a bridge and kissing gate. The line of trees is on the Salt Line embankment. Bear slightly left across the field to cross the 'line'. Then go ahead to Sandbach Road and left back to the Horseshoe.

# Walk 16
# BESIDE THE DEE
### Length : 4 miles (or 3 miles)

*Holt Castle.*

**GETTING THERE:** Farndon is about 7½ miles south of Chester, near the junction of the B5130 with the A534 Nantwich to Wrexham road.

**PARKING:** There is parking for patrons at the Greyhound and the Farndon Arms, and on-street parking in the High Street.

**MAP:** OS Landranger – Chester 117 (GR 413546).

Farndon and Holt are twin villages – one on either side of the Dee, which here forms the border between England and Wales. So peaceful are they that they could easily compete with some better known villages a little further along the border for the title of 'the quietest places under the sun'. This was not the case, however, in the Civil War of the 1640s, when the Royalists garrisoned Holt castle and the Parliamentarians holed up in Farndon church.

Holt Castle, built in 1281 by John,

Earl de Warenne, is now in ruins but you have a good view of it across the river shortly after leaving Farndon. At the end of the walk there is the chance to explore Farndon church. It was so much damaged during the Civil War that it was almost completely rebuilt in 1658. Go inside and into the chapel to the right of the high altar, where you will see a fascinating little window depicting local gentry who had supported the Royalist cause ranged round a central panel of weapons and armour.

This lovely walk offers history, a riverside path and peaceful villages. Those more intrepid walkers who do not mind negotiating ploughed-up paths can take an alternative route to pass the relic of an earlier, medieval Cheshire–the site of a moated house.

If you would like another short walk in the area, cross the bridge to Holt and buy a village trail leaflet at the post office. You may then tread in the steps of H.G. Wells, who was a teacher in Holt and began his writing career there.

## THE WALK

**1** Turn left out of the Farndon Arms car park or right from that of the Greyhound and head towards Farndon bridge, turning left on reaching it. Do take a good look at the bridge before moving on; it was built in 1345. Across the river is Holt's beautiful perpendicular church of St Chad, rebuilt in 1490 by Sir William Stanley, who five years earlier had helped put Henry Tudor on the throne at Bosworth.

Walk past the Boat House along the wooded riverside path of duckboard. When this swings left carry on along the riverbank. Continue parallel to the river to cross a stile into a meadow. Now there is a good view of what remains of Holt castle. Cross a further stile and walk alongside a cornfield where there is the welcome sight of poppies. Ignore the path on the left and go under the modern bridge which carries the Farndon bypass.

**2** You will see a line of trees fringing the riverbank as it bends to the right. On reaching them pass over another stile and take the second path on the left. Keep to the edge of the field. The obscure path eventually becomes a narrow overgrown lane where the most noticeable vegetation is pink-flowered balsam. The track becomes more discernible as it begins to climb the hill, where keen-eyed children may spot conkers in early autumn.

*Holt's 15th-century church.*

**3** A large barn is visible to the left. Shortly before reaching it, cross a stile on the left and head across the meadow towards a large metal gate. Find a kissing gate to its left and exit onto a lane. Here is the tiny hamlet of Crewe – not the famous Cheshire railway town! Pause to admire the pretty pot plants in the yard of the little Methodist chapel of 1858, and then turn right along the lane to pass the village pump and some picturesque cottages with Gothic windows.

**4** On reaching the crossroads you have the option of turning left and taking a short cut to point 7 or of braving the hardest but not the least interesting part of the route. For this,

walk ahead along the lane until just before the farmhouse on the right. Here the really adventurous will continue past the farm, go round the bend and look for a footpath sign on the left. You may then like to use your map to negotiate the maize crop and find your way past the moat of a vanished medieval house, tentatively identified as Stretton Hall.

**5** Your guide chickened out and took the overgrown track on the left before the farm. This is an ancient green way used by the ox carts of our medieval ancestors and by farmers of long ago to take their herds to market. It may indeed be as old as the Romans, for the name Stretton usually means the place

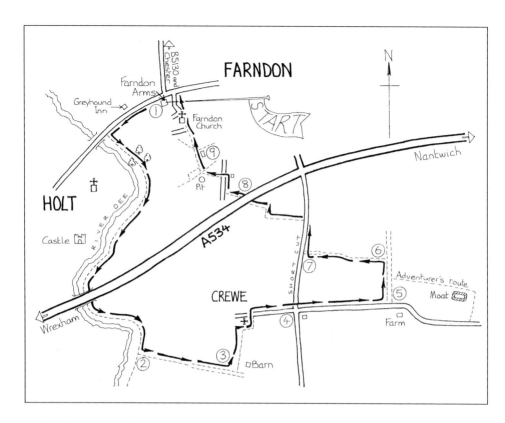

on the Roman road.

**6** Look out for a footpath sign on the left, and cross the laneside ditch by a plank bridge. Follow the line of trees to your left over the large open field. The field is rich in fungi, including that most delicious of mushrooms, the leopard-spotted parasol mushroom. Do, however, be careful to check the toxicity of anything you are tempted to pick. Cross a stile and follow the right-hand edge of the field. Cross a plank bridge on the right and then turn left, passing through or over a series of gates until you reach a lane.

**7** Turn right and walk along the lane until, at a footpath sign, you turn left to follow a line of oaks along a field's edge to its far boundary. Do not cross the boundary here, but bear right to pass, on the left, over two stiles and a plank bridge. Here you will enter a field where you may be greeted by two friendly ponies. Go diagonally right to a stile and down some overgrown steps to the bypass.

**8** Crossing the road with care, walk left along the verge to pass up a met-alled slope which becomes a lane. On reaching a bungalow, go left through a kissing gate. There is a large pit on the left which appears to have dried up but is still wet enough to attract moorhens. Follow the line of houses on the right to reach a narrow sunken lane.

**9** Look out for a small wooden gate. It is somewhat obscured by vegetation, so if you miss it go left along the lane until you come to a gap in the hedge on the right. Pass through the gap and bear right along the hedge until you see a sign for Farndon. Follow the sign and climb up the once fern-clad hill which gave Farndon its name, passing the gardens of some newish houses on the right. Pause for a moment to enjoy the view across the river, then, when the main path swings to the right, bear left down two or three steps, ignoring the long flight to your left. Take the first path on the right and keep ahead through a small gate into the churchyard. Go into the church to see the window commemorating the Civil War struggle.

## PLACES of INTEREST

The main point of natural interest in the Farndon area is not its flora or its fauna but its geology, more particularly the nature of the riverbank. Indeed, the sandstone cliffs on the Farndon side are designated a Site of Special Scientific Interest. A board close by tells their story over many millions of years. And the cliffs behind the castle, where there has been extensive quarrying, are a Regionally Important Geological Site.

Go west from Farndon on the A534 and A5152 and you will find **Farmworld**, a working farm where children can feed new born lambs, have pony rides, visit the deer paddock and amuse themselves in the adventure playground. Telephone 01978 840697 for details.

Leave the church by the north door, and go straight ahead down Church Lane. At the junction with the High Street, notice the attractive Georgian building housing the pharmacy and then turn left to return to the car.

# Walk 17
# RAVENSMOOR
### Length : 5 miles (or 4 miles)

*Sound Oak.*

**GETTING THERE:** Ravensmoor is about 2 miles south-west of Nantwich and a similar distance from the A534 and A51(T) Wrexham and Chester roads.

**PARKING:** There is ample parking for patrons at the Farmers Arms Inn. Alternatively park in Chapel Lane, 100 yards north of the pub off Swanley Lane, but do leave room for residents' cars and farm vehicles to pass.

**MAP:** OS Landranger – Stoke-on-Trent 118 (GR 621505).

This walk is in the Cheshire cheese-producing region which centres on the lovely old town of Nantwich. Do go into the town, both to enjoy its picturesque old buildings and to buy some cheese fresh from the farm. Its 14th century church is splendid too, like a miniature cathedral.

Do not expect hills at Ravensmoor. 'Moor' here means an open stretch of land or heath, which today is both arable and pasture. Do not expect

of the Mainwarings of Baddiley Hall.

---

**FOOD and DRINK**

The Farmers Arms (tel: 01270 623522) sells Greenall's mild and Boddington's bitter and serves food lunchtimes and evenings. Alternatively, there are lots of eating places in Nantwich. Particularly worth visiting is the Crown Hotel (tel: 01270 625283), a wonderful example of a Cheshire timber-framed building, dating from 1585. Here you will find a lunchtime carvery, where in addition to the joint of the day, the reasonably priced meals include home-made pies and pork chops served with the perfect apple fritter. The coffee is good too.

---

ravens either, though you will probably see crows, and house martins taking insects on the wing!

The walk is an exceptionally pleasant one along the lanes and across the fields of one of the most delightful but least known parts of the Cheshire countryside, passing picture postcard cottages and timbered and thatched farmhouses.

Some of the field gates may be locked along your route, so this walk could involve some climbing. It is worth the effort!

Part of the route follows the towpath of the Llangollen branch of the Shropshire Union Canal, opened in 1805, with lovely views across the countryside. Baddiley church is well worth a visit. It is a timber-framed medieval building, though the nave and tower were encased in brick in 1811. Inside there are box pews, a three-decker pulpit and a rare tympanum above the chancel screen painted with the arms of Charles II and those

## THE WALK

**1** Turn right out of Chapel Lane or left out of the pub car park to enter Sound Lane. This odd name may simply be a dialect form of 'sand', a reference to the nature of the soil. You should not meet much traffic but what there is travels at quite a pace so take care. There are wild roses in the hedge as you cross a little tributary of the river Weaver. Look out on the left for the unusual sign of the Friesian cow at Field's Farm. There is now a wide verge on the right where you may find horses being exercised. Here look out for a track leading to a very lovely timbered house called Sound Oak, and turn right into it.

**2** Follow the track between the house and its farm buildings. There is a notice here asking you politely to keep to the footpath, yet there is no obvious

---

**PLACES of INTEREST**

**The Cheshire College of Agriculture** at Reaseheath, a mile or so north of Nantwich off the A51, has an annual open day in May. In addition to the farming attractions, there is a nature trail to explore. The college (tel: 01270 625131) also offers accommodation for individuals and groups in its Georgian farmhouse, which could make an excellent base for a walking holiday. Also about a mile from Nantwich (on the A534) are the woodland gardens at **Dorfold Hall**, which can be visited on Tuesdays and bank holiday Mondays between April and the end of October (tel: 01270 625245).

*The interior of Baddiley church.*

footpath. You should turn left immediately after the farm and head for the right-hand end of a line of trees, where you will find a stile. Cross it and keep along the left-hand side of the field to another stile. Now head towards a white house. Pass along the left-hand side of the house along a track lined with oaks and turn right into a metalled road.

**3** You are now in the delightful hamlet of Wrenbury Heath and have a choice of routes. To walk by the canal, turn immediately left and head down the lane, ignoring the first footpath on the right. On reaching a junction turn right into the trees and then right again onto a slope leading to the canal towpath. At first the path is in a cutting, but after a shaded section beyond the first bridge views open up on the left towards Cholmondeley castle and distant Larkton Hill. Pass under another bridge and leave the towpath at the third, turning left onto the road to reach point 4. The alternative, if you fear the towpath may be muddy, is to bear right at the road junction and walk along a very pleasant lane where, having crossed the canal, you will pass a particularly pretty timber-framed cottage on the left.

**4** Look out for a pair of semi-detached cottages at an easily missed road junction. Here turn into Baddiley Hall Lane. This is a quiet lane, hedged with hawthorn and holly. Notice the splen-

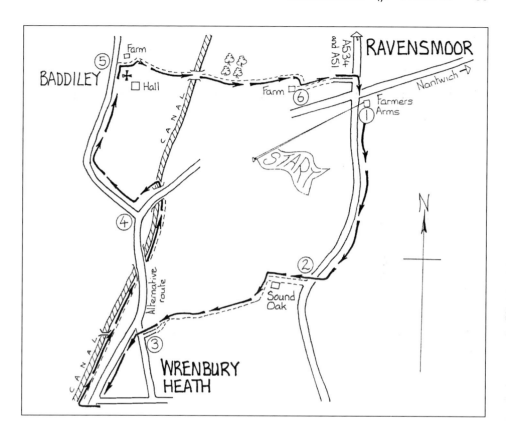

did outbuildings as you turn sharp right at a house called Baddiley Hulse (hulse means hollows). Eventually you will come to Baddiley church. Do borrow the key from the bungalow next door. All four dogs have a bark far worse than their bite!

**5** Before leaving the churchyard have a look over the wall at the 18th century Hall, and then head up the lane towards another bungalow. This is Baddiley Hall Farm. Turn down its right-hand side, then bear slightly left towards a stile. Climb it and head across a large field towards a prominent bridge. Cross it and aim towards the right-hand edge of the wood ahead. Pass through one metal gate and cross the field to pass through or over another. You will see a farmhouse ahead and slightly to the right. Go forward, keeping to the left of the house, to cross a stile. Now look for another stile in the hedge on the right. This will give access to a lane.

**6** Walk away from the house along the lane. This is Chapel Lane. If you have not parked here, turn right at the end to return to the Farmers Arms.

# *Walk 18*
# INTO THE ENGLISH LORDSHIP
## Length : 3½ miles (or 3 miles)

*Threapwood church.*

**GETTING THERE:** Threapwood is just south of the B5069 Malpas to Bangor-on-Dee road, about 5 miles west of the A41 and 7¼ miles from the A49. **PARKING:** Parking at the village inn, the Queen's Head, is limited and the pub is on a blind bend, so the best spot is probably outside Threapwood church, and the walk starts from there.

**MAP:** OS Landranger – Chester 117 (GR 439454).

Threapwood, on Cheshire's south-western border, covers a sizeable area but is more a scattering of houses than a real village. The nearby Welsh village of Tallarn Green bears the mark of Georgina and Henrietta, the spinster daughters of Victorian landowner Lord Kenyon. They lived in the big house called The Gelli (or The Grove) and they built the church, its timbered vicarage and the picturesque Kenyon Cottages – two

## FOOD and DRINK

The Queen's Head (tel: 01948 770244) is a Marston's house with a delightful streamside garden. But, being in such a remote spot, it only opens in the evening on weekdays. However, the Crown at Malpas (tel: 01948 860474) offers acceptable pub food such as gammon and eggs, grilled chicken or scampi, while baguettes, sandwiches and toasties are also available. These can be enjoyed by the waterfall in the pub's pleasant lavender-scented garden.

single-storey ones for estate workers' widows and a larger labourer's house in-between.

This walk starts and ends in Cheshire, and therefore can claim a place in this book, but it is also an exploration of that mysterious land known historically as Maelor Saesneg – the English Lordship. It was probably so called because it was the king's land, unlike the neighbouring Maelor Cymraeg, the great Welsh marcher lordship of Bromfield and Yale. When North Wales was divided into counties Maelor Cymraeg became part of Denbighshire while Maelor Saesneg became a detached part of distant Flintshire, another area where the Crown had lands.

The walk is quite a short one along what is for the most part level ground and therefore suitable for all ages. Do not let the fact that it is mainly along lanes put you off. The lanes are very quiet and it is possible to complete the full circuit without coming across a single moving motor vehicle! The ini-

tial stages of the walk are along a footpath anyway, and here do make sure you are well-shod, for in wet weather this path can be muddy. Finally, this is a walk for those who love blackberrying and jam-making, for in late September and early October there are hedges all along the way which are covered with fruit.

## THE WALK

**1** From the church gate turn right and walk along Barn Road. Opposite its junction with Back Lane you will see a litter bin. Here turn left along what is at first a metalled road and then, at Middle Wood Farm, a green way. Looking slightly to the right, the hills you can see in the distance as you approach the farm are the Clwydians. Keep to the right of the farm buildings, where the path becomes narrower, and make sure the nettles don't sting you. If they do, there are lots of dock leaves to rub on the sting for relief! Eventually you will see the edge of a wood to the left. This is Caenant Wood, its name an indication that you have crossed the border.

An English translation would be Brookfield, the wood being bisected by the Wych Brook. A wych is of course a type of elm, but perhaps we should look for another meaning for the stream's name, for many of the trees here are silver birches, unusually tall for their species. It may be derived from an Old English word for a dairy farm, for this has long been dairying country.

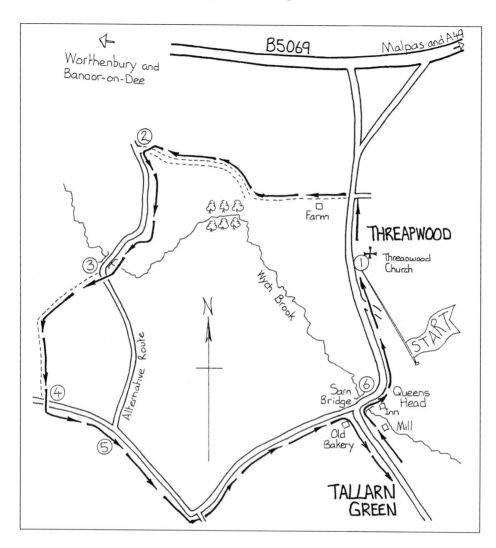

**2** Turn right, away from the wood, onto a broader track. Follow it till it reaches a metalled road, Mulsford Lane. Here turn left down to a bridge over the brook. This is an idyllic spot and it is worth pausing awhile to enjoy the peaceful scene.

**3** You now have a choice of routes. If the weather is reasonably dry, go straight ahead onto a bridlepath which, judging from its overgrown condition, is probably little used by horses. Otherwise continue along the lane, which too sees little traffic. Over to the right is the brooding mass of

Ruabon Mountain, 1,648 feet at its highest point.

**4** & **5** At the end of lane or bridlepath, turn left along a lane which will eventually bend sharply to the left. Beyond the bend is a road junction. Here go straight ahead, following the sign for Sarn Bridge. When you reach the Old Bakery, which now sells some rather esoteric ornaments, you may either turn left to the bridge or, if you have the energy, go right to briefly explore the village of Tallarn Green.

**6** Sarn is the Welsh for a paved road or causeway. Have a look at the bridge for the various dates from the 17th to the 20th century at which it and the road were reconstructed. Then cross the bridge back into England and, as you pass the Queen's Head, look across the brook to see Tallarn Green's lovely old mill, still with its waterwheel. Threapwood, whose name appropriately for a border settlement means disputed wood, has a disused windmill.

Soon you are back at Threapwood church, which dates from Regency times. Judging from the way the Virginia creeper, rich red in autumn, covers most of the windows, it must be seldom used, although it is fully furnished for worship. Do wander through the wrought iron gates into

> **PLACES of INTEREST**
>
> To continue the blackberrying theme, if the walk across the border has whetted your appetite and you have time to go a little further into the Principality, travel by the B5069, B5426 and south on the A483 to the Tŷ **Mawr Country Park**. Both blackberrying and jam-making feature amongst the activities organized by the rangers of this lovely park on the banks of the Dee, along with guided walks and talks about its flora and fauna. For details, contact them on 01978 822780. Alternatively you can go east via Malpas and visit **Cholmondeley Castle Gardens** and their adjacent parkland. Here you will see red deer, meres rich in fish and waterfowl, and magnificent trees including cedar of Lebanon, oak, lime, sweet chestnut, beech and plane. Do, however, check on opening times before setting out by telephoning 01829 720383.

the still well-kept churchyard. There can be few lovelier or more peaceful last resting places.

# Walk 19
# BELL O' TH' HILL
## Length : 3 miles

*The Blue Bell inn, possibly the oldest inn in Cheshire.*

**GETTING THERE:** Bell O' Th' Hill lies just off the A41(T), Chester to Whitchurch road, about 3 miles north of its junction with the A49.

**PARKING:** Walkers are welcome to park at the Blue Bell Inn. Alternatively park on the lane which is very quiet.

**MAP:** OS Landranger – Chester 117 (GR 523454).

Bell O' Th' Hill is a hamlet apparently named after a pub, the Blue Bell, though its name may be a corruption of 'bowl of the hill'. It is actually in the parish of Tushingham, though there is no village of that name. There are, however, two Tushingham churches, one of which we shall be visiting on the walk.

This is known as Old Chad to distinguish it from the present St Chad's on the main road, and was built in 1689. A replacement for an earlier timber building, it was the gift of a

London merchant, a local boy made good in the Dick Whittington tradition. You can see its interesting period fittings by looking through the windows, but if you want a closer look, telephone the rector on 01948 685328 before setting out.

You will see the date 1667 over the door of the Blue Bell, but there is a record of a licence being granted in 1650 and part of the building is thought to date from the 14th century, making the Blue Bell the oldest inn in Cheshire. Before you go inside look out for the mounting block, which doubled as a dog kennel.

The 'hill' is part of the sandstone ridge which runs the whole length of the county, and you will be crossing its own long-distance footpath, the Sandstone Trail. The route of the walk takes you down the hill onto Willey Moor, a flat expanse of drained mossland, and to the towpath of the Llangollen canal before climbing back onto the hill again.

The canal was built to link the Welsh town of Llangollen with the main line of the Shropshire Union Canal at Hurleston near Nantwich. The latter connected with the Mersey at Ellesmere Port, so called because much of the finance for the canal was raised in and around the Shropshire town of Ellesmere, which is on this branch.

This is a walk for those who enjoy the wide open spaces – the views are very extensive, particularly on a bright frosty morning.

## FOOD and DRINK

The Blue Bell (tel: 01948 662172) is a freehouse providing ale from Hanby's brewery at Wem across the Shropshire border and from Nottingham's Castle Rock brewery. The satisfying meals served under the watchful eye of Bear, the German Shepherd, include homemade steak and kidney pie, ham and eggs and various salads. The Willeymoor Lock (tel: 01948 663274) is also a free house and serves meals lunchtimes and evenings, though its opening times are somewhat erratic.

## THE WALK

**1** From the Blue Bell car park turn right onto the lane. Ignore the track through the tunnel and turn right at the next track. Cross the main road with care to enter a made-up but muddy lane. There are splendid views over south Cheshire and Shropshire to the right, and blue tits flit amongst the trees at the laneside.

Go ahead through the kissing gate and follow the track through the field, heading towards the church.

Notice the unusual external staircase to the church's gallery, and do look through the window of the small building in the corner of the churchyard to see the parish hearse of 1880. Believe it or not, hearses still come up to the church the way we have walked, for this is still the parish cemetery. By the way, if you saw a lady in red along the lane, she was one of Tushingham's several ghosts!

**2** From the church gate turn right

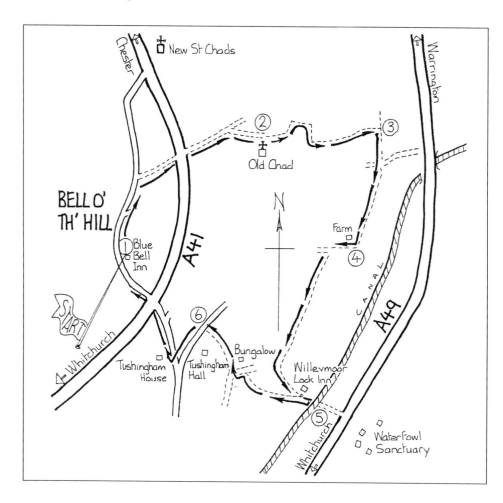

along the churchyard wall to cross a stile, from where there is another great view. Go straight ahead, looking for a metal gate, and then go forward on a path through the crop.

Cross the stile and a plank bridge into a field where you are likely to have rabbits for company, and go straight ahead to cross a further stile. Head for the left-hand corner of the new field and another stile/bridge.

Then walk along the left-hand field edge, alongside a drainage ditch, to yet another bridge.

**3** Turn right onto the bridleway, which has Scots pines along its left-hand side. Be careful the brambles do not scratch or trip you. Pass through a metal gate and continue ahead along a track lined with willows, hawthorns and young beeches, where you are likely to be accompanied by the trill of greenfinches.

**4** At the end of the bridleway turn right and pass through a gate to walk past a barn and the front of a farmhouse. Cross a stile in the fence on the left, marked Marches Way, and walk down the right-hand edge of the field. After the next stile, cross the drive of a thatched house to reach a further stile. Go half-left across the meadow to a kissing gate and walk alongside the garden fence to the canal. Here is the Willeymoor Lock Tavern, the tables by the lock a pleasant place to break one's journey with a refreshing drink on a summer's day.

**5** Retrace your steps away from the towpath and take the left-hand of the two stiles. Pass under electric wires and head for a stile to the right of the bungalow. Pass the bungalow and bear slightly right, passing some tall oaks on the left.

**6** At the road junction turn left and as you climb the hill look across the parkland to the gleaming white, Regency period, stucco façade of Tushingham Hall. Look out for the impressively

> ### PLACES of INTEREST
>
> Some undrained mossland remains at **Brown Moss** near Whitchurch, 3 miles south of the Blue Bell. It is home to 30 rare plant species and a haven for woodland birds and wildlife. For details contact Whitchurch Tourist Information Office on 01948 664577. Do not be surprised to see foxes on your walk. Ducks and geese are given refuge from them at **The Waterfowl Sanctuary** at Bradeley Green, just west of the Willeymoor Lock on the A49, where live birds and eggs can be purchased. Self-catering holidays are available for walkers in the adjacent cottages, but, for obvious reasons, dogs are only allowed by prior arrangement (tel: 01948 663442).

carved inscription on the lodge, built in 1867. At the junction ignore the tempting footpath ahead and turn right past the handsome Victorian front of Tushingham House. Its owners, the Vernons, had a comfortable box pew up at Old Chad, while the peasantry sat on the simple forms we still see there today. The Vawdreys from the Hall had the gallery as their private pew.

Walk along the lane past the windpump and cross the main road to return to the Blue Bell.

# Walk 20
# ABOVE THE RIVER WEAVER
### Length : 5¾ miles (or 5¼ miles)

*The pond on Hankelow green.*

GETTING THERE: Hankelow is on the A529 Nantwich to Market Drayton road, about 1½ miles north of Audlem.

PARKING: There is parking for customers at the White Lion Inn. Alternatively park on one of the lanes which cross Hankelow green, or in the free car park at Audlem, starting the walk at point 6.

MAP: OS Landranger – Stoke-on-Trent 118 (GR 671453).

Hankelow is a charming place – a scattering of houses around a large green, complete with duck pond. Its name means Haneca's hill and it stands on a rise above the river Weaver at a point where the undulating sheep pasture of the Shropshire border meets the dairying lands of the Cheshire Plain, though arable farming also has a presence here. There is no ancient church but there are some large and handsome old

## FOOD and DRINK

The White Lion (tel: 01270 811288) is a well-run house selling Theakston's mild and Wells' Bombardier bitter. Food is available every day except Monday. There is a reasonably priced three-course lunch, while main courses include a pot roast and Cumberland sausage and mash. Vegetarian meals, lite bites and a children's menu are also available. In Audlem's Old Priest House the friendly proprietor of Beaman's Coffee Shop (closed Tuesday) serves home-made cakes, good coffee, tea and hot chocolate, as well as home-made ice cream, while on most summer afternoons you can also get a cup of tea in Audlem church.

houses, including 18th century Hankelow Hall.

The parish church is in Audlem, a village you visit on the walk. It is a sleepy place which has the air of having seen better days. Indeed, up to the First World War it was a market town as well as a flourishing canal port. It still has some imposing buildings which help give it an urban character, including the George hotel and the 17th century grammar school, though both have changed their function. And some still regard it as Cheshire's most southerly town.

The walk is one of the longest in the book but it is not a difficult one. There are, however, places where mud churned up by cows' hooves may have to be negotiated and boots will be an advantage.

There is so much to see and enjoy in the way of scenery, old buildings, flora and fauna that you may wish to make a leisurely day of it, starting with morning coffee in Audlem, stopping at Hankelow for a pub lunch or a picnic on the green, and returning to Audlem for tea.

## THE WALK

**1** From the White Lion car park turn right, past the old smithy. This is a pleasant lane where rabbits may be your companions, but what motor traffic there is can come at speed, so take care, especially where the hedges are high. You are walking through a predominantly pastoral landscape, but the presence of bracken and gorse here and there suggests that it was once heathland.

Bear left at each junction to pass the tower of an old windmill. Soon you will cross a stream to enter the village of Buerton, where the wide, well-kept verges lend beauty to a place of nondescript modern housing.

**2** You will see on the right a sign pointing to Audlem and, unusually, giving you a time for the walk – 40 minutes. However, the path is overgrown, so ignore it and take the next turning on the right, down Festival Avenue. Enter the field at the end of the road and walk down its left-hand edge, looking for a stile on the left. Cross the stile and stream, and now bear right until you come to a stile which will enable you to recross the stream. Look for another stile across the field. Cross it and, turning half-left, aim for a further stile in front of a bay-windowed, red-brick house. This will give you access to a lane at a road junction.

**3** Go straight ahead, following the sign for Bunsley Bank, but bear left soon afterwards to approach Gorsecroft Farm. By the cricket pavilion, cross over a stile and skirt the farm buildings to cross two further stiles and turn left onto a farm track. This is one of the most pleasant parts of the walk, through a lovely pastoral landscape. Savour it.

At the end of the track look for a stile on the right. Cross it and continue in the same direction, noticing the attractive Victorian farmhouse at Mount Pleasant on the left. Also on the left are two stiles. Take the second, in the corner of the field, to enter a narrow pathway which passes some picture-postcard cottages.

**4** Turn right into a lane. Look over to the left to see the unusual and handsome Baptist chapel of 1840. The lane is called Salford, which means willow ford, and you will see why as you cross the bridge, where you should bear left. Do not climb the hill!

**5** Turn right and walk into the centre of Audlem, enjoying the lovely old houses on the way. Soon the church is in sight. At its gate is the early 18th century Buttercross (a miniature market hall), and a stone to which animals were once secured for the cruel sport of bear-baiting. The oldest part of the church is its prominent 13th century tower. The building is usually open and is worth a brief visit to see its medieval font and chest and, unusually, a Roman funeral urn. The churchyard was a Celtic, possibly pre-Christian burial ground. Opposite the church, and now a teashop, is the medieval priest house. Go down its side to see the old grammar school and what is reputedly the smallest house in Cheshire.

**6** Returning to the village square, where the lamp post is a memorial to a local surgeon, bear right along Cheshire Street. Pass the free car park and then, immediately after the cemetery, turn left into Moss Hall drive. When that beautiful, early 17th century building comes into view, cross a stile on the left and walk straight ahead to cross another stile. Climb the bank to a further stile and turn right onto the canal towpath.

**7** This is the main line of the Shropshire Union Canal. Begun in 1791, its barges once carried local cheese to market in Nantwich, Middlewich, Chester and even Manchester. Notice the old stables for the barge horses as you pass under the bridge and out onto the aqueduct over the river Weaver, here a narrow stream rippling amongst the trees.

**8** Leave the towpath through the gate on the far side of the next bridge, and turn left onto a cart track. Where the main track bends to the left, go through a gate into a field, turn left and cross four stiles to reach a metalled

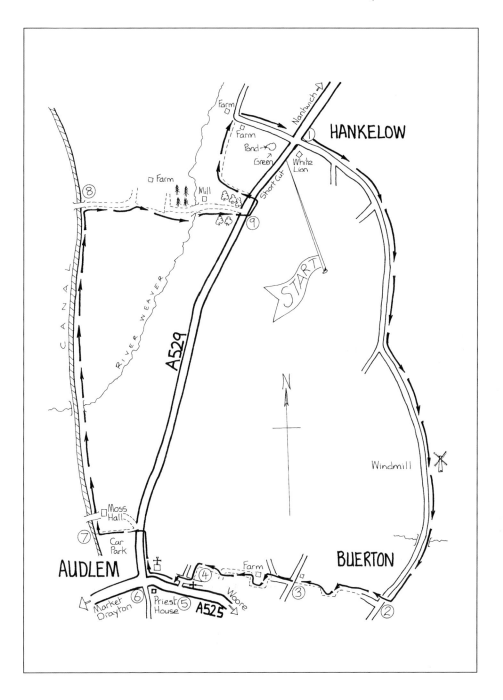

lane. Go straight on, passing a small pine plantation which provides a home for grey squirrels. Just beyond it is an old water-mill and its dam, the mill stables and the mill-owner's house – altogether a delightful spot. You will now enter an area of mixed deciduous and evergreen woodland providing some welcome shade on a hot day.

**9** Turn left onto the main road. Here you have the option of continuing back to the White Lion along the road, which can be very busy, or almost immediately climbing some steps on the left. Taking the latter option, walk along the right-hand edge of a ploughed field until you reach a gap in the hedge from where you can see a large, imposing farm house – Hankelow Manor. Continue past the gap, cross the stile and head for the left-hand side of the farm buildings. You will emerge onto a lane by a house

> ### PLACES of INTEREST
>
> While you are in the area you might like to slip over the Staffordshire border to **The Dorothy Clive Garden** at Willoughbridge (tel: 01630 647237) with its lovely views of three counties. It is easily reached from Hankelow and Audlem by going east on the A525 and turning south on the A51 at Woore. Two miles north of Hankelow on the B5071 is **Dagfields Crafts and Antiques Centre** (tel: 01270 841336) with its Animal Village, where children can cuddle rabbits, calves, piglets and lambs.

with impressive gateposts, the aptly named Ball House Farm. Here turn right. Over to the left is a fine example of late-Victorian Cheshire timbering – Hankelow Grange. On reaching the green, do pause to enjoy the birds on and around the pond, which include Canada geese and pintail, mandarin and mallard ducks. The White Lion is straight ahead.